CHINA'S EURASIAN CENTURY?

Political and Strategic Implications of the Belt and Road Initiative

CHINA'S EURASIAN CENTURY?
Political and Strategic Implications of the Belt and Road Initiative

Nadège Rolland

THE NATIONAL BUREAU of ASIAN RESEARCH

Published in the United States of America by
The National Bureau of Asian Research, Seattle, WA, and Washington, D.C.
www.nbr.org

Copyright © 2017 by The National Bureau of Asian Research

All rights reserved. No part of this publication may be reproduced, stored in a retrieval system, or transmitted in any form or by any means, electronic, mechanical, photocopying, recording, or otherwise, without prior permission of the publisher.

Front cover image: Movement of trains in ways of evening twilight fog spring © Vladimir_Timofeev/iStock

Back cover images (left to right): Beijing highway at night © bjdlzx/iStock; Chinese temple in desert, Mingsha Shan, Dunhuang, China © Nithid/iStock; and Large container vessel unloaded in Port of Rotterdam © Serbek/iStock.

ISBN (print): 978-1-939131-50-8

ISBN (electronic): 978-1-939131-51-5

NBR makes no warranties or representations regarding the accuracy of any map in this volume. Depicted boundaries are meant as guidelines only and do not represent the views of NBR or NBR's funders.

In loving memory of Lucien Relave
Soldier, mentor, father in everything but name

Contents

Acknowledgments .... *ix*

Executive Summary .... *xi*

Introduction 1

Chapter 1 – Mapping the Silk Roads 7

Chapter 2 – The Belt and Road Initiative: Bigger, Bolder, Better? 43

Chapter 3 – Drivers of the Belt and Road Initiative 93

Chapter 4 – A Vision for China as a Risen Power 121

Chapter 5 – Hurdles on the Way 151

Chapter 6 – Political and Strategic Implications
of the Belt and Road Initiative 177

Appendix: Note on Sources *189*

About the Author *195*

Acknowledgments

There are many people who have accompanied and supported me on this journey along China's 21st-century version of the Silk Road, but I alone am responsible for any errors of fact or interpretation that persist in this book.

My deepest gratitude goes to Richard Ellings, who threw open the doors at the National Bureau of Asian Research and welcomed me three years ago into NBR's incomparable family. I could never have dreamed of working with better and more engaging people than the NBR team. I would like to extend a special thanks to Roy Kamphausen, whose unflappable character, professional scrupulousness, and intellectual rigor have been an inspiration throughout this project. I benefited greatly from his guidance while drafting the manuscript. I would also like to give special thanks to Brian Franchell, who assisted me in the research process, unearthed key materials from abstruse Chinese databases, and took care of all the nitty-gritty administrative and logistical details so that I could focus on reading and writing. I want to acknowledge the terrific work of NBR's editorial team, including Joshua Ziemkowski, Jessica Keough, and Craig Scanlan, the magicians who smoothed my gawky sentences into something readable to native English speakers. I would also like to express my sincere gratitude to Daniel S. Markey from the Johns Hopkins School of Advanced International Studies, who kindly agreed to read the manuscript's draft and share his comments. His perceptive observations and judicious remarks helped me sharpen my own thinking and polish the rough edges of my ideas.

This project would not have been possible without a generous grant provided by the Smith Richardson Foundation. I am most grateful for the foundation's commitment to support research and would like to extend a special thanks to Allan Song, whose assistance has been invaluable throughout the project.

Finally, I am deeply grateful for the enduring love and support of my husband, Aaron, and children, Alexandre, Claire, and Hadrien. Their enthusiasm and encouragement throughout the last two years have given me strength, confidence, and fortitude. I am thankful for their patience and toleration of the creeping intrusion of China's Belt and Road in our family discussions. Each page of this book is a token of my profound affection for them.

Executive Summary

China's Belt and Road Initiative (BRI) has become the organizing foreign policy concept of the Xi Jinping era. The 21st-century version of the Silk Road will take shape around a vast network of transportation, energy, and telecommunication infrastructure, linking Europe and Africa to Asia and accompanied by strengthened monetary cooperation and increased people-to-people exchanges. Beijing sees physical infrastructure as a first step toward Eurasian integration, thanks in part to the creation of economic corridors that will enable greater regional policy coordination and foster a vibrant "community of common destiny."

Drawing mostly from the work of Chinese official and analytic communities who are striving to make BRI a reality, this study examines the concept's origins, drivers, and various component parts, as well as the accompanying ideational narrative and domestic and international objectives, as seen through Beijing's eyes. While Beijing is selling the promise of economic development, its main focus is on the benefits that it hopes BRI will bring to China, not simply in the realm of economics but most importantly in the geopolitical domain. More robust engagement of the entire Eurasian continent through BRI is intended to enable China to better use its growing economic clout to achieve its ultimate political aims without provoking a countervailing response or a military conflict. BRI thus serves the Chinese leadership's vision of a risen China sitting at the heart of a Sinocentric regional order, the essence of Xi's "dream of the great rejuvenation of the Chinese nation." This vision reflects Beijing's desire to shape Eurasia according to its own worldview and its own unique characteristics. More than a mere list of revamped infrastructure projects, BRI is a grand strategy that advances China's goal of establishing itself as the preponderant power in Eurasia and a global power second to none.

Introduction

China's Belt and Road Initiative (BRI) has become the organizing foreign policy concept of the Xi Jinping era.[1] From London to Canberra, Moscow to Cairo, Astana to Jakarta, cooperation under the BRI umbrella is now the main theme of discussions between Chinese officials and their local counterparts. And the initiative is making rapid progress. Merely one year after President Xi announced the creation of the Silk Road Economic Belt and the 21st Century Maritime Silk Road at the end of 2013, Beijing identified BRI as a top national priority, created specific financial institutions to fund it, and promised to spend hundreds of billions of dollars on infrastructure projects across Eurasia.[2]

China's 21st-century revival of the Silk Road harkens back to an era when ancient trade routes connected the Chinese and Roman empires through Mesopotamia and Central Asia.[3] Along with goods that merchants carried from country to country, ideas, religion, scientific discoveries, inventions, and art also traveled in both directions along the Silk Road.[4] Its closing in 1453 following the defeat of the Byzantine Empire by the Ottomans forced merchants to look for alternative routes on the sea. This search initiated the Age of Discovery and marked the dawn of commercial and civilizational interaction on a truly global scale. The term Silk Road conjures up images of camel caravans loaded with rare and precious goods, traveling across deserted areas from one opulent empire to another. For China, it evokes memories of glorious times when Chinese civilization was flourishing, and the Chinese empire was dominant and stood at the center of the known world—as *Zhongguo* (literally "middle kingdom"), its own given name, suggests. It should therefore come as no surprise that President Xi,

---

[1] This monograph adopts the official English translation of *Yidai Yilu* approved by the State Council of the People's Republic of China (PRC)—"Belt and Road." This term is often translated as "One Belt, One Road." See National Development and Reform Commission, Ministry of Foreign Affairs, and Ministry of Commerce (PRC), "Vision and Actions on Jointly Building Silk Road Economic Belt and 21st-Century Maritime Silk Road," March 28, 2015, http://en.ndrc.gov.cn/newsrelease/201503/t20150330_669367.html.

[2] The "belt" expands across the Eurasian continental landmass through Central Asia, Russia, the Caucasus, the Levant, and Eastern Europe and branches out to Southeast and South Asia. The "road" comprises a string of ports connecting China with Southeast Asia, South Asia, Africa, the Middle East, and Europe through the South China Sea, the Indian Ocean, and the Mediterranean Sea.

[3] Not just one but many different routes stretched from China through India, Mesopotamia, and the African continent to Greece and Rome. The term Silk Road was coined by German geographer Ferdinand von Richthofen in 1877. Although all sorts of merchandise traveled along the Silk Road, the name comes from the popularity of Chinese silk in the West, especially with Rome.

[4] Peter Frankopan, *The Silk Roads: A New History of the World* (New York: Alfred A. Knopf, 2016).

the promoter of the "dream of the great rejuvenation of the Chinese nation," chose the reference to the Silk Road for his vision of renewed regional interactions, as a symbol of China's resurgence as a world power.

Of course, the 21st-century version of the Silk Road will not bring back camel caravans. It will take shape instead around a vast network of transportation (railways, roads, and port facilities), energy, and telecommunication infrastructure, linking Europe and Africa to Asia and accompanied by strengthened monetary cooperation and increased people-to-people exchanges. Beijing sees physical infrastructure as a first step toward Eurasian integration, thanks in part to the creation of vast economic corridors that will enable greater regional policy coordination. Eventually, the BRI countries will be tied tightly to China in a vibrant and prosperous "community of common destiny." If this vision can be fulfilled, then all roads will eventually lead to Beijing, both literally and figuratively.[5]

To the 21st-century global citizen and denizen of the cyber age, Eurasian transportation construction might seem passé and reminiscent of the transcontinental railway projects of the 19th century. Yet the logic of physical connectivity is as powerful today as it was 150 years ago. The impact of more and better transcontinental links on the regional landscape could be huge, not only by boosting trade and commerce but also by easing flows of energy and other resources, stimulating technological development, influencing culture and politics, and shaping strategic choices. At the turn of the 20th century, observing the railroad lines being built across North America, the British geopolitician Halford Mackinder noted that "transcontinental railways are transmuting the conditions of land power."[6] Railways helped convert a patchwork of disparate rural and wild territories into a unified, powerful industrial nation. Transportation costs dropped, manufactured products flooded into remote areas, exploitation of natural resources increased, technical innovations were born, growth accelerated, and modern management methods were developed. Transportation connectivity can reduce psychological as well as physical space, changing what Chinese scholar Gan Junxian describes as "the way people live in their country and the mental map they have of

---

[5] "Yi zhang tu kandong 'Yidai Yilu'" [A Map to Understand the "Belt and Road"], Yicai, http://www.yicai.com/show_topic/4591483; and "Yidai Yilu yuanjing yu xingdong wenjian fabu" [Belt and Road Vision and Action Plan Revealed], Caixin, March 28, 2015, http://economy.caixin.com/2015-03-28/100795672.html.

[6] H.J. Mackinder, "The Geographical Pivot of History," *Geographical Journal* 170, no. 4 (1904): 434.

their region."[7] In post–Civil War America, railroads helped forge a renewed and strengthened sense of national identity. For countries along China's belt and road, newfound proximity could reinforce feelings of "Asian awareness."

After the end of the Cold War, several Western countries, including the United States, tried to promote infrastructure interconnectivity and economic development in the hope that prosperity would transform post-Communist Eurasia into a democratized and stable region. With BRI, China has now assumed the lead in promoting Eurasian integration, using similar arguments about the relationship between connectivity and development, but with very different economic, political, and strategic objectives in view. Beijing hopes to recycle some of its accumulated foreign reserves, utilize its overcapacity in construction materials and basic industries, and boost the fortunes of its state-owned enterprises by opening new markets. Promoting regional development is seen not as a way to encourage political liberalization but, to the contrary, as a means of strengthening and stabilizing existing authoritarian regimes around China. Both increased economic dependence on and tighter political ties to Beijing serve Chinese strategic interests. Transcontinental infrastructure will help hedge against possible disruptions to maritime supply in the event of conflict. Deepening China's strategic space will help counter alleged U.S.-led efforts to contain the country's rise. Above and beyond these concrete objectives, BRI is also meant to serve the broader regional ambition of building a Sinocentric Eurasian order. It reflects Beijing's newfound willingness to play a leading role in reshaping the world, starting with its extended periphery.

Despite the initiative's significance and the importance that Chinese policymakers clearly attach to it, the study of BRI in the West lags behind a rapidly emerging reality.[8] Moreover, most of the available studies look at BRI from the outside in and tend to focus on its observable physical manifestations, drawing conclusions about its viability and purposes without examining the motivations and calculations of its architects. In order to fully understand BRI, it is necessary to study more closely how the initiative is described by those who are working hard to make it a reality—in other words, the Chinese official and analytic communities.

The purpose of this monograph is to offer a comprehensive assessment of the Chinese conception of BRI, drawing mainly from Chinese-language sources and from field research in China. The chapters that follow will

---

[7] Gan Junxian, "'Sichouzhilu' fuxing jihua yu Zhongguo waijiao" [The Plan for "Silk Road" Revival and China's Diplomacy] *Northeast Asia Forum* 19, no. 5 (2010).

[8] Please refer to the appendix for an overview of available Western reports dedicated to BRI.

examine the origins of the concept, its drivers, and its various component parts, as well as its accompanying ideational narrative and domestic and international objectives—all as seen through Beijing's eyes. Although BRI has both a land and a maritime component, this study focuses mainly on the Eurasian continent. For most of China's long history, its identity has primarily been that of a continental power. Given the constraints and opportunities that China faces on both its land and sea frontiers, BRI's continental dimension will likely once again emerge as particularly important. On the other hand, China's maritime and naval expansion is relatively recent and has received disproportionate attention in the West, both because of its novelty and because it has brought China into direct contact with the United States and its Asian allies.[9]

This study relies on official Chinese sources that speak for the Chinese leadership, as well as on what Carnegie researcher Michael D. Swaine classifies as "non-authoritative" sources—i.e., Chinese media and academic publications.[10] In order to gain a full appreciation of BRI, it is necessary to look beyond the official rhetoric relayed by China's propaganda machinery and pay close attention to "how the text can be understood in terms of the hidden content it discloses."[11] Public discussions are essential to gaining an understanding of that hidden content. Far from being remote from current affairs and isolated from the world of decision-makers, Chinese public intellectuals inform and contribute directly to the leadership's thinking about foreign policy.[12]

What follows is divided into six chapters. The recent publicity around China's BRI has overshadowed a number of earlier initiatives to improve

---

[9] The U.S. literature related to China's maritime and naval developments is extensive. See, among others, Andrew S. Erickson, Lyle J. Goldstein, and Carnes Lord, eds., *China Goes to Sea: Maritime Transformation in Comparative Historical Perspective* (Annapolis: U.S. Naval Institute Press, 2009); Bill Hayton, *The South China Sea: The Struggle for Power in Asia* (New Haven: Yale University Press, 2014); Peter A. Dutton, "China's Maritime Disputes in the East and South China Seas," testimony before a hearing of the U.S. House Foreign Affairs Committee, January 14, 2014; Bonnie S. Glaser, "Conflict in the South China Sea: Contingency Planning Memorandum Update," Council on Foreign Relations, April 2015; and Toshi Yoshihara and James Holmes, "Responding to China's Rising Sea Power," *Orbis* 61, no. 1 (2017): 91–100. See also the National Bureau of Asian Research and Sasakawa Peace Foundation USA, Maritime Awareness Project, http://maritimeawarenessproject.org.

[10] Michael D. Swaine, "Chinese Leadership and Elite Responses to the U.S. Pacific Pivot," Hoover Institution, China Leadership Monitor, no. 38, Summer 2012, http://carnegieendowment.org/files/CLM38MS.pdf. Please refer to the appendix for a context-setting analysis of the Chinese sources used in this monograph.

[11] Michael J. Shapiro, *Studies in Trans-Disciplinary Method: After the Aesthetic Turn* (New York: Routledge, 2013), 29–30.

[12] David M. Lampton, ed., *The Making of Chinese Foreign and Security Policy in the Era of Reform* (Stanford: Stanford University Press, 2001); and Linda Jakobson and Dean Knox, *New Foreign Policy Actors in China*, SIPRI Policy Paper, no. 26 (Stockholm: Stockholm International Peace Research Institute, 2010).

regional infrastructure connectivity, some of which have been going on for decades. These will be described in chapter 1. Chapter 2 pulls together the various pieces of BRI as they have emerged since its launch, describing the initiative's top-level supervision, the financial and intellectual resources devoted to its success, and the early-harvest projects visible in each of the proposed economic corridors. Chapter 3 analyzes why Beijing launched BRI and examines both the economic and strategic drivers. Chapter 4 presents the initiative as an effort to shape Eurasia according to China's broader objective of achieving regional preponderance, in both material and normative terms, and speculates about what a new Sinocentric Eurasian order created by BRI might look like. Chapter 5 describes what Chinese policy experts see as the main challenges and discusses the solutions they envisage to avoid pitfalls. The concluding chapter analyzes BRI's overall political and strategic implications and considers the options that the United States and its allies have for dealing with the initiative.

Chapter 1

Mapping the Silk Roads

The idea of integrating Eurasia by developing regional transportation networks is not a new one. Before 2013, when Xi Jinping first aired the concepts of a Silk Road Economic Belt across Eurasia and a 21st Century Maritime Silk Road linking Southeast Asia with Europe, several infrastructure projects to expand regional transportation networks had already been launched and partially completed. Through projects ranging from the oldest and most ambitious plan, led by the United Nations, to connect the entire Asian continent to Europe via road and rail, to the more recent and narrowly focused South Korean Iron Silk Road or U.S. New Silk Road initiative, transportation connectivity has been encouraged both by individual states and multilateral institutions. Although not necessarily publicly avowed, the hope not only that physical links created on the ground would stimulate economic development by increasing flows of goods and people, but that trade and growth would eventually ease the recipient countries toward societal change and political liberalization was common to all the earlier projects set in motion after the end of the Cold War.

Over the years prior to the launch of Xi's Belt and Road Initiative (BRI), infrastructure building maintained a prominent role in China's domestic territorial development and was a preferred option for the Chinese government's national economic and development planning.[1] Initially limited to the coastal regions where Deng Xiaoping's opening-up policy first focused, infrastructure building gradually expanded westward to the continental depth of the country. The main purpose was not only to facilitate trade flows and the efficient movement of goods and people but also to reduce regional development disparities. During both the 1997–98 and 2008 financial crises, infrastructure building was amply used as a way to stimulate growth despite regional or global slowdowns.

---

[1] As explained in the introduction, this monograph adopts the official English translation of *Yidai Yilu* approved by the State Council of the People's Republic of China (PRC)—"Belt and Road." See National Development and Reform Commission, Ministry of Foreign Affairs, and Ministry of Commerce (PRC), "Vision and Actions on Jointly Building Silk Road Economic Belt and 21st-Century Maritime Silk Road," March 28, 2015, http://en.ndrc.gov.cn/newsrelease/201503/t20150330_669367.html.

Chinese investment in cross-border transportation infrastructure remained limited until the end of the twentieth century, both for geographic and political reasons. The Himalayas and sparsely populated desert areas to the west and southwest provided natural obstacles to the construction of seamless highways and railroads. For decades, China's connection to the Trans-Siberian Railway was its only link to a broader regional network. It was not until Beijing started to normalize relations with its Soviet and Southeast Asian neighbors that it began to understand the need for adequate physical infrastructure to facilitate bilateral and regional commercial exchanges. In most cases, however, China was mainly at the receiving end, not at the leading position, of cross-border transportation network projects initiated by multilateral organizations.

The current chapter situates BRI in its larger historical context by focusing on the regional projects predating 2013. It first examines several major regional infrastructure projects set in motion by multilateral institutions such as the United Nations, the European Union, and the Asian Development Bank (ADB), as well as by individual countries such as Japan, South Korea, and the United States. The next section then describes the importance of infrastructure construction for China's growth and surveys the country's initial attempts to connect to cross-border infrastructure networks.

Older Silk Roads

The idea of a Eurasian regional infrastructure network began to emerge back in the 1960s under the auspices of the United Nations. However, it was not until the end of the Cold War that several projects were rolled out, each of them facing a different set of difficulties, but all moved by the same ambition and hope for a seamlessly interconnected Eurasian continent.

On September 4, 1990, Soviet foreign minister Eduard Shevardnadze opened his speech at the second international conference on the Asia-Pacific region as follows:

> Europe and Asia, West and East, have long reached out toward each other, overcoming the walls of division, self-imposed isolation of individual countries, the nightmares of colonial occupation and enslavement, regional conflicts and material inequality. The great silk road transcended wars and violence, the thin silk thread of history linked together time and space. What was possible in the past appears all the more attainable in the present, with slow moving silk

caravans giving way to optical cable technology and electronics that can bring together in one single entity the formerly divided worlds.²

Shevardnadze went on to underline at great length the role Moscow could play, now that the Cold War had come to an end, in the "integration and development of a single Eurasian entity of security and stability." The Soviet Union enjoyed a unique strategic location, had extensive existing transportation infrastructure, and was willing to approach the issue of Asia-Europe integration with "respect, trust and cooperation" as guiding principles. It is one of history's mischievous twists that, two decades after Russia saw itself at the heart of Eurasian integration, China is now taking the lead in the same endeavor, using almost the same rhetoric.

As in so many other aspects of contemporary history, the end of the Cold War marks a decisive turning point in Eurasia's development of regional infrastructure. With the sudden end of the Cold War, the collapse of the Soviet empire, and the fragmentation of the Soviet Union itself, there was an opportunity for the newly independent Eurasian states to become integrated into the global economy. After decades of isolation behind the iron curtain, these nations would now be physically linked to their Western neighbors, opening new possibilities for commercial exchange. References to the revival of the historical Silk Road became commonplace at this time, and projects designed to consolidate a seamless trans-Asian transportation network, connecting the Far East with Western Europe, began to give a concrete shape to the idealized vision of an interconnected and economically successful Eurasian continent.

The following section will describe, in broad terms, the various cross-border Eurasian infrastructure development projects that have been put forward since the early 1990s. The purpose here is to show that, although they may have attracted less publicity than China's BRI, a number of transcontinental infrastructure projects—both multilateral and unilateral—have already been designed and, for the most part, completed (see **Table 1** for a summary of these projects).³

Multilateral Projects

Asian Land Transportation Infrastructure Development program. The UN Economic and Social Commission for Asia and the Pacific (UNESCAP)

---

² "Eduard Shevardnadze's Statement at Conference on Asia-Pacific," Soviet News, September 5, 1990, 298, http://www.t-k-p.net/yayinlar/cddrt/sovietnews/sovietnews%201990/sovietnews_6542_0990.pdf.

³ The programs related to South Asia and Southeast Asia are beyond the scope of this monograph and will not be addressed in this section.

TABLE 1 Multilateral and unilateral projects to promote an integrated Eurasian continent

Leader	Area covered	Project name	Objectives
UNESCAP	Entire Eurasian continent, from East Asia to Europe	• Asian Land Transportation Infrastructure Development Program (launched in 1992)	• Upgrade rail and roads • Build missing links • Harmonize cross-border regulations
TRACECA	Caucasus and Central Asia	• TRACECA (launched in 1993) • Silk Wind Project (launched in 2012)	• Upgrade rail and roads • Build missing links • Harmonize cross-border regulations
CAREC	Mostly Central Asia	• CAREC (formed in late 1990s)	• Promote economic development through transportation infrastructure and trade
Japan	Mostly Southeast and Central Asia	• "Eurasian diplomacy" efforts (since late 1990s) • Arc of freedom and prosperity (announced in 2006)	• Create transportation, telecommunication, and energy supply networks
South Korea	Korean Peninsula and beyond	• Trans-Korean railway (since 2000) • Iron Silk Road (announced in 2004) • Eurasian Initiative (announced in 2013)	• Integrate South Korea in Eurasian road and rail network
The United States	Afghanistan, Pakistan, and Central Asia	• Silk Road Strategy Act (introduced in Congress in 1997, 1998, 1999, and 2006) • New Silk Road Initiative (announced in 2011)	• Create a regional energy market • Facilitate trade and transportation • Improve border procedures • Enhance people-to-people relations

Table 1 continued

Leader	Funding	Goal	Results
UNESCAP	• World Bank • UN Development Programme (UNDP)	Promote economic development	Project is still ongoing, with some missing links; local cooperation has not been totally achieved.
TRACECA	• EU • European Bank for Reconstruction and Development (EBRD)	Facilitate recipient countries' integration into the world economy	Project has been slowed by a lack of commitment by both EU and TRACECA countries.
CAREC	• ADB • IMF • EBRD • Islamic Development Bank • UNDP • World Bank	Facilitate recipient countries' integration into the world economy	Lack of elite commitment has slowed project; soft linkages have been difficult to achieve.
Japan	• Official development assistance (ODA) • Japan International Cooperation Agency	Promote economic development leading to democratization and freedom	Initiatives were short-lived due to government instability; ODA was slow and complicated.
South Korea	• South Korea • Russia	Achieve Korean reunification	North Korea has been unwilling to cooperate.
The United States	• World Bank • ADB	Stabilize Afghanistan post-2014	Project has been thwarted by a lack of high-level and financial commitment.

has been promoting the idea of a trans-Asian railway, connecting Asia to Europe (Singapore to Istanbul), since the 1960s.[4] Because of the Cold War, this vision could not be realized, and it was not until the profound economic and political changes brought to the region in the 1990s that a new impetus to build such a transportation network was created. More outward-looking governments in Asia now recognized the potential for increased trade, not only with Europe but also among themselves. Taking advantage of this newly favorable situation, UNESCAP launched its Asian Land Transportation Infrastructure Development program in 1992, which comprised two main components: the Trans-Asian Railway and the Asian Highway networks. Between 1994 and 2002, UNESCAP's secretariat carried out studies of existing networks, identifying the routes of international importance linking regional capitals or major industrial and commercial hubs, pondering the project's economic feasibility, and reviewing the necessary technical standards and requirements. UNESCAP also sought to generate regional dialogue among the potential participants in order to minimize some of the politically induced local difficulties. The Intergovernmental Agreement on the Asian Highway Network was finally adopted in November 2003, and the Intergovernmental Agreement on the Trans-Asian Railway Network was adopted in April 2006.

When UNESCAP began its studies, the commission was faced with a composite of national road and rail networks, each primarily designed to serve domestic needs. There were great disparities in development among the existing networks as well as several missing links that prevented them from connecting seamlessly from one end of the continent to the other. UNESCAP decided to focus on maximizing the use of existing land transportation infrastructure and optimizing the use of limited available resources.[5] In particular, a new trans-Asian railway would offer four main routes for freight traffic between Asia and Europe: the northern corridor (China-Mongolia-Kazakhstan-Russia-Korea), the southern corridor (Thailand-Myanmar-Bangladesh-India-Pakistan-Iran-Turkey), the Southeast Asian corridor (ASEAN region and Indochina), and the north-south corridor (Northern Europe–Russia–Caucasus–Central Asia–Persian Gulf). UNESCAP's expert group meeting in Bangkok in 1995

---

[4] UNESCAP was established in 1947 as the Economic Commission for Asia and the Far East to assist in postwar reconstruction. For further details on the Asian Land Transportation Infrastructure Development program, see Pierre Chartier, *The Northern Corridor of the Trans-Asian Railway* (Niigata: Economic Research Institute for Northeast Asia, 2004), 10–19; and UNESCAP, *Review of Developments in Transport in Asia and the Pacific 2007: Data and Trends* (New York: United Nations, 2008).

[5] Keizo Kasuga, "Trans-Asian Railway," *Japan Railway and Transport Review*, June 1997, 31–35.

concluded that rail container traffic along the northern route to Europe not only was possible but could be highly competitive with the sea routes "if a proper package of transit times, tariffs and services [were] offered."[6]

Today, the Asian Highway network covers 143,000 kilometers (km) of roads and highways through 32 countries, while the Trans-Asian Railway counts 117,500 km of railway lines serving 28 countries, including 11,000 km of sections that have yet to be constructed.[7] More progress needs to be made in terms of upgrading the quality of some of the existing networks, developing intermodal facilities such as dry ports or inland container depots, and better using the region's extensive railway network for international freight movement. Moreover, physical links will need to be accompanied by a set of harmonized regulations for cross-border transit to facilitate trade and transportation while at the same time enabling control and preventing smuggling.[8] But the Asian Land Transportation Infrastructure Development program has already created a basic physical skeleton that supports smoother regional connectivity. Ultimately, however, the main driving force behind such regional connectivity is the political will of national governments. The next step, from UNESCAP's point of view, is to encourage strong institutional cooperation and coordination at different levels so that a transcontinental network can be fully achieved.[9] This process is ongoing.

Transport Corridor Europe-Caucasus-Asia. As UNESCAP was revisiting the idea of a trans-Asian transportation network, the EU also developed its own vision of an integrated subregional infrastructure system. As part of its greater neighborhood diplomacy and attempts to reach out to its newly independent Eastern neighbors, the European Commission launched the Transport Corridor Europe-Caucasus-Asia (TRACECA) assistance program in May 1993. The initial hope was that the development of a transportation link connecting the South Caucasus and Central Asian countries with Europe would strengthen regional cooperation, increase international investment in the region, and ultimately enable the related countries' effective participation in the world economy. Between 1996 and 1998, Ukraine, Mongolia, and Moldova joined the existing eight participants (Armenia, Azerbaijan, Georgia, Kazakhstan, Kyrgyzstan, Tajikistan, Turkmenistan, and

---

[6] Kasuga, "Trans-Asian Railway," 34.

[7] Maps of the Trans-Asian Railway and Asian Highway networks are available at http://nbr.org/research/activity.aspx?id=771. The maps have been reproduced with the permission of UNESCAP.

[8] UNESCAP, *Regional Connectivity for Shared Prosperity* (New York: United Nations, 2014), 25–26.

[9] Ibid., 74–75.

Uzbekistan), followed by Bulgaria, Romania, and Turkey in March 2000; by Lithuania as an observer in June 2009; and by Iran in July 2009.

In September 1998 the international conference "TRACECA—Restoration of the Historic Silk Route" was held in Baku, home of TRACECA's Permanent Secretariat in Azerbaijan. At this event, the participants expressed a collective interest in restoring a Silk Road rail route. The Basic Multilateral Agreement on International Transport for Development of the Transport Corridor Europe–the Caucasus–Asia was signed, laying the foundation for further institutionalized regional cooperation on railway and road transportation and commercial maritime navigation, as well as the unification of customs and documentation procedures.[10] The EU participates as an observer and as a source of funding: over the years, it has invested 180 million euros in 80 projects in the areas of infrastructure development, legal harmonization, safety and security in transportation, and trade facilitation and logistics.[11] The European Bank for Reconstruction and Development also financed a series of projects to modernize transportation infrastructure in some of the TRACECA countries.[12] Several projects aimed to develop and rehabilitate telecommunication systems in the region, in particular by laying down fiber-optic cables along rail lines. Approximately 15 million euros were allocated for the purchase and installation of equipment, with additional financing for system testing and personnel training.[13]

TRACECA nations quickly took the lead in promoting their own vision of what a subregional transportation network should look like. In 2012, they launched the Silk Wind Project, a multimodal rail-sea-rail network linking Kazakhstan to Turkey via the Caspian Sea and through the Baku-Tbilisi-Kars (Azerbaijan-Georgia-Turkey) rail link.[14] Over time, TRACECA's prospects for success appear to have declined for three main reasons. First, while the Silk Wind Project's Caspian link made some progress, financial, political, and

---

[10] Seçil Özyanik, "TRACECA: Restoration of the Silk Road," *Journal of Caspian Affairs* 1, no. 2 (2015): 1–12.

[11] "Central Asia—Transport," European Commission, https://ec.europa.eu/europeaid/regions/central-asia/eu-support-transport-development-central-asia_en.

[12] Teimuraz Gorshkov and George Bagaturia, "TRACECA, Restoration of Silk Route," *Japan Railway and Transport Review*, September 2001, 50–55.

[13] Levan Buchukuri, "The Role of Telecommunications in Supporting Regional Cooperation and the New Silk Road," MagtiCom, http://www.magticom.ge/magazine/2000-1/2000-1-13.html.

[14] A map of the Silk Wind Project is available from the TRACECA website at http://www.traceca-org.org/uploads/media/14_Presentation_Silk_Wind_07-11-12_eng.pdf. See also Richard Weitz, "Silk Wind Project in Central Asia and South Caucasus Gains Speed," Jamestown Foundation, Eurasia Daily Monitor, December 2012, http://www.jamestown.org/single/?tx_ttnews%5Btt_news%5D=40217&no_cache=1#.V6Ili00UXcs; and Sergey Radzhabov, "Silk Wind Railway Project Pulls in to Astana," Silk Road Reporters, April 2, 2014, http://www.silkroadreporters.com/2014/04/02/silk-wind-railroad-takes-kazakhstan.

geographic problems caused ongoing delays in the construction of the rail link, and its completion date has been repeatedly postponed.[15] Second, the EU and TRACECA countries have accused each other of a lack of interest in and support for the initiative. For example, in 2015, TRACECA's national secretary in Azerbaijan, Akif Mustafayev, told European representatives that in response to their perceived lack of engagement, TRACECA countries were considering working instead with Asian partners such as China and Japan. The European Commission, for its part, lamented the TRACECA countries' passivity and delay in preparing subsidized tariffs and simplified customs procedures.[16] Finally, the Silk Wind Project faces competition from China's faster new Eurasian land bridge line, which promises to outperform a multimodal link in terms of both cost and transit time.[17]

Central Asia Regional Economic Cooperation. The Central Asia Regional Economic Cooperation (CAREC) emerged in the late 1990s from a regional initiative for Central Asia led by ADB, modeled on its other subregional project, the Greater Mekong Subregion initiative. Following the same logic of spurring economic development through improved transportation and expanded trade, ten countries (Afghanistan, Azerbaijan, China, Kazakhstan, Kyrgyzstan, Mongolia, Pakistan, Tajikistan, Turkmenistan, and Uzbekistan) partnered with six multilateral institutions (ADB, the European Bank for Reconstruction and Development, the International Monetary Fund, the Islamic Development Bank, the UN Development Programme, and the World Bank). After a period of dialogue and confidence building among the regional partners—more than half of which were struggling to find their footing as independent nations in the aftermath of the Soviet Union's disintegration—the first CAREC senior officials meeting was held in 2001 and a comprehensive action plan was signed in 2006. The plan marked the beginning of dedicated cooperative efforts and investments focusing on three main areas: transportation (e.g., road maintenance and upgrades, as well as the construction of new highways), energy (e.g., electricity transmission and hydropower), and trade facilitation (e.g., customs

---

[15] Alexandros Petersen, "Kazakhstan Puts Components in Place for Caspian Shipping," Jamestown Foundation, Eurasia Daily Monitor, July 2012, http://www.jamestown.org/programs/edm/single/?tx_ttnews%5Btt_news%5D=39709&cHash=3e1a6a9852fe53b885ec7650c2d3281d#.V6Imbk0UXcs; and Vasili Rukhadze, "Completion of Baku-Tbilisi-Kars Railway Project Postponed Again," Jamestown Foundation, Eurasia Daily Monitor, March 2016, http://www.jamestown.org/single/?tx_ttnews%5Btt_news%5D=45159&no_cache=1#.V6DnFE0UXcs.

[16] Azad Hazanli, "TRACECA May Refuse to Cooperate with European Commission," *Trend* (Azerbaijan), August 15, 2015, http://en.trend.az/azerbaijan/business/2424645.html.

[17] "China Together with Russia Killed TRACECA Transport Corridor and Silk Wind Block Train," Azerbaijan Business Center, http://abc.az/eng/news/85650.html. Maps of TRACECA routes can be viewed at http://www.traceca-org.org/en/routes/gis-database-maps-downloads.

cooperation and trade policy). Increased cooperation in these domains is intended ultimately to reorient the region's economic links from an almost exclusive focus on Moscow to intensified interactions with each other and beyond. To transform the region "from landlocked to land-linked," CAREC invested $16 billion in 84 transportation projects, 26 energy projects, and 10 trade projects between 2001 and 2011.[18] By 2013, CAREC listed 108 transportation projects—32 ongoing projects (mainly focused on road improvements) and 76 new projects (mainly focused on railway construction and upgrades)—with a total cost estimated at $38.8 billion.[19]

Despite some improvements in the development of physical infrastructure, progress on the CAREC agenda has been much slower in the building of "soft" linkages, such as harmonizing the legal, regulatory, and administrative aspects of transportation, energy, and trade. Regional powers' extreme sensitivity about sovereignty and intraregional competition are some of the obstacles now facing CAREC. Under Chinese and Uzbek pressure, for example, the management of water resources has not been included in the program's agenda, and tensions between Tashkent and Dushanbe over the Rogun Dam hydropower project have been stirring tensions that are not conducive to increased regional cooperation. Poor local governance and accountability, pervasive corruption, and the lack of genuine commitment by regional leaders also create a bundle of challenges that appear difficult to overcome in the short term.[20]

CAREC's *Transportation and Trade Facilitation Strategy 2020*, endorsed in October 2013, sought to address these challenges and vowed greater efficiency and sustainability. However, as with the other regional cooperation schemes discussed above, the success of CAREC is hindered not so much by inadequate financial resources as by a lack of political commitment to regional cooperation on the part of current elites.[21]

---

[18] Asian Development Bank (ADB), *From Landlocked to Linked In: The Central Asia Regional Economic Cooperation Program* (Mandaluyong City: ADB, 2012); and ADB, *The New Silk Road: Ten Years of the Central Asia Regional Economic Cooperation Program* (Mandaluyong City: ADB, 2011), 116–19.

[19] ADB, *CAREC Transport and Trade Facilitation Strategy 2020* (Mandaluyong City: ADB, 2014), 19–20, http://www.adb.org/sites/default/files/institutional-document/34107/files/carec-ttfs-2020.pdf.

[20] Johannes F. Linn, "Central Asian Regional Integration and Cooperation: Reality or Mirage?" in *Eurasian Integration Yearbook*, ed. Evgeny Vinokurov (Almaty: Eurasian Development Bank, 2012), 96–117, http://www.eabr.org/general//upload/CII%20-%20izdania/Yerbook-2012/a_n5_2012_full%20version.pdf.

[21] For a map of the CAREC corridors, see ADB, *CAREC Transport and Trade Facilitation Strategy 2020*, 14.

Unilateral Projects

The idea of Eurasian regional integration has not been pushed only by multilateral institutions. Since the end of the Cold War, a number of individual countries also have sought to encourage greater subregional integration. In most cases, infrastructure building has been seen as a basic step toward promoting a stable and peaceful Eurasian continent by creating a physical connection that would encourage enhanced regional cooperation, much-needed economic development, and greater integration with the wider international community. Plans for a physically interconnected Eurasian continent, however, have usually run up against an array of political challenges. Much progress still must be made before, to paraphrase former Indian prime minister Manmohan Singh, one will be able to have "breakfast in Amritsar, lunch in Lahore, and dinner in Kabul."[22] The following discussion will examine unilateral efforts by Japan, South Korea, and the United States to improve regional integration.

Japan. Japan has been one of the most active countries in promoting infrastructure building across Asia. Following the so-called "Fukuda doctrine" presented in 1977 and backed financially by both ADB and Japan's official development assistance (ODA) program, Tokyo's assistance policy focused primarily on Southeast Asia. Economic aid was to be deployed around the region, regardless of the recipient's ideology, to create "heart to heart" relations between Japan and its Southeast Asian neighbors in order to benefit its geopolitical interests.[23] By the mid-1990s, Japanese diplomats started to recognize that the focus of diplomacy in a post–Cold War world had shifted from a transatlantic axis to an "axis spanning the Eurasian landmass," where newly independent nations were, in the words of Prime Minister Ryutaro Hashimoto, "making great efforts to establish affluent and prosperous domestic systems under a new political and economic structure."[24] The Caucasus and Central Asia's geopolitical importance, energy resources potential, and critical position at the crossroads between Asia and Europe nudged the Ministry of Foreign Affairs to pay more attention to the Silk Road region. This is in essence what Prime Minister Hashimoto told a corporate audience in July 1997. Japan, he said, "has a deep-rooted nostalgia

---

[22] "Breakfast in Amritsar, Lunch in Lahore, Hopes PM," *Hindu*, January 9, 2007, http://www.thehindu.com/todays-paper/breakfast-in-amritsar-lunch-in-lahore-hopes-pm/article1780445.ece.

[23] Gilbert Rozman, "Japan's Approach to Southeast Asia in the Context of Sino-Japanese Relations," *Asan Forum*, October 17, 2014, http://www.theasanforum.org/japans-approach-to-southeast-asia-in-the-context-of-sino-japanese-relations.

[24] "Address by Prime Minister Ryutaro Hashimoto to the Japan Association of Corporate Executives," Prime Minister of Japan and His Cabinet, July 24, 1997, http://japan.kantei.go.jp/0731douyukai.html.

for this region stemming from the glory days of the Silk Road," and he called for enhanced political dialogue, economic cooperation, and encouragement of democratization. Japanese private businesses were called on to play a role in creating "a transport, telecommunications and energy supply system," as well as to help with the development of regional energy resources.[25]

Japan's first foray into "Eurasian diplomacy" proved short-lived: Hashimoto stepped down in 1998, and the Japanese officials who had initiated the proposal moved elsewhere. At the same time, Japan entered an economic recession and had to revise its budget priorities.[26] Despite these changes, Japanese assistance to Central Asia and the Caucasus continued to increase: in 2003 the region received 5.8% of Japan's total bilateral ODA, compared with only 0.6% in 1995.[27]

A decade after Hashimoto's elusive Eurasian diplomacy, Foreign Minister Taro Aso embarked on an entirely new strategic direction for Japan's foreign policy. In late November 2006, he delivered a speech on Japan's expanding diplomatic horizons through the creation of an "arc of freedom and prosperity" spanning the outer rim of Eastern Eurasia.[28] Japan would deploy its economic and diplomatic resources and extend its development assistance to countries transitioning from autocracy to democracy across the entire Eurasian continent, helping Southeast Asia, the Caucasus, and Central Asia move down the road to "peace and happiness through economic prosperity and democracy."[29] The "arc of freedom and prosperity" label gradually faded, as it failed to gain domestic support for fear of antagonizing China and as Japan entered yet another period of governmental instability.[30] But Japan's overall approach has remained constant in its fundamental belief that socioeconomic assistance can help foster an environment that

---

[25] "Address by Prime Minister Ryutaro Hashimoto to the Japan Association of Corporate Executives."

[26] Kawato Akio, "What Is Japan Up To in Central Asia?" in *Japan's Silk Road Diplomacy: Paving the Road Ahead*, ed. Christopher Len, Uyama Tomohiko, and Hirose Tetsuya (Singapore: Central Asia–Caucasus Institute and Silk Road Studies Program, 2008), 18, http://www.silkroadstudies.org/resources/pdf/Monographs/2008_12_BOOK_Len-Tomohiko-Tetsuya_Japan-Silk-Road-Diplomacy.pdf.

[27] Yuasa Takeshi, "Consolidating 'Value-Oriented Diplomacy' towards Eurasia? The 'Arc of Freedom and Prosperity' and Beyond," in Len, Uyama, and Hirose, *Japan's Silk Road Diplomacy*, 58.

[28] Taro Aso, "Arc of Freedom and Prosperity: Japan's Expanding Diplomatic Horizons" (speech at the Japan Institute of International Affairs Seminar, November 30, 2006), http://www.mofa.go.jp/announce/fm/aso/speech0611.html.

[29] Ibid. See also Tomohiko Taniguchi, "Beyond 'The Arc of Freedom and Prosperity': Debating Universal Values in Japanese Grand Strategy," German Marshall Fund of the United States, Asia Paper Series, 2010, 2.

[30] Taro Aso left office in August 2007, while Shinzo Abe, then serving his first term as prime minister, resigned only a month later.

will ultimately lead to recipient countries' further democratization.[31] In particular, Japan's 2012 white paper on foreign aid reiterated that "expanding support for countries that share strategic interests and the universal values of freedom and democracy with Japan is crucial in attaining a free, prosperous and stable international community with the goal of securing peace and stability in developing countries."[32]

More recently, Shinzo Abe's government has seen infrastructure building as a potentially useful contribution to Japan's "revitalization strategy" to help the country's economic recovery. Infrastructure export occupies a dedicated section in the related official document issued in June 2013. Companies are called on to "use Japan's advantageous technology and know-how" and to "actively take into the world's huge demand for infrastructure" by raising sales from 10 trillion yen in 2011 to 30 trillion yen by 2020. Three regions are identified as deserving priority: the first comprises China and ASEAN; the second comprises Southwest Asia, the Middle East, Russia, the Commonwealth of Independent States, and Central and South America; and the third is Africa.[33] Asia remains the top priority for Japan's infrastructure investment, as shown by the Partnership for Quality Infrastructure launched in May 2015. The initiative promises to spend $110 billion in the region over the coming five years (half from Japan's ODA though the Japan International Cooperation Agency and half through ADB). Japan intends to leverage its comparative advantage and insist on "high quality" projects—clearly with the idea of challenging China's own regional infrastructure investments. Japan's projects claim to be environmentally friendly, disaster-resilient, based on each country's development plan, and built with local labor.[34] India and Southeast Asia are areas where Japan is still the most active in terms of development assistance, including infrastructure.[35]

---

[31] Maiko Ichihara, "Japan's Approach to Democratic Support," Carnegie Endowment for International Peace, March 7, 2014, http://carnegieendowment.org/2014/03/07/japan-s-strategic-approach-to-democracy-support-pub-54816.

[32] Ministry of Foreign Affairs (Japan), *Japan's International Cooperation 2012* (Tokyo, March 2013), 3, http://www.mofa.go.jp/policy/oda/white/2012/pdfs/all.pdf.

[33] Office of the Prime Minister (Japan), *Japan Revitalization Strategy—Japan Is Back* (Tokyo, June 14, 2013), 130, http://www.kantei.go.jp/jp/singi/keizaisaisei/pdf/en_saikou_jpn_hon.pdf.

[34] "Partnership for Quality Infrastructure," Ministry of Foreign Affairs (Japan), May 21, 2015, http://www.mofa.go.jp/files/000117998.pdf; "Follow-Up Measures of the 'Partnership for Quality Infrastructure,'" Ministry of Foreign Affairs (Japan), November 2015, http://www.mofa.go.jp/files/000112838.pdf; and "Towards Strategic Promotion of the Infrastructure Export," Keidanren (Japan Business Federation), November 17, 2015, http://www.keidanren.or.jp/en/policy/2015/105.html.

[35] C. Raja Mohan, "Raja-Mandala: Japan's Counter to China's Silk Road," *Indian Express*, November 24, 2015, http://indianexpress.com/article/opinion/columns/raja-mandala-japans-counter-to-chinas-silk-road.

South Korea. The Republic of Korea's efforts in cross-border infrastructure building stem principally from its desire to reunify the Korean Peninsula, but progress has been very slow due to North Korea's repeated refusal to cooperate. Article 19 of the Agreement on Reconciliation, Non-aggression and Exchanges and Cooperation between South and North Korea signed in December 1991, which theoretically provides the basis for increased bilateral cooperation, stipulates that the South and the North should link disconnected railways and roads and open sea and air routes.[36] But since the signature of the basic agreement, inter-Korean cooperation on transportation infrastructure has followed the ebbs and flows of the overall precarious relationship between the two Koreas. As part of UNESCAP's trans-Asia transportation network program, discussions started in 1996 regarding the possible construction of a northern line to link the Korean Peninsula to Europe via China or Russia. For this project to materialize, severed inter-Korean rail and road links would need to be restored and opened to enable the free flow of passengers and material goods. Following President Kim Dae-jung's 1998 announcement of a new Sunshine Policy to ease tensions with the North, Seoul submitted a set of concrete proposals to Pyongyang in different domains, such as humanitarian aid, business cooperation, and family reunions. Thanks to this momentary bilateral thaw, and following the historic summit between Kim Dae-jung and Kim Jong-il in Pyongyang in June 2000, the two Koreas agreed to reconnect the missing transportation links across the demilitarized zone (DMZ).

On paper, the Gyeongui rail and road lines are meant to eventually connect the peninsula from south to north—starting by traveling from Busan to Seoul, crossing the DMZ at Munsan in the South to Kaesong in the North, then passing through Pyongyang and extending northwest to China through Sinuiju/Dandong or northeast to Russia through Rajin/Khasan (see **Figures 1** and **2**). The 27 km missing link between Munsan and Kaesong opened in 2003. The Donghae line runs along the peninsula's eastern coastline, allowing South Korean tourists to take the train to the Mount Kumgang Tourist Region. The reconstruction of the 11.1 km cross-border section between South Korea's Jejin and North Korea's Gamho was completed in 2006, but North Korea's military authorities canceled

---

[36] "Agreement on Reconciliation, Non-aggression and Exchanges and Cooperation between the South and the North," December 13, 1991, available at http://nautilus.org/wp-content/uploads/2011/12/CanKor-VTK-1991-12-13-agreement-on-reconciliation-non-agression-exchanges.pdf.

the initial test run. Service was briefly restored to the railway in May 2007 before being closed down again in 2008.[37]

Seoul's primary goal is to establish a trans-Korean railway, and beyond that to connect with the Russian Trans-Siberian Railway and the

FIGURE 1   Rail connections between North and South Korea

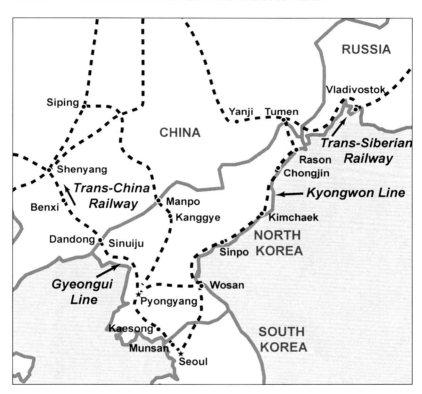

SOURCE: Jonathan Tennenbaum, "The New Eurasian Land-Bridge Infrastructure Takes Shape," *Executive Intelligence Review*, November 2, 2001, http://www.larouchepub.com/eiw/public/2001/eirv28n42-20011102/eirv28n42-20011102_016-the_new_eurasian_land_bridge_inf.pdf.

---

[37] Ko Chang-nam, "Present Status of Trans-Korean Railways and Plan for Connection with Trans-Siberian Railway," UNESCAP, http://www.unescap.org/sites/default/files/Rep%20of%20Korea%20-%20Present%20Status%20of%20Trans-Korean%20Railways.pdf; and Kevin Smith, "Sowing the Seeds for Railway Reunification," *International Railway Journal*, August 28, 2014, http://www.railjournal.com/index.php/asia/sowing-the-seeds-for-railway-reunification.html.

FIGURE 2 North Korea–South Korea rail network if connected

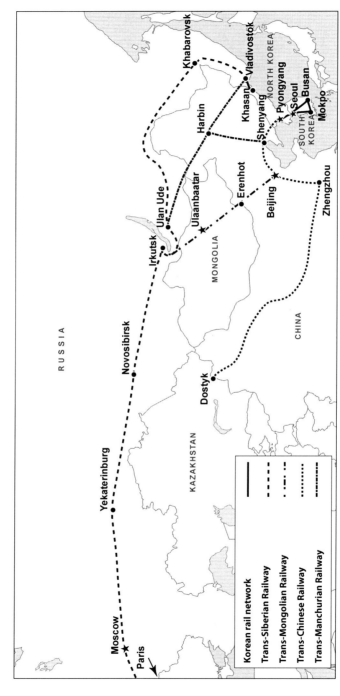

SOURCE: Ser Myo-ja, "Inter-Korean Railroad Faces Huge Obstacles," *Korea Joongang Daily*, May 21, 2007, http://koreajoongangdaily.joins.com/news/article/article.aspx?aid=2875760.

Chinese new Eurasian land bridge networks. This is the Iron Silk Road vision advocated by South Korea during the June 2004 Asia-Europe Meeting symposium auspiciously called "Iron Silk Road: Overcoming the Land Divide between Asia and Europe."[38] Being connected to the broader trans-Eurasian network would benefit South Korea economically. As the fifth-largest export economy in the world, the country currently relies heavily on cargo shipping, and train freight would cut transit time to Europe by half. Because of its geographic position next to one of the world's most isolated countries, South Korea is physically cut off from the continent, making it difficult to access natural resources, including energy, and markets in landlocked Eurasia. The trans-Korean railway is the central missing link to South Korea's land connectivity with the rest of the continent. Aside from the economic benefits, South Korean authorities also hope that interconnected transportation infrastructure could gradually encourage North Korea's opening up, eventually "recovering ethnic homogeneity based on increased personal exchanges between the two Koreas."[39]

President Park Geun-hye's Eurasia Initiative expanded on the basic idea of the Iron Silk Road. At an October 2013 international conference on Eurasian cooperation, Park put forward the slogan "one continent, creative continent, peaceful continent," which encapsulates South Korea's priorities with regard to its physical integration with the Eurasian continent: "one continent" is about unified land connectivity, "creative continent" is about encouraging a new type of growth for the country's sluggish economy by insisting on innovation and information and communications technologies, and "peaceful continent" is about reducing the security threats that linger over the Korean Peninsula, in particular.[40] The initiative envisioned a seamless transportation, energy, and trade network across Eurasia, supported not only by the construction of railways and roads but also by the opening up of Arctic sea routes and the gradual elimination of trade barriers, leading eventually to the realization of a regional trade area. A "Silk Road express" transcontinental high-speed railway crowned the vision. However, aside from the estimated $3.5 billion it would take to modernize the obsolete

---

[38] Na Hee-seung, "ASEM Symposium on an Iron Silk Road: Overcoming the Land Divide between Asia and Europe," Presidential Committee on Northeast Cooperation Initiative, June 2004, http://nabh.pa.go.kr/board/data/archive/337/329.pdf.

[39] Hwang Sang-kyu and Kim Gunyoung, eds., *50 Praxes for Better Transport in Korea* (Gyeonggi-do: Korean Transport Institute, 2014), 150–53.

[40] Park Geun-hye (remarks at the 2013 International Conference on Global Cooperation in the Era of Eurasia, Seoul, October 18, 2013).

North Korean railroad, the key precondition for the trans-Korean railway plan to be realized is peace on the Korean Peninsula.[41]

The United States. The Silk Road Strategy Act was introduced in Congress in 1997, 1998, 1999, and 2006. The act called for the United States to support the "economic and political independence of the countries of the South Caucasus and Central Asia" through strengthening democracy and the development of civil society, assisting in developing and maintaining border guards and customs controls capacity, promoting reconciliation of regional conflicts, providing economic assistance to allow the growth of private-sector and market-based economies, and developing physical infrastructure while removing impediments to cross-border trade. Although the act was never passed by the Senate, its different iterations and updates reveal a strong willingness to promote liberal values such as democracy, human rights, accountability, and market-based economics. Physical interconnectivity was seen as an important step toward the wider objective of bringing the Central Asian and South Caucasus republics more fully into the international system. As S. Frederick Starr explains, it was not until after the Taliban government was toppled in 2001 that Washington began to consider Afghanistan as part of Central Asia, and from then on U.S. policy emphasized Afghanistan to the detriment of the five Central Asian republics.[42]

As Operation Enduring Freedom got under way, building infrastructure that connected Afghanistan with its neighbors became a top priority for the immediate purpose of enhancing military logistics. In 2009, as the route passing through Pakistan became more vulnerable to attacks and disruption, the Northern Distribution Network became NATO's primary overland supply route (see **Figure 3**). Central Asia suddenly became critical to the military transit routes into and out of Afghanistan. Trucks loaded with fuel, food, and hardware would deliver their cargo to NATO troops through either Uzbekistan-Turkmenistan or Tajikistan-Kyrgyzstan-Kazakhstan. Immediately after the death of Osama bin Laden, President Barack Obama, acknowledging that "the tide of war [was] receding," announced in June 2011 his intention to incrementally withdraw U.S. troops from Afghanistan

---

[41] Ser Myo-ja, "Inter-Korean Railroad Faces Huge Obstacles," *Korea Joongang Daily*, May 21, 2007, http://koreajoongangdaily.joins.com/news/article/article.aspx?aid=2875760; and "Park Proposes 'Silk Road Express' to Connect Eurasian Nations," Yonhap, October 28, 2013, http://english.yonhapnews.co.kr/national/2013/10/18/16/0301000000AEN20131018003200315F.html.

[42] S. Frederick Starr, "A Regional Approach to Afghanistan and Its Neighbors," in *Strategic Asia 2008–09: Challenges and Choices*, ed. Ashley Tellis, Mercy Kuo, and Andrew Marble (Seattle: National Bureau of Asian Research, 2008), 335.

FIGURE 3   The Northern Distribution Network

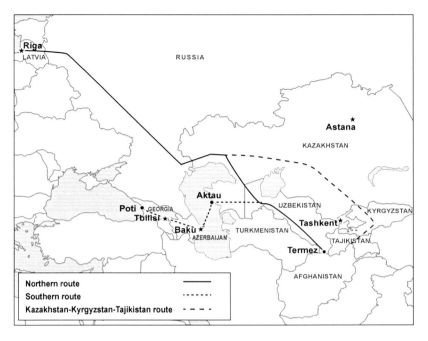

SOURCE: International Institute for Strategic Studies cited in Rayhan Demytrie, "Why Tajik Security Matters to Nato," BBC, December 14, 2011.

with the goal of ultimately handing over the country's security to the local authorities by 2014.[43]

Despite the impending drawdown in NATO forces, Afghanistan would still have to be stabilized, and one way to help advance this objective, as then secretary of state Hillary Clinton suggested in October 2011, was to integrate the country within a broader new Silk Road network. Afghanistan would be put "at the crossroad of economic opportunities" created by the 360-degree integration of the South and Central Asian economies around it. A "network of transit and trade connections" would open up new markets for natural resources and agricultural products, while trade barriers would

---

[43] Barack Obama, "Remarks by the President on the Way Forward in Afghanistan," White House, Office of the Press Secretary, June 22, 2011, https://obamawhitehouse.archives.gov/the-press-office/2011/06/22/remarks-president-way-forward-afghanistan.

come down, and more investment would be attracted.[44] The reasoning was that economic benefits would generate revenue that governments would in turn use to improve the overall security situation.[45]

The U.S. New Silk Road initiative has four prongs: (1) building a regional energy market by linking Central Asian suppliers to South Asian customers, (2) facilitating trade and transportation by reconstructing roads and railways broken by years of conflict, (3) improving customs and border procedures, and (4) enhancing people-to-people relations.[46] Its flagship projects are the Central Asia–South Asia electricity transmission line, which is supported by the World Bank and eventually will allow for the export of surplus electricity from Tajikistan's and Kyrgyzstan's hydroelectric dams to Afghanistan and Pakistan, and the Turkmenistan-Afghanistan-Pakistan-India gas pipeline, which is supported by ADB and expected to be operational by 2019.[47]

But efforts to improve Afghanistan's physical connectivity with its neighbors, reform counterproductive trade and border regulations, and promote free-market principles face a number of enduring challenges, including the lack of political support for U.S. initiatives in the region and local legal frameworks not conducive to business. The most critical issue remains Washington's own lack of financial commitment to projects not exclusively related to Afghanistan.[48] The United States' perceived disregard for its own New Silk Road initiative seems to be widely considered in the region as the root cause of its failure to make significant progress. As one panelist stated during an international conference organized in Istanbul in October 2013, "the New Silk Road was a strategy, then an initiative, now I guess it is a vision. It should be called an illusion and ignored. It was created by outsiders without reference to what is going on in the region."[49]

---

[44] Hillary Rodham Clinton, "Town Hall with Women, Youth, and Civil Society," U.S. Department of State, October 22, 2011, https://2009-2017.state.gov/secretary/20092013clinton/rm/2011/10/175985.htm.

[45] Malou Innocent and Tridivesh Sing Maini, "Bumps on the New Silk Road," Huffington Post, May 18, 2012, available at http://www.cato.org/publications/commentary/bumps-new-silk-road.

[46] "U.S. Support for the New Silk Road," U.S. Department of State, https://2009-2017.state.gov/p/sca/ci/af/newsilkroad/index.htm.

[47] James McBride, "Building the New Silk Road," Council on Foreign Relations (CFR), CFR Backgrounder, May 25, 2015, http://www.cfr.org/asia-and-pacific/building-new-silk-road/p36573; and Nate Bills, "Powering a New Silk Road: Helping Connect Supply with Demand in South and Central Asia," Frontlines, November/December 2014, https://www.usaid.gov/news-information/frontlines/afghanistan/powering-new-silk-road-helping-connect-supply-demand-south.

[48] Richard Weitz, "U.S. New Silk Road Initiative Needs Urgent Renewal," Central Asia–Caucasus Institute and Silk Road Studies Program, Central Asia–Caucasus Institute Analyst, March 4, 2015, http://www.cacianalyst.org/publications/analytical-articles/item/13155-us-new-silk-road-initiative-needs-urgent-renewal.html.

[49] Myles G. Smith, "While Central Asia Deintegrates, Washington Policy Crowd Envisions Integrated Future," EurasiaNet, October 29, 2013, http://www.eurasianet.org/node/67692.

China's Infrastructure Projects before BRI

Before it started to think about regional infrastructure connectivity, the Chinese government largely used infrastructure construction as a way to better connect its own large national territory, to promote domestic economic development, and to link the emerging Chinese economic powerhouse with the rest of the world. The following section will describe how infrastructure building inside China has been concomitant with the country's opening up and how it has progressed over time from the coasts westward and finally across China's borders.

The Role of Infrastructure in China's Economic Success Story

Before the reform era, Mao Zedong's pursuit of autarkic economic development resulted in the expansion of a transportation network in Northeast China, where heavy industries were located. Rail was chosen over roads to carry huge quantities of raw materials from resource-rich provinces to the country's Manchurian "rust belt." Under the central government's impulse, the railway network's length more than doubled between 1952 and 1978, from 22,900 km to 48,600 km.[50] After the Sino-Soviet split in 1963, Mao pushed for the establishment of a "third front" in the country's strategic interior, to provide for a possible fallback in the event of a Soviet attack. Hundreds of large and medium industries were established in remote areas in China's northwest and southwest, away from Russia's reach but also far from any suppliers or potential markets and isolated from the more vibrant coastlines. Major military bases were established in those areas, dispersed across the inaccessible regions, tucked between mountains, or hidden in caves. The 1,134 km Chengdu-Kunming railway was built between 1958 and 1970 across some of China's roughest terrain as part of this national inward pushback, but China's infrastructure network remained embryonic during the Maoist period.

With his opening-up policy, Deng Xiaoping took the opposite approach and gave clear priority to the development of China's coastal regions. At the beginning of the 1980s, a central investment plan designated energy and infrastructure as priority sectors. Yet it was not until a decade later, when the government acknowledged that chronic transportation congestion and bottlenecks hampered the smooth flow of raw materials to industrial centers

---

[50] Sylvie Démurger, "Infrastructure Development and Economic Growth: An Explanation for Regional Disparities in China?" *Journal of Comparative Economics* 29, no. 1 (2001): 98.

and goods to consumers, that it started to invest heavily in infrastructure.[51] Since 1992, China has invested an average of 8.5% of its GDP on domestic infrastructure, as the government has launched a series of landmark projects, one more grandiose than the next.[52] The Three Gorges Dam on the Yangtze River, now the world's largest power station, was approved by the National People's Congress in 1992 and became fully operational seventeen years later. The development of highways also soared. China's first expressway project, a link measuring over 17 km between Shanghai and Jiading, was completed in 1988. By 2002, the national expressway network had reached 25,130 km, representing an average annual growth rate of 44%. That same year, Chinese roads totaled 1.77 million km, carrying 14.7 billion passengers and 11.1 billion tons of goods.[53]

Transportation networks and hubs, electrical and telecommunication grids, and oil and gas pipelines have supported China's opening up, helped sustain its export-driven growth model, and transformed its landscape. In addition to policy reforms, cheap labor, and improvements in human capital, the expansion of the domestic transportation network has been identified as one of the major engines for China's economic growth and as a key factor in poverty alleviation in rural areas.[54] Farmers in extremely poor rural provinces have participated in construction projects such as road and irrigation development in exchange for government-provided vouchers for basic products and food.[55]

The People's Liberation Army (PLA) has also actively participated in building infrastructure throughout the country, using the experience and skills that its engineering corps acquired in national economic reconstruction after 1949, when one of its missions was to build bridges, railroads, factories, and irrigation canals, often through remote and inaccessible areas.[56] The PLA's Railway Engineering Corps only separated from the military in January 1984, when it was merged into the Ministry of Railways. The latter was dissolved in 2013 and replaced by three new entities: the Ministry of

---

[51] Barry Naughton, *Growing Out of the Plan: Chinese Economic Reform, 1978–1993* (Cambridge: Cambridge University Press, 1996).

[52] Yougang Chen, Stefan Matzinger, and Jonathan Woetzel, "Chinese Infrastructure: The Big Picture," *McKinsey Quarterly*, June 2013.

[53] Shenggen Fan and Connie Chan-Kang, *Road Development, Economic Growth, and Poverty Reduction in China* (Washington, D.C.: International Food Policy Research Institute, 2005), 17.

[54] Ibid.

[55] Shenggen Fan, Linxiu Zhang, and Xiaobo Zhang, *Growth, Inequality and Poverty in Rural China: The Role of Public Investments* (Washington, D.C.: International Food Policy Research Institute, 2002), 17.

[56] Dennis J. Blasko, *The Chinese Army Today: Tradition and Transformation for the 21st Century* (New York: Routledge, 2006), 172.

Transport, the China Railway Construction Corporation, and the State Railway Administration. Yet the link between the PLA and infrastructure building persists through some of China's major state-owned construction enterprises. Like its distant cousin, the telecommunication giant Huawei Technologies, state-owned China Railway Construction and its affiliated companies are direct descendants of the PLA.[57] Per its 2015 annual report, China Railway Construction—listed as number 100 on the Fortune Global 500 list—is the successor of the PLA Railway Engineering Corps.[58] The website of its subsidiary, China Railway Material Group, proudly declares that the company is descended from the Logistics Department of the PLA Railway Engineering Corps, which "made great contribution[s] in the War of Liberation and the War to Resist U.S. Aggression and Aid Korea by building the 'unbreakable transportation line.'"[59]

Since the beginning of the 1990s, expansion of domestic transportation infrastructure has been a preferred option for the Chinese government's national economic development planning. In the early stages of reform, the government gave preferential treatment to coastal regions in the hope that the country's backward interior provinces would benefit over time from growth spillovers. Deng had declared in 1984 that "egalitarianism will not work" and that it was alright to have some areas become rich first, as long as the leadership made sure that all would prosper eventually and that there was no polarization of society.[60] The coastal development strategy adopted in March 1988 called for economic development to extend progressively from the special economic zones to coastal cities, then to coastal regions, and finally to interior areas. But whereas the coastal provinces attracted massive FDI and developed rapidly, the rest of the country lagged behind, creating growing inequalities in regional per capita income. Nearly a quarter of the Chinese population lives in the western regions, which cover two-thirds of the country's land. Such development disparities have become a major challenge, not only for economic reasons but because of the resulting heightened risk of social conflict, complicated by ethnic, religious, or political factors in areas such as Tibet and Xinjiang. The Chinese leadership

---

[57] For some historical background, see Sheng Hong, Zhao Nong, and Yang Junfeng, *Administrative Monopoly in China: Causes, Behaviors and Termination* (Singapore: World Scientific Publishing, 2015), 219–20.

[58] China Railway Construction Corporation Limited, "2015 Annual Report," 2016, http://english.crcc.cn/s/1108-3817-1428.html.

[59] "About Us," China Railway Material Group Hong Kong and Macao, https://www.crmg-imex.com/en/aboutus.php?id=6.

[60] Deng Xiaoping, *Selected Works of Deng Xiaoping* (Beijing: Foreign Language Press, 1994), 45, 163.

sees regional imbalances as possible threats to the political stability and the unity of the nation and has long been looking for ways to close the development gap within the country for fear of social and political turmoil.[61] As will be explained in greater detail in chapter 3, BRI is the most recent iteration of the idea that infrastructure will help close the development gap and thus perpetuate stability across the country, including in its most backward provinces.

As Asia faced the 1997–98 financial crisis, the Jiang Zemin government, with Premier Zhu Rongji at its head, started to look for solutions to help boost economic growth and stimulate domestic demand, while at the same time addressing the growing problem of imbalances in regional development.[62] Investment in domestic infrastructure, coupled with preferential policies to boost industrial development by attracting more foreign investment, seemed to be a one-size-fits-all answer. The Chinese government consequently pledged to spend $1.2 trillion over three years on infrastructure development, relying on domestic spending rather than increased exports to promote future economic growth. It issued $12 billion in bonds in 1998 to fund new infrastructure projects.[63] The following year, the leadership launched its campaign to "open up the west" (*xibu da kaifa*), intending to promote economic growth in the remote western provinces. The State Council set up the Leading Group for Western Region Development in January 2000, led by Premier Zhu. Writing in 2007, Jane Golley, an economist at the Australian National University, noted that "virtually every policy document on the western region stresses the need to build infrastructure, which is clearly recognized as an essential aspect of the region's industrial capacity and competitiveness."[64]

During this period, most of the central government's capital investment went to developing transportation, communication, and urban infrastructure in these areas.[65] As a result, major western Chinese cities were connected to each other through a dense local, provincial, and regional

---

[61] David S.G. Goodman, "The Campaign to 'Open-Up the West': National, Provincial-Level and Local Perspectives," in *China's Campaign to 'Open-Up the West': National, Provincial-Level and Local Perspectives*, ed. David S.G. Goodman (Cambridge, Cambridge University Press, 2004), 3–20.

[62] Yongnian Zheng and Minjia Chen, "China's Regional Disparity and Its Policy Responses," University of Nottingham, China Policy Institute, Briefing Series, no. 25, September 2007.

[63] Wayne M. Morrison, "China's Response to the Asian Financial Crisis: Implications for U.S. Economic Interests," Congressional Research Service, CRS Report for Congress, 98–220, March 3, 1999.

[64] Jane Golley, *The Dynamics of Chinese Regional Development: Market Nature, State Nurture* (Cheltenham: Edward Elgar, 2007), 155.

[65] Hong Yu, "The Rationale, Prospects, and Challenges of China's Western Economic Triangle in Light of Global Economic Crisis," *Asian Politics and Policy* 2, no. 3 (2010): 442.

highway network spanning over 650,000 km with 150,000 km of roads linking local towns and villages. The railway network was also extended from east to west through the construction of the Chongqing-Huaihua section in 2000 and the Qinghai-Tibet line in 2001. In 2002 the vice minister of railways pledged that 40% of total spending on construction would be devoted to the west over a period of five years. Airports in Xi'an, Chengdu, Kunming, Lanzhou, and Urumqi started to be upgraded and expanded in 2000 in order to become regional transportation hubs.[66] Between 1999 and 2008, China implemented the largest domestic road and rail network expansion of any Asian country.[67] In 2006, Tibet was the last province to be connected to the national rail network upon completion of the 1,100-km-long Golmud-Lhasa line, which climbs to a maximum height of over 5,000 meters above sea level. The highest railway in the world officially cost $4.1 billion, a sum that many commentators saw as hard to justify in economic terms alone. The central government's main objective appears to have been to enhance economic and military control over Tibet and further exploit its mineral resources. By comparison, investment in other needed infrastructure, such as roads to connect local towns and electrification of rural villages, remained a lower priority.[68]

China's predilection for domestic infrastructure construction stands out as a favorite solution to stimulate growth in times of crisis. When the country was hit by the 2008 global financial crisis, the Chinese government planned to offset decreased global demand with proactive fiscal and monetary policies but also turned again to infrastructure investment as part of its $586 billion stimulus package.[69] Issued in late 2008, Central Document no. 18 laid out a ten-point emergency plan to increase domestic demand and thereby economic growth. Four points specifically identified infrastructure projects, including water, gas, and electricity projects as well as roads, railways, airports, and various other types of construction and reconstruction projects.[70] The stimulus package both financed new projects

---

[66] Hongyi Harry Lai, "China's Western Development Program: Its Rationale, Implementation, and Prospects," *Modern China*, no. 28 (2002): 432–66, http://www.case.edu/affil/tibet/tibetanNomads/documents/ChinasWesternDevelopmentProgram_000.pdf.

[67] Jonathan Holslag, "China's Roads to Influence," *Asian Survey* 50, no. 4 (2010): 641–62.

[68] Joseph Kahn, "Last Stop, Lhasa: Rail Link Ties Remote Tibet to China," *New York Times*, July 2, 2006.

[69] Barry Naughton, "China and the Two Crises: From 1997 to 2009," Japan International Cooperation Agency (JICA), Working Paper, no. 53, January 2013, 15–17.

[70] Liu Zebang, "Guanyu Zhonggong Zhongyang 18 Hao Wenjian" [About CCP Central Committee Document No. 18], November 26, 2008, http://liuzebang.2000.blog.163.com/blog/static/42248892008102644556842.

and accelerated the completion of projects already included under the 11th Five-Year Plan (2006–10).

As a consequence of the central government's stimulus measures, infrastructure investment, especially in urban areas, increased sharply in 2009. More than 60,300 km of expressways were built in 2008 alone, compared with 8,600 km in 2007, making China's expressway network second only to that of the United States in terms of length.[71] The "7-11-18" expressway network was set to eventually crisscross the country, with 7 roads radiating from Beijing, 11 running vertically from north to south, and 18 running horizontally from east to west. In 2008, China's railway system was already the world's third-largest network, with 6% of the world's track length, but the Ministry of Railways announced its ambition to expand the network from 78,000 to 120,000 km by 2020 and to lay 16,000 km of high-speed rail track, a target that was raised to 30,000 km in the 13th Five-Year Plan (2016–20).[72] To move the rapidly growing tonnage of cargo around the country and to keep pace with the needs of an increasing number of outbound Chinese travelers, the government also decided to develop and upgrade the existing airport network, with plans to expand the number of civilian airports in operation from 159 in 2008 to 244 in 2020.[73]

Cross-Border Infrastructure Building

China's appetite for infrastructure building has not been contained within its own domestic boundaries. Since the beginning of the 1990s, it has been involved in several cross-border infrastructure projects, mainly with its Southeast Asian and Central Asian neighbors. Although some of these projects were not initiated, financed, or led by Beijing, the central and provincial governments have seized the opportunity to increase regional connectivity, especially to the landlocked Yunnan Province and Guangxi Zhuang Autonomous Region in the south and to the Xinjiang Uighur Autonomous Region and Gansu Province in the west. The following discussion surveys the most significant projects.

Greater Mekong Subregion Economic Cooperation. The first such cross-border project was initiated in 1992 by ADB a year after China normalized relations with Vietnam. The Greater Mekong Subregion (GMS) Economic Cooperation program was designed to enhance economic

---

[71] Kai Yuen Tsui, "China's Infrastructure Investment Boom and Local Debt Crisis," *Eurasian Geography and Economics* 52, no. 5 (2011): 689–90.

[72] "Infrastructure in China: Foundation for Growth," KPMG, September 2009, 6.

[73] Ibid., 14.

relations among Cambodia, China (specifically Yunnan and Guangxi), Laos, Myanmar, Thailand, and Vietnam. The program focuses on high-priority subregional projects in transportation, energy, telecommunications, environment, human resource development, tourism, trade, private-sector investment, and agriculture.[74] The ADB philosophy motivating this project is that the increase in the flow of goods and people as a result of a highly efficient transportation system will further promote economic growth, stimulate regional development, and thus contribute to poverty reduction—an approach consistent with China's own.

The 1997–98 Asian financial crisis strengthened the GMS countries' resolve to cooperate and accelerate the pace of subregional economic development. The 1998 GMS eighth ministerial meeting, held in Manila, proposed that China and other member states build three vertical and two horizontal transportation corridors. The three vertical transportation lines would all connect to Kunming, Yunnan's provincial capital, starting from Myanmar, Thailand, and Vietnam. The east-west economic corridor, running through Vietnam, Laos, Thailand, and Myanmar, would eventually extend from the Andaman Sea to the port of Da Nang, on the shores of the South China Sea. A series of transportation links connecting major towns across the southern part of the GMS, via Myanmar, Thailand, Cambodia, and Vietnam, completed the project (see **Figure 4**).

The development of these transportation networks was subsequently designated as a flagship initiative under the ten-year strategic framework endorsed by the leaders of the GMS countries during their first summit, held in Phnom Penh in 2002. In March 2008, GMS leaders stressed the importance of transforming these transportation links into economic development corridors, maximizing benefits from improved physical connectivity in the subregion. According to ADB, around $11 billion in priority infrastructure projects either have been completed or are under construction.[75] The infrastructure connections created by the GMS initiative have helped the participating countries expand their cross-border trade. For example, by the end of 2012, Myanmar's transportation link connecting Yangon and Mandalay with China was recognized as the country's main trade corridor and a critical lifeline for its future development.[76]

---

[74] "Overview of the Greater Mekong Subregion," ADB, https://www.adb.org/countries/gms/overview.

[75] Ibid.

[76] Christian Ksoll and John Quarmby, "Private Sector Views on Road Transport along the Yangon-Mandalay-Muse/Ruili-Kunming Corridor," Greater Mekong Subregion Freight Transport Association, December 2012, 9, http://www.gms-cbta.org/uploads/resources/15/attachment/Private_Sector_Views_on_Road_Transport_in_Myanmar.pdf.

FIGURE 4   Greater Mekong Subregion economic corridors

SOURCE: "Greater Mekong Subregion Economic Cooperation Program," ADB, 2015, https://www.adb.org/sites/default/files/publication/29387/gms-ecp-overview-2015.pdf.

NOTE: Black lines represent economic corridors. Dashed lines represent possible extensions.

The Asian financial crisis marked the beginning of a decade-long effort on China's part to improve its relations with Southeast Asia, a period often referred to as China's "charm offensive." The first ASEAN +3 summit meeting (involving the ten ASEAN countries plus China, Japan, and South Korea) took place in Kuala Lumpur in December 1997 and was followed by incremental progress toward the creation of the China-ASEAN Free Trade Agreement.[77] It was during this decade of enhanced diplomatic engagement with ASEAN that China initiated the idea of a regional cooperation mechanism based on the development of transportation infrastructure—the Pan-Beibu Gulf Economic Cooperation project.

Pan-Beibu Gulf Economic Cooperation. The Pan-Beibu (Greater Mekong) Gulf Economic Cooperation (PBGEC) is another major subregional transportation infrastructure project, launched in July 2006 at the initiative of the Guangxi provincial government with the support of China's central government and ADB. At an inaugural forum in Nanning, the government of Guangxi proposed the idea of a "one axis, two wings" network, the axis being formed by the Nanning-Singapore corridor and the wings constituted by the GMS and the PBGEC.[78] Although the one axis, two wings terminology was abandoned because of negative reaction in Beijing, the central government approved the blueprint of a Beibu Bay economic zone plan in 2008.[79] In addition to China, the Pan-Beibu countries include Vietnam, Malaysia, Singapore, Indonesia, the Philippines, and Brunei—in other words, all the ASEAN countries (with the exception of Vietnam) that were not included in ADB's earlier GMS project.

The PBGEC's original objective was to give China a leading role in preparing the way for further economic integration via the China-ASEAN Free Trade Agreement, which was scheduled to go into effect in January 2010. The first stage of this new regional mechanism was to create a network of land, maritime, and air transportation infrastructure that would enhance trade and facilitate further cooperation at the institutional level. Despite China's ambitions, the initiative slowly lost momentum as the other Pan-Beibu countries showed a lack of engagement and commitment. Some evidently feared expanded engagement with their larger neighbor and wanted to be convinced that the Chinese initiative was "really a win-win scheme, not by words but by facts."[80] These misgivings were soon reinforced

---

[77] The initial framework agreement for the China-ASEAN Free Trade Agreement was signed in 2002 and went into effect in January 2010.

[78] Gu Xiaosong and Li Mingjiang, "Nanning-Singapore Corridor: A New Vision in China-ASEAN Cooperation," S. Rajaratnam School of International Studies, Commentary, October 24, 2008.

[79] Li Mingjiang, "Local Liberalism: China's Provincial Approaches to Relations with Southeast Asia," *Journal of Contemporary China* 23, no. 86 (2014): 275–93.

[80] Daisuke Hosokawa, "Pan-Beibu Gulf Economic Cooperation: China's New Initiative in Cooperation with ASEAN," *Osaka Keidai Ronshu* 60, no. 2 (2009): 76.

by rising tensions between China and some ASEAN nations over territorial issues and China's acceleration of its naval modernization programs. The other Pan-Beibu countries perceived these developments as being contradictory with China's professed desire for peaceful and prosperous relations with its neighbors. Still, four years after the project's launch, progress had been made, thanks mostly to China's own efforts. A number of expressways linking Guangxi to Vietnam were opened to public traffic, and an international passenger train from Nanning to Hanoi began operation on January 1, 2009. By this time, the Nanning-Singapore railway, estimated at 5,000 km in length, was almost complete.[81]

For their part, the ASEAN countries liked the idea of a seamless regional transportation network, but not necessarily under China's auspices. In October 2010 the seventeenth ASEAN Summit launched the Master Plan on ASEAN Connectivity, aimed at facilitating the creation of an ASEAN Community by extending the vision of an infrastructure network to building institutional and people-to-people connectivity.[82] Seeking to encourage an alternative to Chinese-led infrastructure development efforts, the Japan International Cooperation Agency offered strong support for the Master Plan on ASEAN Connectivity and its two main projects, which run in parallel from east to west across Southeast Asia. One project links Da Nang (Vietnam) to Mawlamyaing (Myanmar), and the other links Ho Chi Minh City (Vietnam) to Dawei (Myanmar) through Phnom Penh (Cambodia) and Bangkok (Thailand). The Maritime ASEAN Economic Corridor completes the picture of a subregion interconnected horizontally—in contrast with the vertical corridors envisaged by the GMS. The Japanese government also proposed an "Asia cargo highway," to be realized by 2020, and offered assistance in building cross-border operability, modernizing customs administrations, strengthening people-to-people relations (especially through the ASEAN University Network established in 2001), and sharing experiences in disaster management and maritime safety.[83]

---

[81] Lan Xinzhen, "Nanning-Singapore Economic Corridor," *Beijing Review*, August 2010.

[82] ASEAN, *Master Plan on ASEAN Connectivity: One Vision, One Identity, One Community* (Jakarta: ASEAN Secretariat, 2010), http://www.asean.org/storage/images/ASEAN_RTK_2014/4_Master_Plan_on_ASEAN_Connectivity.pdf.

[83] "JICA's Regional Cooperation in ASEAN," JICA, November 2012, https://www.jica.go.jp/english/publications/brochures/c8h0vm0000avs7w2-att/jica_asean.pdf. Uneven efforts and lack of experience by the recipient countries may prove major obstacles to the success of the Master Plan on ASEAN Connectivity. See Duong Anh Nguyen and Thanh Tri Vo, "Enhancing East Asian Connectivity: What Can ASEAN and Japan Do?" in *Navigating Change: ASEAN-Japan Strategic Partnership in East Asia and in Global Governance*, ed. Rizal Sukma and Yoshihide Soeya (Tokyo: Japan Center for International Exchange, 2015), 99–113.

New Eurasian land bridge. China's efforts to develop transportation links with its neighbors were not limited to its southeastern border. In addition to the connection to the north through the Russian Trans-Siberian Railway (via Manzhouli in northeast China) completed before 1949 and the Trans-Mongolian Railway (from Erenhot, at the Sino-Mongolian border, to Siberia's Ulan-Ude via Ulaanbaatar) completed in 1961, China's railway system eventually connected to the Soviet rail network to the west in September 1990. Because of the deterioration of Sino-Soviet relations in the mid-1960s, it had taken 36 years to finally complete the 20-km-long track linking Xinjiang's border town of Alashankou to Dostyk (Druzhba in Russian) in the Kazakh Soviet Socialist Republic. Freight trains began running across the border in July 1991, followed by passenger trains in June 1992. From that point on, Urumqi was directly connected by train to the then capital of newly independent Kazakhstan, Almaty.[84] With the establishment of this link, China and Kazakhstan signed an agreement in 1995 permitting Kazakhstan to use Lianyungang as its primary trade seaport.[85]

This cross-border railway was an extension of China's uninterrupted east-to-west line, connecting Lianyungang port in Jiangsu to Alashankou in Xinjiang, and became one of the two main transcontinental train routes linking China to Europe—the other being the Trans-Siberian Railway, or first Eurasian land bridge (see **Figure 5**). Thanks to China's connection with Kazakhstan and Kazakhstan's Soviet-era rail connection to Eastern Europe via Russia and Belarus, the new (or second) Eurasian land bridge was now open. Freight trains began operating on a regular basis, transporting produce and manufactured goods from China's eastern shores all the way to Rotterdam in the Netherlands. Several additional transcontinental routes linking China with Europe across Eurasia followed. Along the Trans-Siberian route, the Zhengzhou-Hamburg line opened in 2008 and the Suzhou-Warsaw line was launched in September 2011. Along the new Eurasian land bridge route, the Chongqing-Duisburg line was inaugurated in January 2011, and the Chengdu-Lodz line started operating in April 2013. With the exception of the Yiwu-Madrid line, which was inaugurated in December 2014 and is the longest rail link in the world to date, all these transcontinental Eurasian railways predate the Belt and Road Initiative.

---

[84] Shigeru Otsuka, "Central Asia's Rail Network and the Eurasian Land Bridge," *Japan Railway and Transport Review*, September 2001, 42–49.

[85] "JSC NC KTZ Has Signed an Agreement on Cooperation and Coordination with the National Government of Lianyungang City, China," Kazakhstan Temir Zholy, September 7, 2013, http://www.railways.kz/en/node/5544.

FIGURE 5 Eurasian land bridges

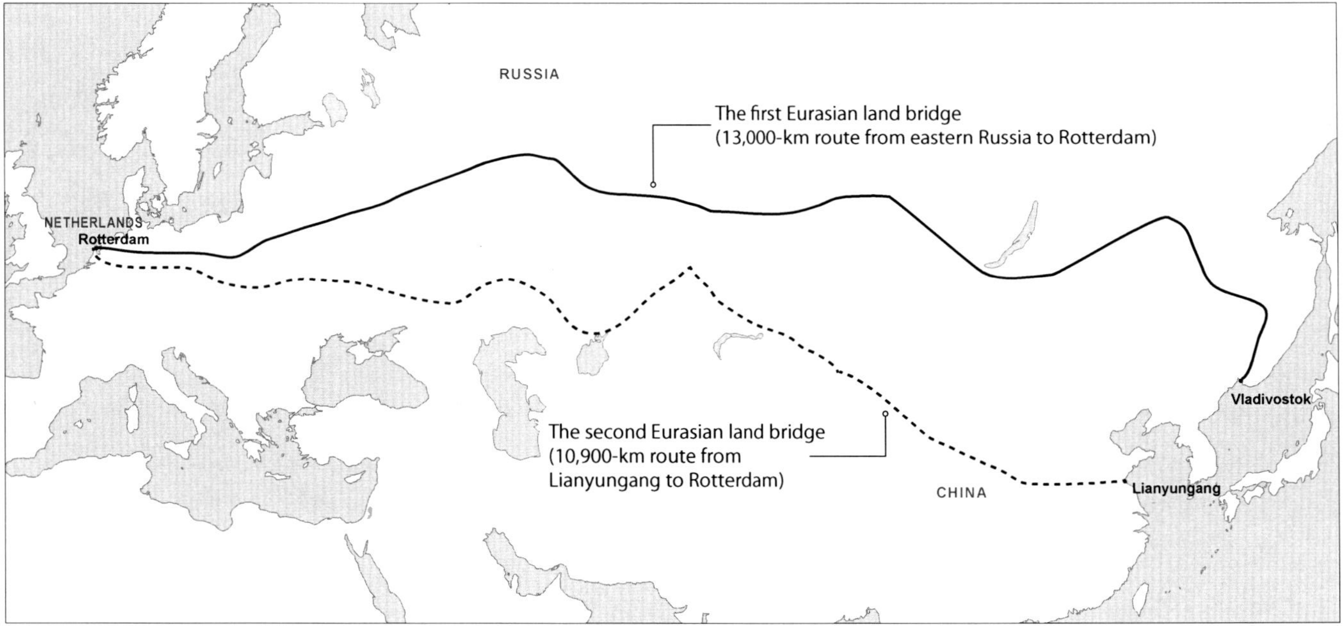
RUSSIA
The first Eurasian land bridge
(13,000-km route from eastern Russia to Rotterdam)
NETHERLANDS
Rotterdam
The second Eurasian land bridge
(10,900-km route from
Lianyungang to Rotterdam)
CHINA
Lianyungang
Vladivostok

SOURCE: Yunnan Academy of Economics.

With the establishment of the Eurasian Customs Union in 2010, which includes Russia, Belarus, and Kazakhstan, and the resulting gradual disappearance of border controls starting in July 2011, trains were no longer immobilized for several days for physical inspections. The transit time for container trains between Asia and Europe was reduced to only ten to seventeen days, 50% faster than ocean freight. Because of the difference in gauge width, one train cannot physically travel the entire route. Containers are transferred onto different trains when they leave China and connect to the former Soviet network and again when they reach Europe. This process generally takes less than an hour.[86]

A second China-Kazakhstan rail link, this time connecting Khorgos in Xinjiang to the Zhetigen logistics center near Almaty, was inaugurated in December 2011 as a result of a bilateral agreement on the Khorgos International Center of Boundary Cooperation signed in 2005 to simplify cross-border trading.[87] This second border-crossing point was expected to match the Alashankou-Dostyk line's freight volume, with up to 15 million metric tons a year initially and a long-term target of 30 million metric tons.[88]

As China started to normalize relations with its neighbors in the beginning of the 1990s and to accelerate its economic opening up, the construction of cross-border infrastructure emerged as a natural way to enhance exchanges with the region (see **Figure 6** for a map of the transcontinental Eurasian rail network). But laying rail tracks and asphalt does not automatically create regional prosperity. Progress is also necessary in logistics, infrastructure security, tariff harmonization, and the professionalization of customs administration.

Conclusion

Infrastructure is the physical manifestation of globalization. Roads, railways, pipelines, bridges, and airports are the vital sinews of trade and commerce—the conveyors of goods, materials, produce, and people; the epitome of openness; and the supposed antidote to economic isolation and backwardness. Several attempts have been made over the last three decades

---

[86] Wade Shepard, "Why the China-Europe 'Silk Road' Rail Network Is Growing Fast," *Forbes*, January 28, 2016, http://www.forbes.com/sites/wadeshepard/2016/01/28/why-china-europe-silk-road-rail-transport-is-growing-fast/4/#57f46b6c471a.

[87] Clare Nuttall, "Building the New Silk Road," *Business News Europe*, December 2012, available at http://www.mcps-khorgos.kz/en/smi-review/building-new-silk-road.

[88] "Second China-Kazakhstan Rail Link Inaugurated," *Railway Gazette*, December 24, 2012, http://www.railwaygazette.com/news/infrastructure/single-view/view/second-china-kazakh-link-inaugurated.html.

FIGURE 6 Transcontinental Eurasian rail network

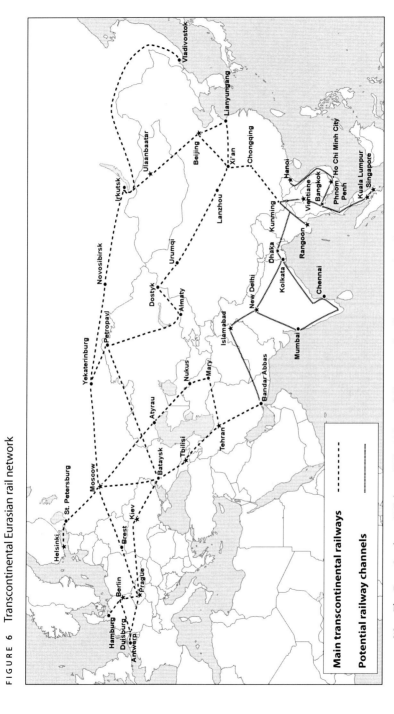

SOURCE: Wang Zhe, Dong Suocheng, Li Zehong, Li Yu, Li Jun, and Cheng Hao, "Traffic Patterns in the Silk Road Economic Belt and Construction Modes for a Traffic Economic Belt across Continental Plates," *Journal of Resources and Ecology* 6, no. 2 (2015): 79–86, http://www.jorae.cn/article/2015/1674-764x-6-2-79.html.

to build transcontinental or subregional transportation networks across Eurasia. It is not by chance that the great majority of these initiatives were launched right after the end of the Cold War. Whether led by a multilateral institution or under a regional country's unilateral helm, they all stem from the same hope that physical infrastructure would ultimately dissipate the remnants of Soviet-era autarky and unlock the socioeconomic potential of the newly independent states. The overarching vision and ultimate objective of all these programs was to enable the recipient countries' eventual integration into the liberal international order. Roads and railways crisscrossing Eurasia are not just meant to facilitate cargo transportation; they have a strong political component. Upstream, they suppose a level of cooperation and agreement among contiguous countries based on a shared will to open up and abide by liberal norms of free trade, reduced customs restrictions, and unimpeded people-to-people exchanges. Downstream, the proponents of these earlier programs hoped and assumed that the economic development brought by increased commercial and business activity would foster further liberalization and societal changes and eventually lead to democratization.

Many countries have been resistant to transregional projects predating the Belt and Road Initiative due to their reluctance to fully embrace the openness and liberalization subtext that came attached to infrastructure development as it was envisaged by the United Nations, the EU, or ADB. Because of the utterly political nature of transregional infrastructure projects, technical, geographic, bureaucratic, and even funding issues pose much smaller challenges to concrete progress than political resistance. Across Eurasia, rivalries among neighbors, the lack of high-level commitment, elites' reluctance to give up revenue generated by illicit trafficking, and their fear that opening their country to foreign passage will loosen their grip on power constitute the biggest roadblocks to transcontinental interconnectivity.

As described in this chapter, China has relied on infrastructure building for its own national development—notably as a tool to stimulate growth in times of financial and economic crises but also as a way to consolidate the central government's control over the country's remote frontiers. Since the beginning of the 1990s, China has also assumed an increasingly active role in subregional cross-border infrastructure projects launched by ADB as a way to help bring economic development to its own landlocked provinces. However, China has mostly remained focused on its own infrastructure network and has been a latecomer in the regional ventures.

China's BRI is the latest of an impressive list of ambitious projects to promote Eurasia's integration since the end of the Cold War. It bears similarities to some of the previous projects but also exhibits subtle, yet consequential, differences. The next chapter will look in detail at the initiative: its birth, its drivers, and its promises.

Chapter 2

The Belt and Road Initiative: Bigger, Bolder, Better?

China's "belt and road" was not announced with great fanfare, but almost inconspicuously, and separately, in the course of two speeches by Xi Jinping at the end of 2013—in Astana and then Jakarta. At first, even the Chinese media did not appreciate the importance of his reference to the need to create a 21st-century version of the historical Silk Road. Xi's poetic evocation of ancient caravans traveling across deserted lands was assumed to be a mere rhetorical tribute to an almost mythical time when traders used to be the conveyors of prosperity and the instruments of vibrant cultural exchanges between Asia and Europe. Yet all the key themes of what by March 2015 would officially become the Belt and Road Initiative (BRI) were already laid out in Xi's 2013 speeches: his vision of a Eurasian continent interconnected by "five links" (policy coordination, infrastructure connectivity, unimpeded trade, financial integration, and people-to-people communication), bound by the "Silk Road spirit," striving to build a "community of common destiny."

Xi's vision is not original. As seen in chapter 1, over the past 30 years, various plans for an interconnected Eurasian continent have been announced and, to varying degrees, implemented. Some of the Chinese-led projects that are now labeled part of BRI would have happened anyway, as a consequence of Beijing's standard practice of regional diplomacy and outreach. Is BRI just a repackaging of past policies or a relabeling of things that China has already tried more or less successfully? Is it just an empty slogan, now conveniently applied to every contract or agreement that Chinese government agencies or companies had been negotiating for years and would eventually have signed anyway?

As will become clear in the following pages, BRI cannot be compared with past regional connectivity projects. It is not just a series of engineering and construction plans linked together to complete a fragmented Eurasian transportation network but a thoroughly considered and ambitious vision for China as the rising regional leader, in which Xi has invested great personal capital, and which is backed up by considerable financial and human resources. As we have seen, post–Cold War attempts to connect

Eurasia through infrastructure development had the political objective of promoting liberalization in the former Soviet republics. As will be described in chapter 3, BRI has political motivations of its own. For now, the present chapter will focus on describing the initiative's many tangible manifestations since its launch in 2013, in the process demonstrating the scope and importance of BRI as an essential piece of Xi's domestic and foreign policy programs.

Only a few months after Xi's speeches, Beijing had created new financial institutions to back up BRI. It had rallied international support and begun to secure significant financial resources, created a central supervisory group, published a roadmap, mobilized the very best Chinese experts and intellectuals, embarked on an aggressive soft-power campaign, and dispatched Chinese diplomats, government officials, and business representatives to sign hundreds of agreements and memoranda of understanding (MOU) promising more trade opportunities and Chinese investment in neighboring economies. While some international commentators were tempted to dismiss BRI as an unachievable fantasy that would stall at the first frontier change in railway gauge, the Chinese central government's initiative has generated a substantial degree of interest, both across China and in potential recipient countries. Motivated by the prospect of getting a piece of the desirable pie, Chinese state-owned enterprises, provincial governments, media, and academic institutions have all quickly jumped aboard the BRI bandwagon. But their enthusiasm is not just the result of pure self-interest. Whereas efforts from such a diverse group of actors might at first give an impression of dispersion, a closer look reveals that they all converge in the same direction: serving the goals defined by the top leadership.

Across the region, from Finland to Poland, Azerbaijan, Kazakhstan, Pakistan, Malaysia, Thailand, and Hong Kong, businesspeople and policymakers have also started to pay attention to the economic opportunities that China's initiative might bring closer to their countries. Most of Eurasia's landlocked countries have been struggling to modernize their infrastructure networks. From their perspective, if China is willing to "find synergies" with their own development plans and offers realistic funding options, this proposition is worth considering, despite some existing misgivings about China's potential unstated political objectives. For Beijing, there is now a need to reap early harvests so that BRI, portrayed as a long-term plan that cannot transform the regional landscape overnight but will span over 35 years, does not suffer the fate of previous connectivity plans that failed due to lack of financial support.[1]

BRI saturates Chinese official statements and speeches, and Chinese popular culture has picked up on the same theme, inspiring a song depicting the initiative as "a new worldwide tide, mankind's beautiful quest"; a poem dedicated to Xi that rhapsodizes about "following the camel bell on 'One Belt, One Road' and the warm bliss from mighty ships and high-speed trains"; and a ballet performance with the Chinese historic maritime Silk Road as a backdrop for an epic love story.[2]

Yet, despite its omnipresence and top-level supervision, BRI remains—arguably purposely—an amorphous and ambiguous construct that even some Chinese analysts admit having difficulty in grasping. Many uncertainties linger about the initiative's actual content, its objectives, its feasibility, and even its reality. This chapter attempts to put together the most important pieces of this puzzle and to describe its concrete manifestations and broad contours. The first section focuses on how Xi's 2013 speeches portrayed BRI and describes how the initiative is supervised directly by the top leadership. Section two examines the significant financial resources that have thus far been deployed to support the initiative. The third section tracks the activities of Chinese intellectual elites, including members of think tanks, academia, and media, and considers how they have been mobilized to promote BRI both at home and abroad. The final section shows how Xi's vision has taken concrete form in "early harvest" projects along each of the six economic corridors that constitute BRI's backbone.

The Rollout of BRI

Xi Jinping's Astana and Jakarta Speeches

The Silk Road Economic Belt and the 21st Century Maritime Silk Road were both mentioned publicly for the first time by Xi, not together as "One Belt, One Road," but on two separate occasions. He announced the former during an address at Nazarbayev University in Astana on September 7, 2013,

---

[1] "Silk Road Economic Belt Construction: Vision and Path," Chongyang Institute for Financial Studies, Renmin University, Research Paper, no. 4, June 28, 2014.

[2] See Zhou Yanhong, "One Belt, One Road," https://www.youtube.com/watch?v=4ULQk-sM9H0; Hannah Beech, "Ode to Autocracy: Viral Poem Highlights Cult of China's Leader," *Time*, February 19, 2016, http://time.com/4230280/china-xi-jinping-poem-media; and "Guangxi daxing wuju 'Bihai Silu' chongxian 'Haishang Sichouzhi Lu'" [Guangxi Ballet Performance "Blue Sea Silk Road" Evokes "Maritime Silk Road"], news.163.com, April 17, 2016, http://news.163.com/16/0417/10/BKRMOK7H00014JB6.html.

and the latter during a speech given in front of the Indonesian parliament in Jakarta on October 2, 2013.[3] Kazakhstan and Indonesia, sitting respectively at the heart of continental and maritime Asia, were not chosen by mere chance as the official sites for the launch the Chinese "belt" and "road" ideas just one month apart. Xi's half-hour speeches both start with cultural and historical references meant to celebrate each country's bilateral relationship with China over the years. Xi mentions the Han Dynasty's special envoy to Central Asia, Zhang Qian, and the Ming Dynasty's Admiral Zheng He, whose seven naval expeditions all made stopovers in Indonesia. Moreover, setting each country at the heart of its broader regional environment, the two speeches praise the remarkable friendship and deep understanding between China and Central Asia, on the one hand, and China and the Association of Southeast Asian Nations (ASEAN), on the other. Both conclude with expressions of hope that the youth will continue to nurture bilateral ties and bring to life the full potential of enhanced cooperation through exchanges, which Xi promises to encourage by offering thousands of scholarships for local students to study in China.

The two speeches are similar in structure and are designed to convey the same message of China's willingness to cooperate more closely with its neighbors to promote common development and prosperity while respecting "the development paths and domestic and foreign policies chosen independently by the people of every country." The Jakarta speech posits that "the sea is big because it admits many rivers." The region should be tolerant of diversity, and nations should learn from each other. In an implied reference to non-Asian countries, possibly including the United States, Xi called for "other countries [to] also respect our region's diversity."

The Astana speech gives more detail about his vision for an "economic belt of the Silk Road" than the Jakarta speech gives about the Maritime Silk Road, only briefly evoked as China's way to increase connectivity and maritime cooperation with ASEAN. "To forge closer ties, deepen cooperation and expand the development space in the Eurasian region," Xi said, "we should take an innovative approach and jointly build an economic belt along the Silk Road," starting first in "individual areas," which would be linked over time "to cover the whole region." To achieve this aim, he called for policy coordination, infrastructure connectivity, unimpeded trade, financial integration, and

---

[3] For Xi's speech at Nazarbayev University, see Xi Jinping, "Promote Friendship between Our People and Work Together to Build a Bright Future" (speech given at Nazarbayev University, Astana, September 7, 2013), http://www.fmprc.gov.cn/ce/cebel/eng/zxxx/t1078088.htm. For a transcript of his Jakarta address, see "President Xi Gives Speech to Indonesia's Parliament," *China Daily*, October 2, 2013, http://www.chinadaily.com.cn/china/2013xiapec/2013-10/02/content_17007915_3.htm.

people-to-people exchanges. These five links give shape to and are at the heart of BRI's vision: regional policy cooperation and consultation are seen as the basis for regional economic integration, supported by a transcontinental transportation network connecting East Asia, South Asia, and West Asia. This plan encompasses an area "inhabited by close to 3 billion people and represent[ing] the biggest market in the world." People-to-people exchanges in parallel with relations at the state level will facilitate trade and investment, as well as monetary circulation in local and Chinese currency, while nurturing public support for regional cooperation.

The Silk Road, with its semi-mythical evocation of caravans of merchants traveling across Eurasia, is a powerful symbol that is supposed to bear "witness to the history of great glory in Asia" and conjure up the values of "peace, cooperation, openness, inclusiveness, mutual respect and resilience." A March 2014 editorial in the *People's Daily* argues that "if our ancestors could treat each other with respect as equals, work for mutual benefit and rise above occasional hostility 2,000 years ago, it is all the more pressing for us today to carry this invaluable legacy forward." But contrary to the ancient Silk Road, which "was mainly about trade in goods," BRI has "a much wider scope," notes the editorial. Regional integration, which will unleash Asia's formidable potential and "enhance the awareness of a community of shared interest and shared destiny for a harmonious Asia," is "an unavoidable phase towards economic globalization." Such a plan "cannot be done overnight" but will advance incrementally, from early-harvest projects to more difficult ones, from scattered spots to ultimately the entire continent. The initiative will rely on existing bilateral and multilateral mechanisms and build on already ongoing cooperative efforts. Finally, BRI is presented as benefiting not China alone but all participating countries.[4]

The proposed transcontinental belt (fully named the Silk Road Economic Belt) bears a resemblance to the ancient land-based Silk Road trade routes that linked China to Europe through Central Asia and Mesopotamia from antiquity to the beginning of the modern era. As described in official Chinese publications, the new belt will branch out to Southeast and South Asia and expand across the Eurasian landmass. This part of China's massive scheme is supposed to take shape around a network of roads and railways that will stretch across the roughly 11,000 kilometer (km) Eurasian continent. Together with a parallel network of pipelines, fiber-optic cables, and telecommunication links, this transportation infrastructure is seen as

---

[4] Zhong Sheng, "The Silk Road: From Past to the Future," *People's Daily*, March 11, 2014, http://en.people.cn/98649/8562370.html. Zhong Sheng, or "central voice," is a pen name used to convey official Chinese positions on foreign policy.

the first step in the creation of an economic corridor that will integrate the landlocked economies of the Eurasian hinterland and tie them more tightly to China. While the belt links Eurasia by land, the road (fully named the 21st Century Maritime Silk Road) will comprise a string of ports connecting China with Southeast Asia, South Asia, Africa, the Middle East, and Europe through the South China Sea, the Indian Ocean, and the Mediterranean Sea. Although official Chinese publications generally refer to BRI as including more than 60 countries, there is no official map publicly available that shows the exact locations of future projects. The full extent of Beijing's vision of an integrated Eurasian continent is only visible on the map released by China's news agency Xinhua in May 2014 (see **Figure 1**).

Top-Level Supervision

Since its inception, BRI has received extensive political, financial, and intellectual support from the top Chinese leadership. The national mobilization of resources and the hands-on, top-bottom management suggest that the initiative has rapidly become one of Beijing's highest priorities. Sources in China hint that Xi Jinping personally supervised the development plans with a small group of close advisers before his elevation to the post of general secretary of the Chinese Communist Party (CCP) at the 18th Party Congress in November 2012.[5] All major statements related to BRI have been made by Xi himself, and his personal identification with the initiative, similar to his association with the "China dream" or the anticorruption campaign, indicates its political importance.[6]

The Silk Road Economic Belt and the 21st Century Maritime Silk Road were officially endorsed at the CCP level soon after Xi's speeches in Astana and Jakarta—first by the work forum on China's periphery diplomacy (October 24–25, 2013), then by the Third Plenum of the 18th CCP Central Committee (November 9, 2013), and finally by the Central Economic Work Conference (December 10, 2013).[7] The belt and road henceforth

---

[5] During a December 2016 meeting in Beijing, National Development and Reform Commission (NDRC) representatives told the author that the Chinese Ministry of Foreign Affairs and the Chinese Academy of Social Sciences had started to work jointly on the idea in 2011, as the United States was launching its own New Silk Road initiative. Chinese Academy of Social Sciences and Renmin University representatives hinted at the fact that the belt and road strategy had been elaborated by Xi and a close circle of advisers before 2012. Author's interviews, Beijing, November 2015.

[6] Christopher K. Johnson, "China's 'Belt and Road' Initiative: Implications for Global Infrastructure Development" (presentation at the Center for Strategic and International Studies [CSIS], Washington, D.C., March 28, 2016).

[7] Zhong, "The Silk Road: From Past to the Future"; and "Chronology of China's 'Belt and Road' Initiatives," Xinhua, February 5, 2015, http://news.xinhuanet.com/english/china/2015-02/05/c_133972101.htm.

FIGURE 1 China's Silk Road Economic Belt and 21st Century Maritime Silk Road

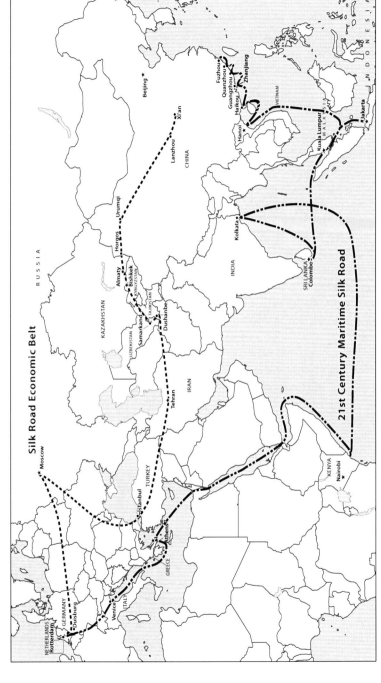

SOURCE: "West China Seeks Fortune on Modern Silk Road, Xinhua, May 15, 2016, http://news.xinhuanet.com/english/2016-05/15/c_135360904.htm. Originally published in Chinese in Xinhua, 2014.

became fully integrated into the central government's foreign and economic policies. From then on, all the government agencies and entities, including their related think tanks and academic centers, started to work on how to give substance to the initiative laid out by the Chinese leadership: Xi, the architect, had painted a vision with broad brushstrokes, and now the rest of the country had to provide bricks and cement to make it spring up from the ground.[8] The process took over a year. It was not until 2015 that BRI started to feature in the State Council's reports on the work of the government and in the 13th Five-Year Plan that lays out China's economic and social priorities and strategies for 2016–20.[9]

A central leading small group on "advancing the development of the belt and road" was set up in March 2015, indicating the central leadership's determination to coordinate all aspects of the initiative and oversee its implementation at the very highest levels.[10] Chaired by vice premier and Politburo Standing Committee member Zhang Gaoli, this new body includes four vice chairmen: Wang Huning, a key policy adviser to Xi and one of the fathers of the BRI idea; Vice Premier Wang Yang, whose portfolio includes trade, agriculture, and tourism; Yang Jiechi, a former minister of foreign affairs and state counselor; and Yang Jing, who serves at key coordinating positions within both the Central Committee and the State Council.[11] The backgrounds, ranks, and experience of these five men and their close ties to Xi provide further evidence of BRI's importance and its diverse facets and orientations: domestic and international, diplomatic and strategic, and economic. Beneath the leadership level, an office has been established within the National Development and Reform Commission (NDRC), China's top economic planning agency, in order to coordinate the work related to the initiative with the Ministry of Commerce and the Ministry of Foreign Affairs.[12]

---

[8] Author's meeting with a Ministry of Commerce official, Yinchuan, December 2016.

[9] Scott Kennedy and Christopher K. Johnson, *Perfecting China, Inc.: The 13th Five-Year Plan* (Washington, D.C.: CSIS, 2016).

[10] Central leading small groups are informal bodies used to advise the CCP Politburo on policy and to coordinate implementation of the Politburo's decisions. They are more important and powerful than the ministries. For further discussion of their role, see Cary Huang, "How Leading Small Groups Help Xi Jinping and Other Party Leaders Exert Power," *South China Morning Post*, January 20, 2014, http://www.scmp.com/news/china/article/1409118/how-leading-small-groups-help-xi-jinping-and-other-party-leaders-exert.

[11] Yi Ming, "Yidai Yilu lingdao banzi 'yizhengsifu' mingdan shou puguang" [Belt and Road Leading Group's 'One Head, Four Assistants' List of Names Published for the First Time], *Caijing*, April 5, 2015, http://finance.china.com.cn/news/gnjj/20150405/3041455.shtml.

[12] Xinyi Yang and David A. Parker, "Buckling Down: How Beijing Is Implementing Its 'One Belt, One Road' Vision," CSIS, cogitASIA, May 7, 2015, http://cogitasia.com/buckling-down-how-beijing-is-implementing-its-one-belt-one-road-vision.

With the release on March 28, 2015, of a document jointly issued by the NDRC, the Ministry of Foreign Affairs, and the Ministry of Commerce, the project was finally officially labeled the Belt and Road Initiative. Entitled "Vision and Actions on Jointly Building Silk Road Economic Belt and 21st-Century Maritime Silk Road," the document reads more like a general roadmap than a concrete and detailed proposal.[13] While clearly an attempt to give some structure to the government's vision, it consists of a laundry list of ideas, mixing ends with means and sometimes putting together concepts that appear contradictory. For example, it claims that BRI is "a positive endeavor to seek *new* models of international cooperation and global governance," while at the same time explaining that it will take "full advantage of the *existing* bilateral and multilateral cooperation mechanisms" (emphasis added). The document alludes to ill-defined concepts, such as the "Silk Road spirit," which is presented as a "historic and cultural heritage shared by all countries around the world," and promises that BRI will bring nothing less than "world peace." General concepts are enumerated to guide China's actions that are part of the government's usual arsenal of international relations jargon, such as "mutual learning," "mutual benefits," "win-win cooperation," and "closer economic ties and deeper political trust." The document proposes to "improve the international communications connectivity" and "strengthen financial regulation cooperation," without explaining how exactly these ideas will be translated into concrete actions. At the same time, it enumerates concrete measures in areas as diverse as cooperation in maritime logistics, civil aviation, ecology, literature, and the translation of television programs.

The "Vision and Actions" document was followed a few months later by a joint statement on standardizing the English translation of BRI, specifically demanding that "initiative" should be in the singular instead of the plural form and that the words "strategy," "project," "program," and "agenda" should not be used.[14] Most of the Chinese-language articles continue to use the word *zhanlüe* (strategy) instead of *changyi* (initiative). As Xie Tao, a professor at Beijing Foreign Studies University, explains, "initiative" conveys the idea of an open "call for action, on behalf of public good," whereas "strategy" implies

---

[13] NDRC, Ministry of Foreign Affairs, and Ministry of Commerce of the People's Republic of China (PRC), "Vision and Actions on Jointly Building Silk Road Economic Belt and 21st-Century Maritime Silk Road," March 28, 2015, http://en.ndrc.gov.cn/newsrelease/201503/t20150330_669367.html.

[14] Xie Tao, "Is China's 'Belt and Road' a Strategy?" *Diplomat*, December 16, 2015, http://thediplomat.com/2015/12/is-chinas-belt-and-road-a-strategy.

that there exists a "deliberate plan of actions" tainted with conspiratorial tones that the Chinese leadership would prefer not to communicate abroad.[15]

Xi Jinping conceived BRI as a new vision for China's foreign policy, one that would be distinct from that of his predecessor Hu Jintao. Although Xi articulated the initiative's general direction, he did not fully work out all of its details from the start. BRI's concrete implementation is an evolutionary process that can be adjusted and adapted over time, with each Chinese entity interpreting the concept to suit its own purposes and objectives. But the central leadership keeps a close watch on all activities related to BRI and works to better coordinate these efforts so as to prevent dispersion that could be detrimental to the initiative's ultimate objectives.[16]

All Aboard

The central government decided in December 2013 that the Silk Road Economic Belt would include the Chinese provinces of Shaanxi, Gansu, Qinghai, Sichuan, and Yunnan; the autonomous regions of Ningxia, Xinjiang, Inner Mongolia, and Guangxi Zhuang; and the Chongqing Municipality. The 21st Century Maritime Silk Road would comprise the provinces of Jiangsu, Zhejiang, Fujian, Guangdong, Shandong, and Hainan.[17] The March 2015 "Vision and Actions" document added to this list Heilongjiang, Jilin, and Liaoning Provinces, which would focus on cooperation with the Russian Far East (whereas Guangxi Zhuang Autonomous Region and Yunnan Province would reach out to South and Southeast Asia), as well as Henan Province and some key cities along the Yangtze River to improve cooperation with Europe.[18]

As a result, these provinces and regions have made BRI a development priority and featured the initiative in their annual work plans.[19] Motivated equally by the financial manna that has been promised for the related projects that will serve their own economic development and by the desire

---

[15] Xie Tao and Paul Haenle, "Is China's Belt and Road a Strategy?" Carnegie-Tsinghua Center for Global Policy, Podcast, January 19, 2016, http://carnegietsinghua.org/2016/01/19/is-china-s-belt-and-road-strategy-pub-62514.

[16] Author's interview with officials in the International Liaison Department of the CCP, Beijing, December 2016.

[17] Shao Yuqun, "Two Roads, but One Destination?" China-U.S. Focus, February 24, 2014, http://www.chinausfocus.com/finance-economy/two-roads-but-one-destination; and "A Score of Chinese Provinces Deploy 'One Belt, One Road' Strategy," Xinhua Finance, January 28, 2015, http://en.xfafinance.com/html/BR/Business_Activities/2015/77765.shtml.

[18] NDRC, Ministry of Foreign Affairs, and Ministry of Commerce (PRC), "Vision and Actions."

[19] "Prospects and Challenges on China's 'One Belt, One Road': A Risk Assessment Report," *Economist Intelligence Unit*, 2015, 6.

not to be left behind, 28 of the 31 Chinese provinces have indicated that they will actively participate in BRI's implementation.[20] Northwestern provinces and autonomous regions, such as Ningxia, Gansu, Qinghai, and Xinjiang, have rediscovered their Silk Road historical heritage and are now pushing their economic development agenda under the BRI umbrella.

The Ningxia Autonomous Region stands out as an interesting example of how a landlocked Chinese province has started to reinvent itself as one of the most dynamic centers for the revitalized Silk Road. Making the most of its Hui (Muslim Chinese) identity, Ningxia intends to become the main trade hub with Arab and Muslim countries, as shown by cooperation in the *halal* (permissible) food industry, the launch of a direct Emirates flight to the provincial capital Yinchuan, and the signing of an MOU with the Dubai Multi Commodities Centre, the United Arab Emirates (UAE) government authority on business and trade. The latter agreement is aimed at encouraging twelve thousand Emirati companies to engage in business with their Ningxia counterparts and link "producing and consuming countries in the West as part of China's 'One Belt, One Road' strategy."[21] The autonomous region expects that its integration in the BRI plan will help double its total import-export volume and foreign investment by 2017 compared with 2013.[22]

It is also a reflection of Ningxia's distinctive identity that, in coordination with the Ministry of Commerce and the China Council for the Promotion of International Trade, the provincial government hosted the China–Arab States Expo in September 2015 under the theme "carry forward the Silk Road spirit."[23] In one of the sessions specifically dedicated to the creation of an "online Silk Road" with Arab countries, Lu Wei, minister of the Cyberspace Administration, described Ningxia as the "pivot of cultur[al] communication

---

[20] "Yidai Yilu: Kaiqi chuhai xin langchao" [The Belt and Road Initiative: A New Tide of Opening Up and Going Out], *Guangming Daily*, February 5, 2015, http://theory.people.com.cn/n/2015/0205/c40531-26511569.html.

[21] For more on Ningxia's halal food industry cooperation, see "Inspired by China's 'One Belt, One Road' Initiative, Ningxia Launches International Cooperation in Halal Food Industry," PR Newswire, July 30, 2015, http://www.prnewswire.co.uk/news-releases/inspired-by-chinas-one-belt-one-road-initiative-ningxia-launches-international-cooperation-in-halal-food-industry-519826001.html. For more on Ningxia's deal with Emirates, see Rajwant Sandhu, "Emirates Launches Services to Yinchuan and Zhengzhou," *Gulf News* (Dubai), May 3, 2016, http://gulfnews.com/business/aviation/emirates-launches-services-to-yinchuan-and-zhengzhou-1.1817844. For more on the attempts to encourage business with Emirati companies, see "Dubai's DMCC and China's Zhongwei Sign MoU to Boost Trade Along the 'One Belt One Road,'" *MENA Herald*, June 23, 2016, https://menaherald.com/en/2016/06/23/dubais-dmcc-chinas-zhongwei-sign-mou-boost-trade-along-one-belt-one-road.

[22] Xu Jing, "'One Belt, One Road' Policy to Boost Ningxia's Cement Industry," China.org.cn, August 7, 2015, http://www.china.org.cn/travel/Ningxia/2015-08/07/content_36249149.htm.

[23] For more information, the China–Arab States Expo prospectus is available at http://en.casetf.org/u/cms/www/201506/15093948w6h9.pdf.

between Arab countries and China" and laid out multiple possibilities for closer digital cooperation.[24] A few months later, the Ningxia Silk Road ePath Company (SRP) signed an agreement with Egypt's Information Technology and Service Company for the joint establishment of a "China-Arab online Silk Road," which includes a trade information technology and service platform and a cross-border Internet payment platform.[25] Ningxia SRP also signed agreements with Dubai and Jordan.[26]

Understandably, BRI stands out as a promise of better opportunities for China's most remote and economically backward areas. For some of them, the initiative also created the prospect for a greater opening to the outside world. Gansu, one of China's poorest provinces, saw its role and objectives in the economic belt defined by the central government by the end of 2014: the blueprint underlines the province's crucial geographic position at the crossroads connecting China with Central Asia, South Asia, and West Asia. It specifies the province's industrial assets, highlights its tourism and cultural potential, and defines its special role as an "ecological protection screen" for the greater region. During a 2014 forum dedicated to the new Silk Road, China's Ministry of Foreign Affairs urged Gansu's provincial government to step up its international role by strengthening its partnerships and exchanges with governments and businesses in Central and West Asia, as well as in Eastern and Central Europe.[27] Xinjiang, too, is trying to burnish its international profile through events such as the Karamay Forum in August 2016, which brought together political and business representatives from Iran, Kazakhstan, Pakistan, and Uzbekistan. For these poorer provinces, greater interactions at the provincial level with foreign countries may create hope that the opportunities for economic development that the older "greater western development" program has failed to deliver will finally reach their frontiers instead of stopping at the coastal regions.

---

[24] "Lu Wei Delivers Keynote Speech to China–Arab States Expo Online Silk Road Forum," *China Daily*, September 10, 2015, http://www.chinadaily.com.cn/business/2015chinaarabforum/2015-09/10/content_21841735.htm.

[25] "Joint Establishment of 'China-Arab Online Silk Road' between SRP and ITSC," Ningxia SRP and Information Technology and Service Company, June 2, 2016, http://en.silkroad.cn/news/detail/109.

[26] "Ningxia to Develop Sino-Arab Cross Border E-commerce," Xinhua, July 20, 2015, http://news.xinhuanet.com/english/china/2015-07/20/c_134427176.htm; "New Deal to Facilitate China Auto Export to Arab Countries," Xinhua, September 12, 2015, http://news.xinhuanet.com/english/2015-09/12/c_134618323.htm; and "Strategic Cooperation Agreement Signing between SRP Company and Aqaba National Real Estate Projects," Ningxia SRP, May 20, 2016, http://en.silkroad.cn/news/detail/106.

[27] Xue Chaohua and Liu Xiangrui, "Gansu Set to Star in 'Belt and Road' Plan," *China Daily*, April 17, 2015, http://www.chinadaily.com.cn/m/gansu/2015-04/17/content_20440357.htm.

Thus, the provinces have embraced the central government's calls for them to play a greater role in BRI-related international outreach. The web of links that provincial governments are starting to create with countries adds to the density of China's overall diplomatic push toward its neighbors. Rather than dispersing the central government's efforts, they reinforce its general objective of greater regional integration. Although the diversity of actors elbowing to promote their own interests or vying for "Silk Road hub" status can lead to disorderly competition, when signs of possible unruly dispersion appear, the central government intervenes. This was the case in October 2016 when, faced with the emergence of a number of competing trans-Eurasian rail projects that would have undermined the potential of the network as a whole, the NDRC announced that only three routes would be pursued. A streamlined trans-Eurasian rail network under the China Railway Express brand will now provide higher-quality service than would have been possible with the plethora of rail services launched by local governments for the existing 39 rail links between China and Europe.[28]

In summary, Xi Jinping's visible personal involvement in designing the BRI vision, the creation of a central leading small group to oversee and provide top-down guidance, the NDRC's supervision of daily coordination and implementation across national agencies and ministries, and the central government's intervention in order to prevent competition among provinces all underscore the top-level nature of the initiative. Only the central leadership is able to mobilize the extensive resources, both financial and human, that are required for BRI's success.

Financial Resources

BRI is backed by the promise of considerable financial resources, some of which will be offered by new financial institutions created through Beijing's initiative on the premise that existing organizations cannot fill Asia's massive infrastructure funding gap. According to an Asian Development Bank (ADB) study published in 2009, $8 trillion would have to be spent on infrastructure during the 2010–20 decade to match the region's needs.[29] The World Bank and ADB, whose capital bases are $232 billion and

---

[28] "China Adds Fuel to Speed Up 'Railway Express' to Europe," Reuters, October 12, 2016, http://www.reuters.com/article/us-china-railway-europe-idUSKCN12C0EJ.

[29] Asian Development Bank (ADB) and Asian Development Bank Institute (ADBI), *Infrastructure for a Seamless Asia* (Tokyo: ADB and ADBI, 2009), 167, https://www.adb.org/sites/default/files/publication/159348/adbi-infrastructure-seamless-asia.pdf.

$160 billion, respectively, each spend roughly $20 billion within Asia every year.[30] Although China alone will obviously not close the entire remaining investment gap, other major lending institutions have welcomed China's efforts in helping finance Asian infrastructure projects that they see as complementing their own.[31] Whereas other lenders, such as ADB, finance a wide array of projects that include poverty reduction, social development, agriculture, education, and health, the China-led organizations will focus only on infrastructure projects, which will then be easily included under the BRI umbrella.

New Institutions: The Asian Infrastructure Investment Bank and Silk Road Fund

The creation of financial institutions outside the existing multilateral framework marks a turning point in China's foreign policy. Beijing's announcement of the creation of the Asian Infrastructure Investment Bank (AIIB) confirmed that Deng Xiaoping's exhortation to keep a low profile had been overturned in favor of a more proactive stance, a move signaled by President Xi himself during a CCP foreign affairs conference in October 2013, when he called for China to "strive for achievement."[32] China has been trying to increase its voting power in global financial institutions to better reflect its economic power, but to no avail. The establishment of such new institutions reflects its frustration over the World Bank and the International Monetary Fund's stalled reforms and its determination to take the initiative in "achieving" something instead of "biding time."[33]

---

[30] "Why China Is Creating a New 'World Bank' for Asia," *Economist*, web log, November 11, 2014, http://www.economist.com/blogs/economist-explains/2014/11/economist-explains-6; and "How China-Led Banks Could Help Plug Asia's Infrastructure Gap," Deutsche Welle, April 15, 2015, http://www.dw.com/en/how-china-led-banks-could-help-plug-asias-infrastructure-gap/a-18384803.

[31] "ADB Chief Welcomes Chance to Work with New China-Led Financier," *Japan Times*, November 27, 2014, http://www.japantimes.co.jp/news/2014/11/27/business/economy-business/adb-chief-welcomes-chance-work-new-china-led-financier/#.V79ewGV_i-8; and Jerin Mathew, "World Bank, IMF, Welcome Asian Infrastructure Investment Bank, Say This Will Boost Global Infrastructure Development," *International Business Times*, March 23, 2015, http://www.ibtimes.co.uk/world-bank-adb-welcome-asian-infrastructure-investment-bank-say-this-will-boost-global-1493112.

[32] Yan Xuetong, "From Keeping a Low Profile to Striving for Achievement," *China Journal of International Politics* 7, no. 2 (2014): 153–84; and Zhibo Qiu, "From 'Game Player' to 'Game Maker': New Features of China's Foreign Policy," Jamestown Foundation, China Brief, July 17, 2015.

[33] David Dollar, "Lessons for the AIIB from the Experience of the World Bank," Brookings Institution, April 27, 2015, https://www.brookings.edu/articles/china-on-the-global-stage; Erik Berglof, "What China's Scaling Up of Global Finance Really Means," Caixin Global, February 29, 2016; and Molly Elgin-Cossart and Melanie Hart, "China's New International Financing Institutions," Center for American Progress, September 22, 2015, https://www.americanprogress.org/issues/security/reports/2015/09/22/121668/chinas-new-international-financing-institutions.

Xi aired the idea of a new investment bank specifically dedicated to infrastructure during his October 2013 speech in Jakarta. One year later, 21 Asian countries signed an MOU in Beijing to establish the AIIB. After a few months of diplomatic back and forth, 57 countries, including 18 European nations but not Japan or the United States, gathered for the official signing ceremony in June 2015. The AIIB approved the membership of 13 additional countries in March 2017. Based in Beijing, the AIIB began operating in January 2016. It took just a little over two years after Xi's first mention of the possibility of a new bank for China to round up major countries' support and to begin operation. The speed of this accomplishment bodes well for the AIIB's promise to be flexible, swift, and lean in comparison with other multilateral lending institutions.[34] China retains 26% of the bank's voting power, enough for a veto on major issues, but in order to attract broad membership, Beijing gave up veto authority on policy and lending decisions. China's success in securing the participation of important extraregional countries helped allay suspicions that the new bank would be used as an instrument for expanding Chinese influence. Additional membership from major industrialized countries also strengthened the AIIB's access to capital markets and expanded its financial capacity.[35] When the AIIB was created, China was sitting on the world's largest foreign exchange reserves, which seemed to be headed toward a record-breaking $4 trillion. The loss of $500 billion in hard currency reserves in 2015 prompted concerns about capital flight and, as a consequence, about China's actual capacity to fulfill its $100 billion commitment to the AIIB. However, China's commitment is equivalent to less than 1% of its total foreign exchange reserves, and almost 70% of the bank's capital is drawn from its 56 other participants, which reduces the risk that the AIIB's plans will stall from a lack of financial resources or lending capacity.[36]

Additional funding for BRI projects is also expected to come from the Silk Road Fund, whose creation was announced by Xi in a speech

---

[34] European countries joined the AIIB despite strong U.S. opposition. This move was considered a major setback for U.S. diplomacy and greatly pleased Beijing. See Simon Denyer, "China Gloats as Europeans Rush to Join Asian Bank," *Washington Post*, March 18, 2015, https://www.washingtonpost.com/world/china-gloats-as-europeans-rush-to-join-asian-bank/2015/03/18/82139f88-9915-4a81-81af-ae6eacf528c7_story.html?tid=a_inl.

[35] Chris Humphrey, "Will the Asian Infrastructure Investment Bank's Development Effectiveness Be a Victim of China's Diplomatic Success?" in *Multilateral Development Banks in the 21st Century: Three Perspectives on China and the Asian Infrastructure Investment Bank* (London: Overseas Development Institute, November 2015), https://www.odi.org/sites/odi.org.uk/files/odi-assets/publications-opinion-files/10097.pdf.

[36] "The AIIB: The Infrastructure of Power," *Economist*, July 2, 2016.

to the Asia-Pacific Economic Cooperation CEO Summit in November 2014 and which became active in February 2015. To date, $40 billion has been promised for infrastructure, resources, and industrial and financial cooperation.[37] The Silk Road Fund receives 65% of its capital from China's State Administration of Foreign Exchange, 15% from China's sovereign wealth fund (China Investment Corporation), and the remainder from two policy banks, the Export-Import Bank of China and China Development Bank (CDB).[38] Unlike traditional aid agencies, the Silk Road Fund is supposed to be driven by profit: its chairman, Jin Qi, declared on the sidelines of the 2015 National People's Congress that "the fund is not an aid agency. We will seek reasonable mid- and long-term investment returns and protect the rights of the shareholders."[39]

Chinese Policy Banks

Aside from these new lending institutions created by Beijing, Chinese policy banks are also expected to help fund infrastructure projects included in BRI through the usual bilateral lending mechanisms. The CDB announced in May 2015 that it will invest over $890 billion in more than nine hundred projects involving 60 countries.[40] Similarly, the Export-Import Bank of China started to redirect its focus to BRI countries in 2015. It reportedly planned to finance more than one thousand projects in 49 countries, covering transportation, electricity, resources, telecommunication, and industrial parks, and has set up three cooperation funds for investment in BRI areas.[41] According to a report by the London-based investment bank Grisons Peak, the majority of the 67 overseas loans committed by the CDB and Export-Import Bank of China

---

[37] Xi Jinping, "Seek Sustained Development and Fulfill the Asia-Pacific Dream" (address to the Asia-Pacific Economic Cooperation CEO Summit, Beijing, November 9, 2014), http://www.apec-china.org.cn/41/2014/11/13/3@2580.htm.

[38] Zhang Yuzhe, "With New Fund, China Hits a Silk Road Stride," Caixin Global, December 3, 2014, http://english.caixin.com/2014-12-03/100758419.htm; and "China to Establish $40 Billion Silk Road Infrastructure Fund," Reuters, November 8, 2014, http://www.reuters.com/article/us-china-diplomacy-idUSKBN0IS0BQ20141108.

[39] Teddy Ng, "China's U.S. $40-Billion Silk Road Fund Will Be Driven by Profit, Says Its Chief," South China Morning Post, March 13, 2015, http://www.scmp.com/news/china/article/1736264/chinas-us40-billion-silk-road-fund-will-be-driven-profit-says-its-chief.

[40] He Yini, "China to Invest $900b in Belt and Road Initiative," China Daily, May 28, 2015, http://usa.chinadaily.com.cn/business/2015-05/28/content_20845687.htm.

[41] "China Exim Bank Boosts Lending to Belt and Road Projects," Xinhua, January 14, 2016, http://news.xinhuanet.com/english/2016-01/14/c_135010331.htm.

since 2013—with a total value of more than $49 billion—have gone to projects and countries along the belt and road.[42]

China-backed banks will not be the only ones to invest in BRI projects. Within four months of its launch date, the AIIB had approved four projects, three of which were jointly financed by existing multilateral banks, investing a total amount of $509 million.[43] The European Bank for Reconstruction and Development will co-finance a road linking Tajikistan's capital Dushanbe with the Uzbek border, and the World Bank will co-finance a $217 million loan focused on developing slums in 154 Indonesian cities.[44] For its part, the AIIB will solely finance a $165 million loan to provide electricity to 12.5 million people in rural Bangladesh.[45]

Other Possible Sources for Funding

Other possible sources for BRI funding include investment from the New Development Bank, established in July 2014 to support infrastructure development in the BRICS countries (Brazil, Russia, India, China, and South Africa). The bank has an authorized capital base of $100 billion and approved its first set of loans of up to $811 million for renewable energy projects in April 2016.[46] It also signed an MOU with the China Construction Bank in June 2016.[47] In the future, and if Beijing's hopes come to fruition, a new Shanghai Cooperation Organisation (SCO) Development Bank,

---

[42] James Kynge, "Chinese Overseas Lending Dominated by One Belt, One Road Strategy," *Financial Times*, June 18, 2015.

[43] "China-Backed AIIB Approves $509 Million for First Four Projects," Reuters, June 24, 2016, http://www.reuters.com/article/us-china-aiib-idUSKCN0ZA1RW.

[44] Svitlana Pyrkalo, "Road Project in Tajikistan Becomes First Joint EBRD-AIIB Investment," European Bank for Reconstruction and Development, June 24, 2016, http://www.ebrd.com/news/2016/road-project-in-tajikistan-becomes-first-joint-ebrdaiib-investment.html; and "Indonesia: Improving Infrastructure for Millions of Urban Poor," World Bank, July 12, 2016, http://www.worldbank.org/en/news/press-release/2016/07/12/indonesia-improving-infrastructure-for-millions-of-urban-poor.

[45] "AIIB Approves Half a Billion USD for Its First Four Projects in Bangladesh, Indonesia, Pakistan, Tajikistan," *China Daily*, June 25, 2016, http://www.chinadaily.com.cn/business/2016-06/25/content_25852075.htm.

[46] "New Development Bank Approves First Loans," South African Government News Agency, April 17, 2016, http://www.sanews.gov.za/business-world/new-development-bank-approves-first-loans.

[47] "New Development Bank Signs MOU with China Construction Bank," BRICS Business Council, BRICS Information Sharing and Exchanging Platform, June 13, 2016, http://www.brics-info.org/new-development-bank-signs-mou-with-china-construction-bank.

based on the SCO Interbank Consortium, will also help provide capital for infrastructure projects under the BRI umbrella.[48]

More generally, China is encouraging foreign investors, at both the government and private-sector levels, to join its BRI efforts. Premier Li Keqiang promoted the idea of joint investment in third countries during meetings with the French and Belgian heads of state, while President Xi welcomed British companies to participate.[49] Gestures have also been made in the direction of potential sponsors from Gulf countries and the Islamic Development Bank. The Chinese government has expressed interest in the possibility of issuing Islamic bonds (*sukuk*) to finance infrastructure projects.[50] During the first China-UAE Conference on Islamic Banking, Cheng Manjiang, chief economist for the Bank of China, explained how Islamic finance could boost cooperation between countries along Silk Road routes in Central Asia, the Arabian Gulf, and the Middle East.[51] In April 2016, International Enterprise Singapore, the first foreign government agency specializing in international trade to officially partner with China in investing in BRI projects, signed an MOU with China Construction Bank (CCB). Under its terms, the bank will provide $22 billion of financing services to support local and Chinese companies investing in BRI projects through Singapore.[52] Finally, international pension funds, private banks, insurance companies, and sovereign wealth funds have become interested in BRI's promise of long-term returns.[53] Realizing that the bulk of investment in infrastructure will not come from the AIIB but from capital markets, Bank

---

[48] Li Keqiang declared in December 2015 that China will consider the establishment of an SCO Development Bank "when the time is ripe." See "China Proposes Six Platforms for SCO Cooperation," Xinhua, December 15, 2015, http://news.xinhuanet.com/english/2015-12/15/c_134920075.htm. The SCO Interbank Consortium, created at the October 2005 SCO Moscow Summit in order to support regional economic cooperation, includes the China State Development Bank, Russian State Corporation Bank for Development and Foreign Economic Affairs, Development Bank of Kazakhstan, Tajikistan State Savings Bank, Uzbekistan National Bank for Foreign Economic Activity, and Kyrgyzstan RSK Bank. The Eurasian Development Bank, National Bank of the Republic of Belarus, and Development Bank of Mongolia became partners in 2008, 2012, and 2016, respectively.

[49] Lucy Hornby, "China Seeks Foreign Investors for One Belt, One Road Push," *Financial Times*, May 25, 2016.

[50] Bernardo Vizcaino, "China Turns to Islamic Finance to Expand Economic Clout," Reuters, September 22, 2015, http://www.reuters.com/article/us-islam-financing-china-idUSKCN0RM08020150922.

[51] "First China-UAE Conference on Islamic Banking and Finance Concludes with Positive Outlook for Future of Islamic Economy," Hamdan Bin Mohammed Smart University, May 30, 2016, https://www.hbmsu.ac.ae/news/first-china-uae-conference-on-islamic-banking-finance-concludes-positive-outlook-for-future-of.

[52] Calvin Hui, "IE Singapore, China Construction Bank Sign MOU for Infrastructure Projects," Channel News Asia, April 25, 2016, http://www.channelnewsasia.com/news/business/ie-singapore-china/2729416.html.

[53] James Kynge, "How the Silk Road Plans Will Be Financed," *Financial Times*, May 9, 2016, https://www.ft.com/content/e83ced94-0bd8-11e6-9456-444ab5211a2f.

of China, DBS Bank, Goldman Sachs, and Standard Chartered Bank have created a joint working group to support the development of a standardized Silk Road bond that could be traded internationally to help BRI countries tap a wider source of funds.[54]

In all, despite volatile market conditions surrounding the Chinese economy and the renminbi, financial support for BRI is growing rather than diminishing.[55] China is trying to leverage its own investments in order to get other governments, international organizations, and private actors to contribute to financing BRI projects.

Intellectual Resources

Aside from money, stunning quantities of gray matter have also been deployed in support of BRI. Intellectuals, scholars, academics, and experts from a wide range of fields have all been mobilized to serve two main objectives. First, these specialists provide analysis and advice to the central government about how to manage, implement, and further develop each concrete aspect of Xi Jinping's strategic vision. Second, they are encouraged to engage foreign counterparts in discussions about BRI. International conferences and roundtables provide opportunities to present the official narrative to an international audience, to cast China's efforts in a positive light, and to collect international reactions that are then reported back home. The importance of such intellectual exchanges for BRI should not be ignored. They are not incidental but play a crucial role in Xi's vision as the embodiment of the fifth link: people-to-people connectivity.

Think Tanks

The intellectual dynamism surrounding BRI reflects Xi's instructions, announced during the 18th Party Congress, to build think tanks "with Chinese characteristics" that would provide the authorities with high-quality expertise.[56] Chinese intellectuals, whether working in think tanks or

---

[54] Liz Mak, "Global Bankers Pledge Expertise to Foster Standardised Silk Road Bond," *South China Morning Post*, September 9, 2016, http://www.scmp.com/business/banking-finance/article/2017992/global-bankers-pledge-expertise-foster-standardised-silk.

[55] Sriram Muthukrishnan, "Financing the Belt and Road Initiative: Four Emerging Trends," HSBC, March 28, 2016, http://www.gbm.hsbc.com/insights/financial-institutions/financing-the-belt-and-road-initiative.

[56] Silvia Menegazzi, "Building Think Tanks with Chinese Characteristics: Current Debates and Changing Trends," Jamestown Foundation, China Brief, December 19, 2014, http://www.jamestown.org/programs/chinabrief/single/?tx_ttnews%5Btt_news%5D=43214&cHash=96ea82ace8eabffc5f9d35d431557923#.V9bA7mV_i-8.

university-based research institutes, are expected to offer consulting services for decision-makers. They are also encouraged to be part of China's overall soft-power effort to improve its international influence and "make its voice louder."[57] Individual scholars and analysts disseminate official policies during conferences and meetings with foreign counterparts and government representatives and bring back information and feedback on how official policies are perceived abroad.

With strong direction from the top, Chinese scholars and academics have taken the study and promotion of BRI to heart: according to the China Academic Journals Full-text Database, more than 8,400 BRI-related articles were published by Chinese scholars in 2015, compared with 492 in 2014. Over one hundred dedicated BRI research institutes and centers have also been founded in Chinese universities and think tanks in order to develop a deeper expertise on BRI countries' political, social, and economic conditions.[58] For example, in December 2013, just after Xi's speeches in Astana and Jakarta, five new think tanks were created in Xinjiang and three in Shaanxi.[59] Even when they are not specifically dedicated to BRI, research centers and institutes sometimes choose to incorporate their programs under the BRI label, including in the most unexpected domains: the Shaanxi Institute of Zoology, for example, is researching the impacts of BRI on the trafficking of endangered species of wild flora and fauna.[60]

International outreach is also substantial. When observed carefully, it is hard not to see an intentional soft-power push in this nationwide effort, driven by the top leadership and mainly aimed at influencing the perceptions of foreign audiences. Quite predictably, China's central government has sponsored the vast majority of BRI-related events that have been organized since 2014.

---

[57] Li Wei, "To Build High-Quality Think Tanks with Chinese Characteristics by Deepening Institutional Mechanism Reform," Development Research Center (DRC), State Council (PRC), January 22, 2015, http://en.drc.gov.cn/2015-02/05/content_19496964.htm.

[58] "China's Belt and Road Initiative Brings Think Tank Boom," Xinhua, March 2, 2016, available at http://english.chinamil.com.cn/news-channels/2016-03/02/content_6937942.htm.

[59] Ruslan Izimov, "Chinese Think Tanks and Central Asia: A New Assessment," Central Asia Program, Voices from Central Asia, no. 23, October 23, 2015, http://centralasiaprogram.org/blog/2015/11/04/chinese-think-tanks-and-central-asia-a-new-assessment. The Central Asian Research Center, Central Asian Center for Agriculture, Central Asian Biological Center, Central Asian Industrial Incubator Center, and Central Asian Information Technology Center were established in Xinjiang, and the Central Asia Institute, Institute for the Study of the Silk Road at Northwestern University, and the Central Asia Institute at the Xi'an Institute of Foreign Languages were established in Shaanxi.

[60] "Officials Receive CITES Enforcement Training Relevant to 'One Belt, One Road Initiative,'" Traffic, July 2016, http://www.traffic.org/home/2016/7/11/officials-receive-cites-enforcement-training-relevant-to-one.html.

President Xi's call for people-to-people exchanges has quickly materialized through increased international cooperation offers from Chinese think tanks to their counterparts in countries along the belt and road, mostly under the auspices of the CCP's International Liaison Department (ILD).[61] Through its in-house think tank, the China Center for Contemporary World Studies (CCCWS), The ILD acts as the national secretariat for the outreach activities both inside China and toward foreign think tanks along the belt and road.[62] The ILD has, for example, sponsored the creation of a "One Belt, One Road think tank alliance council" between the State Council's Development Research Center (DRC), the Chinese Academy of Social Sciences, and Fudan University in order "to promote better understanding of the 'One Belt, One Road' initiative." The alliance is also open to foreign institutes willing to promote the "Silk Road spirit of peace and cooperation."[63] The International Silk Road Think Tank Association was launched in February 2016 in Shenzhen with the support of the Shenzhen municipal government, Fudan University, and CCCWS.[64] Guo Yezhou, the ILD's vice minister, indicated that the association would help conduct "cooperative studies on the Belt and Road Initiative and submit objective research" to relevant countries' decision-makers in order to bring "real positive results."[65] Other intellectual platforms have sprung up, such as Research and Development International (RDI) established in 2015 and chaired by Zhao Baige, vice chairperson of the National People's Congress Foreign Affairs Committee. RDI, composed of the Chinese Academy of Social Sciences and the China Institute of Reform and Development, officially aims at providing "intellectual support to the 'One Belt, One Road' Initiative." RDI has partnered with Pakistan to establish a joint think tank dedicated to research on the China-Pakistan economic corridor (CPEC) and has been involved in discussions with Kazakhstan about possible increased cooperation between BRI and President Nursultan Nazarbayev's

---

[61] The ILD is the CCP's strong arm for foreign affairs. Originally tasked with spreading the revolution and fostering relations with other Communist parties around the world, the ILD now conducts diplomacy with all political parties, including in democracies. It is believed to have gained a greater role in the handling of China's foreign affairs under Xi because of his preference for the party over the state apparatus.

[62] Discussion with a delegation from the China Center for Contemporary World Studies, Washington, D.C., November 15, 2016.

[63] "Think Tanks to Promote 'One Belt, One Road' Cooperation," *Chinese Social Sciences Today*, April 23, 2015, http://www.csstoday.com/Item/1991.aspx.

[64] He Na, "Think Tank to Support Belt and Road Initiative," *China Daily*, February 24, 2016, http://usa.chinadaily.com.cn/epaper/2016-02/24/content_23629041.htm.

[65] "China Launches Cross-Border Think Tank," China Central Television, February 23, 2016, http://english.cntv.cn/2016/02/23/VIDEKMrsJajyb6O6LXPve8PP160223.shtml.

Bright Path (Nurly Zhol) initiative.[66] Together with Tsinghua University and the Shanghai Institute for Strategic Studies, RDI also organized a 21-day seminar sponsored by the Chinese Ministry of Commerce. The seminar gathered government officials from sixteen European countries, including Belarus, Bulgaria, Latvia, Macedonia, Serbia, Slovakia, and Slovenia, to discuss "joint governance" issues along the belt and road.[67]

Finally, Cheng Guoqiang, the director general of the DRC Department of International Cooperation, suggested in 2014 that a network be created jointly by "all think-tanks interested in international development issues and the Belt and Road initiative" in order to "contribute wisdom and offer strategic suggestions" for BRI.[68] The Silk Road Think Tank Network (SiLKS), co-founded by the State Council, the DRC, and the Serbia-based Center for International Relations and Sustainable Development, was established in Madrid in October 2015, with the official objective of promoting "economic cooperation, cultural inclusiveness, peace and development throughout the world." SiLKS claims that it has 43 members and partners, including think tanks and international organizations from 27 countries.[69]

Universities

Chinese universities have also been reaching out and seeking closer cooperation with their counterparts along the belt and road. The University Alliance of the Silk Road, composed of 60 universities from 22 countries, was inaugurated in Xi'an in May 2015. Its declared objective is to "contribute to the common development of civilization and open collaboration in higher education." Xi'an Jiaotong University, which serves as the hub for the new alliance and specializes in science, technology, and engineering, has pushed for increasing student exchanges, developing research partnerships, and establishing joint laboratories through its new Collaborative Innovation

---

[66] For more on cooperation with Pakistan, see "Establishing a New Type of Think Tank Platform, Pooling Resources to Develop 'One Belt One Road' Community: Zhao Baige," *China Daily*, November 9, 2015, http://europe.chinadaily.com.cn/business/2015-11/09/content_22406500.htm. For more on cooperation with Kazakhstan, see "China-Kazakhstan Cooperation Development Seminar Held in Jiangyin," Wuxi China, April 8, 2016, http://en.wuxi.gov.cn/sitePages/subPages/1300350001386793.html?sourceChannelId=23296&did=337393.

[67] "2016 nian Sichouzhi Lu Jingji Dai yu Zhongguo-Zhongdong'ou Guojia Hezuo Duijie Zhili Nengli Yanxiu Ban juxing jieye dianli" [2016 Silk Road Economic Belt Study Course on Chinese-Eastern and Central European Joint Governance Capability Holds Graduation Ceremony], *China Daily*, May 5, 2016, http://caijing.chinadaily.com.cn/2016-05/05/content_25076868.htm.

[68] Cheng Guoqiang, "Deepen Think-Tanks Cooperation and Jointly Build Silk Roads," DRC, December 12, 2014, http://en.drc.gov.cn/2014-12/15/content_19090672.htm.

[69] "Declaration of SiLKS," DRC, http://en.drc.gov.cn/2015-10/30/content_22355908.htm; and "Silk Road Forum Held in Madrid," Center for International Relations and Sustainable Development, October 29, 2015, http://www.cirsd.org/en/news/silk-road-forum-held-in-madrid.

Center of Silk Road Economic Belt Research, launched in January 2015. This emphasis on international cooperation not only boosts Xi'an Jiaotong University's international credentials but clearly serves the party-state's national economic objectives to enhance scientific and technological innovation.[70] Some of Europe's most advanced technological engineering universities, such as France's Supélec, Berlin's Technical University, Milan's Polytechnic University, and Finland's Tampere University of Technology, are part of the alliance, which primarily focuses on "superconnectivity" along the Silk Road route. Technological transfers, joint research, and innovation are crucial elements of the partnerships established under the alliance, which hopes to create 23 research centers and integrate more than twenty thousand professionals around the world.[71] This ambitious program to attract foreign experts under the BRI umbrella is consistent with China's national research and development plan, which partially relies on foreign scientific expertise to enhance China's own high-tech industries.[72] By the same token, China plans to attract more foreign students and to partner with the world's leading universities in programs related to major international science projects.[73]

This nascent "academic Silk Road" is accompanied by Beijing's promise to send 2,500 Chinese students to BRI nations over the next three years. If China plans to venture outside its borders, to areas where neither English nor Chinese is the main vernacular language, Chinese students will have to learn foreign languages such as Turkic, Arabic, and even Polish and Serbian. In anticipation of this upcoming need for linguists, some Chinese universities have already started to offer new "untraditional" foreign-language programs.[74] China has also promised to provide ten thousand new scholarships to students from Silk Road countries over

---

[70] Yojana Sharma, "University Collaboration Takes the Silk Road Route," University World News, June 12, 2015, http://www.universityworldnews.com/article.php?story=20150611130705830.

[71] "Announcement of 'Xi'an Consensus' by University Alliance of Silk Road," Xi'an Jiaotong University, April 9, 2016, http://en.xjtu.edu.cn/info/1043/1917.htm; and Hao Nan and Lu Hongyan, "Xi'an Special: Alliance Unites Higher Education along Silk Road Route," China Daily, May 29, 2015, http://www.chinadaily.com.cn/cndy/2015-05/29/content_20851031.htm.

[72] "China Inaugurates National R&D Plan," Chinese Academy of Sciences, February 17, 2016, http://english.cas.cn/newsroom/china_research/201602/t20160217_159669.shtml; and "The Recruitment Program for Innovative Talents (Long Term)," Recruitment Plan of Global Experts, http://www.1000plan.org/en.

[73] "China Focus: China to Boost Import, Export in Ambitious Education Plan," Xinhua, April 29, 2016, http://news.xinhuanet.com/english/2016-04/29/c_135323984.htm.

[74] Chen Ximeng, "Multilingual Education Gains Rising Popularity in the Middle Kingdom Due to the One Belt, One Road Initiative," Global Times, July 10, 2016, http://www.globaltimes.cn/content/993206.shtml.

the next five years.⁷⁵ Yunnan hopes to become the academic hub for international students from Southeast Asia, including public officials in need of governance and technical training, while Xinjiang aims to serve as a hub for Central, South, and West Asia.⁷⁶ According to China's Ministry of Education, roughly half of the 377,000 international students who studied in China in 2014 came from BRI countries.⁷⁷ Considering the central government's ambition to foster people-to-people bonds under BRI, there is a strong possibility that more students from BRI countries will travel to China to pursue their higher education.

China's use of academic exchange is an effective diplomatic tool for engaging neighbors and enhancing its influence across BRI countries: practical programs in Chinese universities can attract students from regional states that still lack adequate educational infrastructure, while the benign appeal of scholarly discussions conducted during international conferences can help soften possible suspicions about Beijing's growing regional clout. Such exchanges are not just meant to offer high Chinese educational standards to developing countries but also to attract the best of what more developed countries have to offer, especially through technology transfers and joint research projects.

International Events

In addition to scholarly conferences and roundtables, many expos, seminars, fairs, symposiums, and other similar events have been organized since 2014 and will continue to occur in countries along the belt and road to promote and bring visibility to the Chinese initiative. Such events usually bring together a mix of representatives from government and multilateral institutions, corporate executives, business investors, and bankers. The following paragraph provides a brief sample of activities that have been organized over the last three years in order to illustrate the scope and breadth of China's soft-power push.

The first international Silk Road Forum was held in 2014 in Istanbul, followed by Madrid in 2015 and Warsaw in 2016, each time bringing together high-level Chinese and local representatives from government and business. BRI was also given a prominent place in the agenda of various

---

[75] "China's New Scholarship to Sponsor Students from Belt and Road Initiative Nations," Xinhua, August 11, 2016, http://news.xinhuanet.com/english/2016-08/11/c_135587410.htm.

[76] Eugene Sebastian and Rahul Choudaha, "Knowledge Helps Power China along the New Silk Road," *Australian*, August 5, 2015.

[77] Zhao Xinying, "The Belt and Road Initiative Can Provide New Study Routes," *China Daily*, February 24, 2016, http://usa.chinadaily.com.cn/epaper/2016-02/16/content_23505657.htm.

international events around the world. More than twenty world leaders attended the Belt and Road Forum for International Cooperation in Beijing on May 14–15, 2017, which gave Xi Jinping an opportunity to showcase his policy's outcomes and discuss international cooperation measures moving forward.[78]

Media

Like their colleagues from think tanks and academia, journalists have been instructed to contribute to the visibility of BRI. As a result, the government initiative has rapidly gained a prominent place in media broadcasting. For example, several satellite TV channels from Chinese central and western provinces jointly created a Silk Road satellite TV alliance, which will mainly broadcast programs related to the Silk Road.[79] In addition, Xinhua deployed a "convoy" of journalists to explore and report from twelve countries along the continental Silk Road, while China Central Television launched an eight-episode documentary dedicated to stories along the Maritime Silk Road.[80] A news website dedicated to the May 2017 Belt and Road Forum was also launched in March 2017.[81]

During a visit to a Silk Road cultural exhibition in 2015, the head of the CCP Central Propaganda Department, Liu Qibao, made clear that public communication had a crucial role to play in showing BRI in the best possible light. As a "major strategic decision made by the central government," he said, BRI should be "recognized as a mutual beneficial approach, with enhanced propaganda." In order to "establish a strong foundation for the 'One Belt One Road,'" Liu indicated that "cultural exchanges should be strengthened, and activities such as joint exhibitions and films encouraged to demonstrate the historical outputs of cultural and

---

[78] "Welcome to the Belt and Road Forum," *Beijing Review*, February 16, 2017, http://www.bjreview.com/World/201702/t20170214_800087177.html.

[79] "'Sichouzhi Lu Weishi Lianmeng' zai Shan jianli" ["Silk Road TV Alliance" Established in Shaanxi], news.163.com, May 24, 2016, http://news.163.com/16/0524/05/BNQB43NE00014AED.html.

[80] For more on this "convoy," see "Xinhua Convoy Starts 12-Nation Silk Road Journey," Xinhua, August 18, 2016, http://news.xinhuanet.com/english/2016-08/18/c_135612188.htm. For more on the documentary, see "Chuanyue Haishang Sichouzhi Lu: Yong renwu gushi kouwen Haishangsilu qianshi jinsheng" [Crossing the Maritime Silk Road: Using Personal Stories to Explore Yesterday's and Today's Maritime Silk Road], *Beijing Daily*, August 17, 2016, http://culture.people.com.cn/n1/2016/0817/c22219-28642532.html.

[81] "China Opens Belt and Road Forum Website," Xinhua, March 10, 2017, http://news.xinhuanet.com/english/2017-03/10/c_136118554.htm.

commercial communications."⁸² Chinese media attempts to concretize the propaganda apparatus's directives are visible in efforts to reach out to international audiences, especially by targeting Silk Road countries. In April 2016, for example, China's State Council Information Office founded the One Belt, One Road Media Alliance.⁸³ The alliance is dedicated to "promoting the Silk Road brand and facilitating international cultural exchanges." It plans to launch a Silk Road multinational TV network to integrate the media resources of the countries along the Silk Road and to create a "production chain of program making, joint-airing and promoting." The alliance hopes to "use these resources to promote a narrative of mutual prosperity in the Silk Road countries." Cui Yuying, deputy director of the State Council Information Office, states that the alliance is "intended to keep the residents of [BRI] countries informed."⁸⁴ It would be surprising if the information that is broadcast by this new platform provides any views that diverge from the Chinese government's official stance. Meanwhile, Xinhua created a dedicated website called "New Silk Road, New Dream," accessible in Chinese, English, Russian, and Arabic, which provides a collection of articles, infographics, videos, and interviews lauding China's initiative.⁸⁵

All official media outlets have been competing to publish reports on BRI, while at the same time engaging foreign counterparts in discussions about the initiative in the hope that they would then echo the Chinese government's vision.⁸⁶ The Chinese media widely disseminates all positive comments and praise offered by foreigners regarding BRI.⁸⁷

---

[82] "The 'Silk Roads Spirit' and 'One Belt One Road' Emphasised by Mr. Liu Qibao," International Council on Monuments and Sites International Conservation Center, November 12, 2015, http://www.iicc.org.cn/Info.aspx?ModelId=1&Id=972.

[83] The State Council Information Office operates under the direction of the Central External Propaganda Work Leading Small Group, which operates in close coordination with the Central Propaganda Department (CPD). It is mainly responsible for international propaganda, while the CPD is mainly responsible for the domestic side. See Mareike Ohlberg, "Boosting the Party's Voice, China's Quest for Global Ideological Dominance," Mercator Institute for China Studies (MERICS), MERICS China Monitor, no. 34, July 21, 2016.

[84] "'One Belt, One Road' Media Alliance," ChinaGoAbroad, http://www.chinagoabroad.com/en/article/20337.

[85] To view this portal directly, see Xinhua, http://www.xinhuanet.com/world/newsilkway/index.htm.

[86] "Development of China's News Media in 2015," China Daily, April 29, 2016, http://europe.chinadaily.com.cn/china/2016-04/29/content_24959094_13.htm.

[87] For an example of this dissemination, see former French prime minister Jean-Pierre Raffarin's interview with China Central Television at http://newscontent.cctv.com/NewJsp/news.jsp?fileId=326018. See also former Afghan president Hamid Karzai's statement in the China Daily that "there are two global trends at the moment: one is hurting countries, while the other provides jobs, opportunities, progress and presents ideas for the future, such as China's One Belt One Road Initiative." See "Global Powers Need More Mutual Trust, Karzai Says," China Daily, April 23, 2016, http://www.china.org.cn/world/2016-04/23/content_38309603.htm.

One international event worth looking at more carefully is the Media Cooperation Forum on Belt and Road, first organized in 2014 and hosted by the *People's Daily*.[88] During the forum's 2015 iteration, Liu Yunshan, the Politburo Standing Committee member in charge of propaganda and ideology, asked participating Chinese and foreign media to create some "positive energy" for BRI.[89] In 2016, President Xi himself sent a message to attendees of the forum, urging them to cooperate. "Media plays an essential role in communicating information, enhancing mutual trust and building consensus," Xi's message said, adding that the Beijing forum provided "a platform for media from many countries to engage in dialogue and practice cooperation." By using this particular platform, China hoped to "promote the development of international relations, deliver public opinion and deepen mutual trust, as well as to push forward the progress of the Belt and Road Initiative." As one European participant observed, "one would not really imagine the EU inviting journalists from some 100 countries to present its development programs and ask the media to help it promote its projects and external policy," for fear of being accused of "mixing information with spin and trying to impose European views and interests on other parts of the world. But this is exactly what China did."[90] On the sidelines of the forum, *People's Daily* signed the International Coalition for New Media Cooperation for One Belt One Road with fifteen media groups, including some from Portugal and the Netherlands.[91] Among other aims such as "enhancing mutual understanding," the coalition intends to "improve culture harmonization," "establish information sharing," and "persevere in media innovation."[92]

International media cooperation on BRI went a step further during a China-Russia media forum held in St. Petersburg in June 2015. Central Propaganda Department head Liu Qibao, who led the Chinese delegation to the forum, called for closer cooperation between Chinese and Russian media outlets and urged both countries' media organizations to "focus on

---

[88] Yuan Can and Zhang Tianrui, "2016 Media Cooperation Forum on Belt and Road Opens in Beijing," *People's Daily*, July 26, 2016, http://en.people.cn/n3/2016/0726/c98649-9091117.html.

[89] "Senior CPC Official Eyes Closer Media Cooperation along Belt and Road," Xinhua, September 22, 2015, http://news.xinhuanet.com/english/2015-09/22/c_134649321.htm.

[90] Eric Maurice, "The EU and China's Velvet Power," *EU Observer*, August 2, 2016, https://euobserver.com/eu-china/134537.

[91] Amy Spiro, "China Holds Charm Offensive with Foreign Journalists," *Jerusalem Post*, August 7, 2016, http://www.jpost.com/Business-and-Innovation/China-holds-charm-offensive-with-foreign-journalists-463467.

[92] "Int'l Coalition for New Media Cooperation on One Belt and One Road Established in Beijing," *People's Daily*, July 26, 2016, http://en.people.cn/n3/2016/0726/c98649-9091297.html.

major strategic blueprints, initiatives and projects" in order to "serve the construction of the Silk Road Economic Belt and Eurasian Economic Union together."[93] *People's Daily* deputy editor-in-chief Lu Xinning was quoted as saying that the two sides should work together to "provide well-rounded images of their countries to the world" and to find "stories worth telling together."[94] Following the forum, China Radio International and RT agreed to launch and develop a joint Sino-Russian multimedia space to promote information exchanges with each other and for other countries' media. A Silk Road–themed joint reporting project naturally became one of the first priorities for the new platform.[95] As Wu Fei, a senior research fellow and professor of journalism at the Charhar Institute, comments, the joint media outlet will help alleviate both the increasing Western criticism of Russia and the Chinese media's over-reliance on Western sources. It will report on BRI and allow a global audience to "hear more authentic opinions from China and Russia."[96] As "authentic" as these reports might be, considering China's and Russia's past record with regard to freedom of the press, there is little doubt that they will present a very particular version of the facts.

In response to clear directives from the propaganda apparatus, Chinese journalists have made a collective effort to "make China's voice heard." Every day, dozens of media platforms present BRI in the best possible light to a wide Chinese and global audience in multiple foreign languages, carefully channeling the most positive comments while loyally relaying the scripted official narrative. The size and scope of China's media work on the BRI front is matched by that of the think tanks and the academic world: it has become impossible to escape from their effort. Media and intellectuals are part of the Chinese leadership's soft-power push to mitigate potential negative responses to BRI.

From Vision to Action: Early Harvests

Amplified worldwide by China's diplomatic and soft-power push and backed by the promise of resources and rewards, Xi Jinping's grand plan has generated a substantial degree of interest, both across China and

---

[93] Zhao Wei, "Joining Hands in Communication," *Beijing Review*, July 9, 2015, http://www.bjreview.com.cn/world/txt/2015-07/06/content_694787.htm.

[94] Ibid.

[95] Ibid.

[96] Nie Ligao and Wu Zheyu, "Sino-Russian Joint News Agency: A Trial Based on Geopolitics," *China Daily*, December 24, 2015, http://www.chinadaily.com.cn/opinion/2015-12/24/content_22799090.htm.

in potential recipient countries. Motivated by the prospect of Chinese investment, foreign businesses and governments alike have jumped aboard the BRI bandwagon. Speaking at a public conference in Washington, D.C., in April 2016, Wang Wen, dean of the Chongyang Institute for Financial Studies at Renmin University, said that 25 countries had already signed MOUs with China on BRI construction projects, while over 70 high-level foreign officials had publicly expressed their government's support for the initiative.[97] However, this rate of support does not seem fast enough for Xi. During a BRI symposium that he chaired in August 2016, the Chinese president praised the progress already made but also called for more projects in specific domains such as energy resource use and R&D. In particular, Xi stressed the need for pilot projects that would quickly generate benefits for the countries involved.[98]

Notwithstanding Xi's impatience, credit has to be given to BRI's advocates. Since its launch only three years ago, thousands of negotiations have been initiated and a quite impressive list of concrete results has already been delivered in all five domains. These projects, many of which were under negotiation before Xi came to power, are only the early accomplishments of a plan that is meant to fully come to fruition around 2050. The following section describes some of the most noteworthy examples of this "early harvest" along the Silk Road Economic Belt.

Outbound Investments and Trade

BRI has clearly created an impetus for both Chinese outbound investment and trade. According to the Ministry of Commerce, in 2015 Chinese companies' outbound direct investment (ODI) to 49 countries along the belt and road soared 38.6% year on year to $18.93 billion, accounting for 13% of total nonfinancial outbound investment. The deputy international trade representative Zhang Xiangchen indicated that BRI investment had become "essential to the fast development of China's ODI."[99] Meanwhile, China's trade with BRI countries totaled $485.5 billion, or 26% of the

---

[97] Wang Wen (remarks at the CSIS event "Asian Development, the OBOR Initiative, and U.S.-China Relations," Washington, D.C., April 18, 2016).

[98] "Xi Calls for Advancing Belt and Road Initiative," Xinhua, August 18, 2016, http://news.xinhuanet.com/english/2016-08/18/c_135608750.htm.

[99] "China's Investment in Belt and Road Countries Up to 38.6%," China Daily, September 22, 2016, http://www.chinadailyasia.com/business/2016-09/22/content_15499459.html.

value of foreign trade.¹⁰⁰ During the three years following the launch of the initiative, China invested a total of $51.4 billion in BRI countries, accounting for 12% of its total ODI over the same period.¹⁰¹ As noted earlier, a study by Grisons Peak found that BRI countries had received the majority of the 67 overseas loan commitments made by the CDB and Export-Import Bank of China as of June 2015. More than half of the loans pledged were attributed to infrastructure projects, while one-third helped finance trade.¹⁰²

The Ministry of Commerce also indicated that during the first eight months of 2016 Chinese companies in 61 countries along the routes signed nearly four thousand engineering contracts, with a combined contract value of $69.82 billion. Chinese companies also established 52 economic cooperation zones, creating $900 million in local revenue and nearly 70,000 local jobs.¹⁰³ The Grisons Peak report observed that two-thirds of the loans extended under BRI have been tied to the involvement of Chinese corporations, either as suppliers of machinery and materials or as construction and operating partners.¹⁰⁴

Six Main Economic Corridors: BRI's Thoroughfares

Six economic corridors identified in the March 2015 "Vision and Actions" plan have now taken shape and become the specific focus of Beijing's attention since a top-level meeting chaired by Vice Premier Zhang Gaoli in July 2015 (see **Figure 2** for a map of the corridors).¹⁰⁵ These corridors appear to constitute BRI's main arteries on land and, seen on a map, look like the backbone of an integrated continental landmass. China's vision will be incrementally realized through multiple layers of transportation, telecommunication, and energy infrastructure networks as well as financial, trade, political, and economic agreements with its partners. Some of these

---

[100] "Navigating the Belt and Road: Financial Sector Paves the Way for Infrastructure," Ernst and Young, August 2015, http://www.ey.com/Publication/vwLUAssets/EY-navigating-the-belt-and-road-en/%24FILE/EY-navigating-the-belt-and-road-en.pdf.

[101] "Highlights: Early Harvests under China's Belt and Road Initiative," Xinhua, August 22, 2016, http://news.xinhuanet.com/english/2016-08/22/c_135624847.htm.

[102] Kynge, "Chinese Overseas Lending."

[103] "China's Investment in Belt and Road Countries Up to 38.6%."

[104] Kynge, "Chinese Overseas Lending."

[105] NDRC, Ministry of Foreign Affairs, and Ministry of Commerce (PRC), "Vision and Actions"; and "China Intensifies Efforts to Construct Belt and Road," Xinhua, July 21, 2015, http://news.xinhuanet.com/english/2015-07/21/c_134433539.htm.

FIGURE 2   Belt and Road Initiative: Six economic corridors spanning Asia, Europe, and Africa

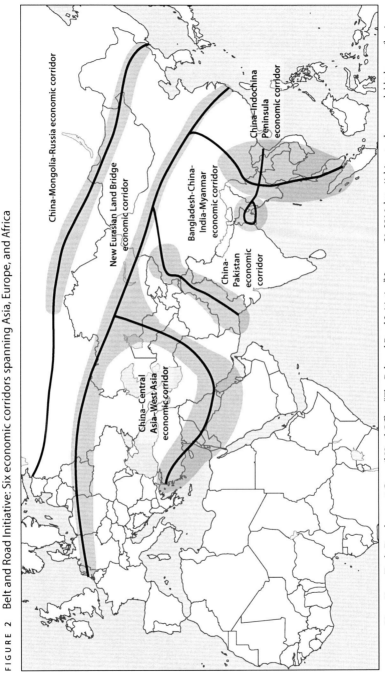

SOURCE: Hong Kong Trade Development Council Head Office, "The Belt and Road Initiative," January 21, 2016, http://china-trade-research.hktdc.com/business-news/article/The-Belt-and-Road-Initiative/The-Belt-and-Road-Initiative-More-Information/obor/en/1/1X3CGF6L/1X0A36H1.htm.

corridors predate Xi's speeches in Astana and Jakarta, but they still have been integrated under the BRI umbrella.[106]

New Eurasian land bridge economic corridor. As seen in chapter 1, the second Eurasian land bridge has effectively operated since the beginning of the 1990s thanks to China's cross-border connection with the ex-Soviet network in Central Asia. Since the launch of BRI, China's relations with Central and Eastern European countries have deepened under this banner.

New railway lines for freight trains have successively opened between China and cities in Europe, such as Warsaw, Duisburg, Madrid, and Hamburg. In 2015, trains made 815 trips between China and Europe, representing a year-on-year increase of 165%.[107] Trains carry goods from China such as clothing and information technology products and often return from Europe with goods such as mechanical equipment and food products—though at this point, one in five eastbound loads is still empty.[108]

Most European countries have reacted positively to China's initiative, seeing it as an opportunity to attract investment at a time when their economies are still struggling to recover from the 2008–9 global financial crisis. With slow growth and European Union funding scarce, many European countries are looking for new capital sources and export markets farther afield. China's diplomatic push for BRI has been particularly effective in Eastern and Central European countries, five of which—Poland, Serbia, the Czech Republic, Bulgaria, and Slovakia—signed agreements with China in November 2015 to jointly promote BRI.[109] In June 2015, Hungary became the first European country to sign an MOU specifically dedicated to bilateral cooperation in developing the new Silk Road. As part of this agreement, it is actively promoting the construction of major projects under the BRI umbrella, such as the Hungary-Serbia railway—the first section of a high-speed rail line that will connect Central Europe to Greece's Piraeus port.[110] Serbia, too, is vying for closer cooperation

---

[106] "Woguo jiang tuijin 'Yidai Yilu' liu da jingji hezuo zuolang jianshe" [China to Promote the "Belt and Road's" Construction of Six Economic Cooperation Corridors], Xinhua, September 24, 2015, http://news.xinhuanet.com/energy/2015-09/24/c_128262923.htm.

[107] Lan Xi, Tang Zhiqiang, and Yan Feng, "China-Europe Freight Trains Bring Vitality to Ancient Silk Road," Xinhua, July 23, 2016, http://news.xinhuanet.com/english/2016-07/23/c_135533595.htm.

[108] John Laurenson, "Laptops and Smartphones on the New Silk Road," *Marketplace*, October 11, 2016, http://www.marketplace.org/2016/10/10/world/laptops-and-smartphones-new-silk-road.

[109] "China, CEE Countries Sign Memo to Promote Belt and Road Initiative," Xinhua, November 27, 2015, http://news.xinhuanet.com/english/2015-11/27/c_134859206.htm.

[110] "Hungary First European Country to Sign Up for China Silk Road Plan," Reuters, June 6, 2015, http://www.reuters.com/article/us-china-hungary-idUSKBN0ON01W20150607.

with China's BRI. Belgrade's Pupin Bridge, inaugurated by Premier Li Keqiang and Serbian prime minster Aleksandar Vučić in December 2014, was China's first big infrastructure investment in Europe. Several additional projects have since been integrated under the BRI banner, such as the construction of a new power plant in the Serbian city of Kostolac, upgrades to sections of the Serbian highway, and the creation of industrial zones for Chinese businesses.[111] Poland, which is China's largest trading partner in Central and Eastern Europe and the only state in that region to be a founding member of the AIIB, has been connected to China since 2013 by transcontinental rail links between Chengdu and Lodz and Suzhou and Warsaw.[112] Further projects defined by Xi could include railway network upgrades, port construction, and industrial zone projects complementing Poland's own historical Amber Road.[113] Finally, under President Miloš Zeman, elected in 2013, the Czech Republic has shown unprecedented support for Beijing's policies.[114] Although no landmark Chinese infrastructure project has been announced so far, given the close links that the China Energy Fund Committee (CEFC) has created with the Czech presidential office, it would not be surprising if the two sides signed new contracts more closely related to BRI.[115]

At the European-wide level, in June 2015 the EU and China committed to create an EU-China connectivity platform and a joint working group to enhance synergies between the EU initiatives and BRI.[116] Both parties want to promote cooperation in areas such as infrastructure, equipment, technologies, and standards, and China has announced a contribution of

---

[111] Dragan Pavlićević, "Chinese Infrastructure Investments in Serbia: Between Politics and Profit," Council for European Studies, December 14, 2015, http://councilforeuropeanstudies.org/critcom/chinese-infrastructure-investments-in-serbia-between-politics-and-profit.

[112] "Business Booms in China-Europe Freight Train Loading Hub," Xinhua, June 19, 2016, http://news.xinhuanet.com/english/2016-06/19/c_135448736.htm.

[113] During the Roman Empire, amber was transported overland from Northern Europe to the Mediterranean. See "In Visit to Poland, Xi Links Silk Road with Amber Road," Xinhua, June 21, 2016, http://news.xinhuanet.com/english/2016-06/21/c_135454640.htm; and "China's Xi Weaves Poland into 'New Silk Road' Plan," *Straits Times*, June 20, 2016, http://www.straitstimes.com/world/europe/chinas-xi-weaves-poland-into-new-silk-road-plan.

[114] "Four Takeaways from President Xi's 49-hour Historic State Visit to Czech Republic," Xinhua, March 31, 2016, http://news.xinhuanet.com/english/2016-03/31/c_135238114.htm.

[115] CEFC's CEO Ye Jianming has been President Zeman's personal adviser on China, and several members of the Czech government, including its former defense minister, have joined CEFC's ranks. "Ye Jianming Appointed as Economic Advisor to Czech President," China Radio International, October 30, 2015, http://english.cri.cn/12394/2015/10/30/2821s901887.htm; and "Czech Presidential Office, Chinese CEFC Personally Merge," *Prague Daily Monitor*, November 20, 2015, http://www.praguemonitor.com/2015/11/20/hn-czech-presidential-office-chinese-cefc-personally-merge.

[116] "China Focus on Belt & Road, Juncker Plan Synergies," Xinhua, February 18, 2016, http://www.chinadailyasia.com/nation/2016-02/18/content_15386616.html.

315 billion euros to the EU's Investment Plan for Europe.[117] The European side is hopeful that these efforts to improve connectivity will benefit both European and Asian countries.[118]

Further east, China and Belarus have pledged to engage in closer cooperation, with Xi calling President Alexander Lukashenko "an old friend of the Chinese people," while the latter hailed how well the two countries have jointly implemented BRI.[119] Approximately twenty Sino-Belarusian projects worth $5.5 billion are underway, with the flagship one being an industrial park called Great Stone next to the Minsk airport.[120]

Bangladesh-China-India-Myanmar (BCIM) economic corridor. Formerly known as the Kunming Initiative, which became the BCIM Forum for Regional Cooperation in 1999, the BCIM economic corridor was given renewed attention when India and China agreed to establish a joint working group during Premier Li's visit to New Delhi in May 2013.[121] The four countries met in Kunming in December 2013 and agreed on the necessity of identifying possible early-harvest projects in transportation, energy, and telecommunication infrastructure, but progress has been slow, especially because of India's misgivings about China's real intentions.[122] New hopes for progress on the corridor have been raised after Xi's visit to Bangladesh in October 2016. The two countries have signed agreements for 27 infrastructure,

---

[117] "Investment Plan for Europe Goes Global: China Announces Its Contribution to #InvestEU," European Commission, September 28, 2015, http://europa.eu/rapid/press-release_IP-15-5723_en.htm; and "EU and China Discuss Trade, Investment, Overcapacity and Cooperation on State Aid Control at the 6th High-level Economic and Trade Dialogue," European Commission, October 18, 2016, http://europa.eu/rapid/press-release_IP-16-3441_en.htm.

[118] Shuai Rong and Yan Lei, "Interview: Europe to Benefit from China's One Belt, One Road Initiative: EC Chief," Xinhua, May 07, 2015, http://news.xinhuanet.com/english/2015-05/07/c_134218780.htm. European think tanks seem to agree with Jean-Claude Juncker's statement. See, for example, Shada Islam, "EU-China Connectivity: Thinking Big, Starting Small," Friends of Europe, June 26, 2015, http://www.friendsofeurope.org/global-europe/eu-china-connectivity-thinking-big-acting-small; and Alicia Garcia Herrero and Jianwei Xu, "China's Belt and Road Initiative: Can Europe Expect Trade Gains?" Bruegel, Working Paper, no. 5, 2016, http://bruegel.org/wp-content/uploads/2016/09/WP-05-2016.pdf.

[119] An Baijie, "China, Belarus to Enhance Cooperation in Several Fields," *China Daily*, September 29, 2016, http://www.chinadaily.com.cn/china/2016-09/29/content_26942061.htm.

[120] "Sino-Belarusian Cooperation Is Not Up to Expectations of Belarusian Authorities," Belarus in Focus, April 22, 2016, http://belarusinfocus.info/society-and-politics/sino-belarusian-cooperation-not-expectations-belarusian-authorities.

[121] "Joint Statement on the State Visit of Chinese Premier Li Keqiang to India," Ministry of External Affairs (India), May 20, 2013, http://mea.gov.in/bilateral-documents.htm?dtl/21723/Joint+Statement+on+the+State+Visit+of+Chinese++Li+Keqiang+to+India.

[122] Ashok Sajjanhar, "Understanding the BCIM Economic Corridor and India's Response," Observer Research Foundation, Issue Brief, no. 147, June 2016, http://www.orfonline.org/wp-content/uploads/2016/06/ORF_IssueBrief_147.pdf.

energy, information, and communication projects, totaling $13.6 billion, and with the signature of an MOU, Bangladesh formally joined China's BRI.[123]

China-Pakistan economic corridor. First mentioned by Premier Li during his visit to Islamabad in May 2013, immediately following a trip to India, CPEC is so far the most advanced of all the BRI corridors.[124] It stands out as China's flagship project, poetically referred to by Foreign Minister Wang Yi as the "sweet melody" of the BRI symphony's first movement, and has been integrated into China's 13th Five-Year Plan (2016–20).[125]

Backed by Xi's April 2015 commitment to Prime Minister Nawaz Sharif to invest $46 billion in Pakistan and a subsequent $5.5 billion loan for the Karachi-Lahore railway in September 2016, CPEC will materialize around a couple of hundred infrastructure projects, including the construction of highways, railways, oil and natural gas pipelines, power plants, a China-Pakistan cross-border fiber-optic network, and the development of Pakistan's Gwadar port. Thus far, 176 projects have been listed for Punjab, 103 for Sindh, 19 for Khyber Pakhtunkhwa, and 8 for Baluchistan.[126] The port is located in Pakistan's least-developed province, where the separatist Baluchistan Liberation Front has described CPEC as "an occupation of Baluch territory" and has threatened to attack anyone working on the project.[127] Islamabad has committed over 12,000 troops to a special security force tasked with protecting Chinese engineers and personnel working on CPEC projects, and

---

[123] Arafat Kabir, "Chinese President Xi Jinping's Visit to Bangladesh Gives Boost to Bilateral Relations," *Forbes*, October 14, 2016, http://www.forbes.com/sites/arafatkabir/2016/10/14/chinese-president-xi-jinpings-visit-to-bangladesh-gives-boost-to-bilateral-relations; and "Bangladesh Formally Joins China's 'One Belt One Road' Initiative," bdnews24, October 15, 2016, http://bdnews24.com/bangladesh/2016/10/15/bangladesh-formally-joins-chinas-flagship-one-belt-one-road-initiative.

[124] "Li Keqiang Urges Development of 'China-Pakistan Economic Corridor,'" *South China Morning Post*, May 23, 2013, http://www.scmp.com/news/china/article/1244267/li-keqiang-urges-development-china-pakistan-economic-corridor.

[125] During a visit to Pakistan in February 2016, Wang Yi declared, "If 'One Belt, One Road' is like a symphony involving and benefiting every country, then construction of the China-Pakistan Economic Corridor is the sweet melody of the symphony's first movement." Quoted in Andrew Small, "The Rebalancing of the China-Pakistan Relationship," testimony before the U.S.-China Economic and Security Review Commission, Washington, D.C., March 10, 2016, http://www.uscc.gov/sites/default/files/Small_Remars%20031016.pdf. See also "CPEC Made Part of China's 13th 5-Year Development Plan," *Pakistan Today*, November 23, 2015, http://www.pakistantoday.com.pk/2015/11/23/business/cpec-made-part-of-chinas-13th-5-year-development-plan-weidong.

[126] Katharine Houreld, "China and Pakistan Launch Economic Corridor Plan Worth $46 Billion," Reuters, April 20, 2015; Khaleeq Kiani, "With a New Chinese Loan, CPEC Is Now Worth $51.5bn," *Dawn*, September 30, 2016, http://www.dawn.com/news/1287040; and Salman Rafi, "'Punjab-Centric' China-Pakistan Economic Corridor Exposes Political Divisions," *Asia Times*, September 14, 2016, http://www.atimes.com/punjab-centric-china-pakistan-economic-corridor-exposes-political-divisions.

[127] Syed Raza Hassan, "To Protect Chinese Investment, Pakistan Military Leaves Little to Chance," Reuters, February 7, 2016.

there are plans for a second security division, which would bring the number of personnel dedicated to CPEC protection to around 30,000.[128]

China-Mongolia-Russia economic corridor. The idea for a China-Mongolia-Russia economic corridor first emerged from a September 2014 meeting between Presidents Xi Jinping, Vladimir Putin, and Tsakhiagiin Elbegdorj at the SCO Dushanbe summit. The three heads of state committed to finding synergies between China's Silk Road Economic Belt, Russia's Eurasian land bridge, and Mongolia's Prairie (or Steppe) Road.[129] A midterm roadmap for development of trilateral cooperation between China, Russia, and Mongolia was adopted on the margins of the 2015 SCO summit in Ufa, and the three leaders reiterated their commitment to making the corridor a reality during the 2016 SCO summit in Tashkent, where they agreed to cooperate on infrastructure building and customs clearance procedures.[130] While the news was overshadowed by the British referendum on EU membership held on the same day, the signing of this trilateral economic partnership agreement is significant. It identifies 32 projects, outlines the creation of a joint investment center to assess their financial requirements, and opens the possibility of future trilateral cooperation in a wide array of domains that include transportation networks, energy, agriculture, tourism, health, food security, scientific and technical cooperation, customs clearance, and environmental protection.[131] Among these projects, construction of a Zamiin-Uud–Ulaanbaatar expressway was launched under the combined auspices of BRI and the Prairie Road initiative in May 2015.[132] High-level tripartite consultations have taken place regarding joint transportation development, and a cross-border freight transportation link

---

[128] Saeed Shah and Josh Chin, "Pakistan to Create Security Force to Protect Chinese Workers," *Wall Street Journal*, April 22, 2015, http://www.wsj.com/articles/pakistan-to-create-security-force-to-protect-chinese-workers-1429701872; and Zofeen T. Ebrahim, "CPEC and Major Unanswered Questions," Third Pole, October 13, 2016, https://www.thethirdpole.net/2016/10/13/cpec-and-major-unanswered-questions.

[129] "Xi Proposes to Build China-Mongolia-Russia Economic Corridor," State Council (PRC), September 12, 2014, http://english.gov.cn/news/photos/2014/09/25/content_281474989434179.htm.

[130] See "Mongolia, Russia and China Approve Mid-Term Development Roadmap for Tripartite Cooperation," MAD Investment Solutions, July 28, 2015, http://mad-intelligence.com/mongolia-russia-and-china-approve-mid-term-development-roadmap-for-tripartite-cooperation. See also "China, Russia, Mongolia Endorse Development Plan on Economic Corridor," Xinhua, June 24, 2016, http://news.xinhuanet.com/english/2016-06/24/c_135461510.htm.

[131] Dulguun Bayarsaikhan, "Over 30 Projects Lined Up for Trilateral Economic Corridor," UB Post, June 29, 2016, http://theubpost.mn/2016/06/29/over-30-projects-lined-up-for-trilateral-economic-corridor.

[132] E. Orgil, "'Altanbulag-Ulaanbaatar-Zamiin-Uud Highway' Project Opens," GoGo Mongolia, May 29, 2015, http://mongolia.gogo.mn/r/146386.

along a 2,152 km road connecting Ulan Ude in Russia to the port of Tianjin via the Mongolian capital of Ulaanbaatar was opened in August 2016.[133]

Under the BRI framework, China has been pushing for closer cooperation with Mongolia in many different areas. In a series of bilateral meetings, Xi insisted that BRI should be linked to Mongolia's development strategies not only with regard to infrastructure building, finance, and trade but also across the mining, agricultural, and security sectors. His position prompted a variety of concerns regarding Mongolia's increasing vulnerability to Chinese demands at a time of extreme economic difficulties due to the global decline in commodity prices.[134] Chinese investment in small and medium-sized projects in Mongolia has largely been driven by government-backed financing in support of BRI.[135] In 2014 the two governments agreed to double the amount of a 2011 currency exchange swap between the People's Bank of China and the Bank of Mongolia to 20 billion yuan.[136] The following year, they signed an MOU calling for the establishment of a cross-border trade area and agreed to sign a separate free trade agreement (FTA) in support of the area in the near future.[137] In Erenhot, on the Chinese side of the border, Inner Mongolia's local government started constructing logistics facilities in preparation for increased trade exchanges.[138] Finally, as part of Xi's call to foster people-to-people cooperation under BRI, Beijing has committed to fund training for 500 Mongolian youths, 500 military officers, and 250 journalists.[139]

The "strategic entente" between China and Russia that has been growing since 2012 may paradoxically have made BRI a less significant framework

---

[133] Alicia J. Campi, "Mongolia, Russia and China Work to Boost Transcontinental Rail Transit," Jamestown Foundation, Eurasia Daily Monitor, April 20, 2015, https://jamestown.org/program/mongolia-russia-and-china-work-to-boost-transcontinental-rail-transit.

[134] For a detailed and well-informed account of China-Mongolia relations and cooperation since 2013 and their implications for Mongolia, see Jeffrey Reeves, "Mongolia's Place in China's Periphery Diplomacy," *Asan Forum*, April 7, 2016, http://www.theasanforum.org/mongolias-place-in-chinas-periphery-diplomacy.

[135] "Sun Weiren: Zhongguo de 'Yidai Yilu' changyi zai zhu Zhong-Meng jingmao hezuo shang xin taijie" [Sun Weiren: China's "Belt and Road" Initiative to Help China and Mongolia to a New Level of Economic and Trade Cooperation], Economic and Commercial Counselor's Office of the Embassy of the People's Republic of China in Mongolia, November 11, 2015, http://www.mofcom.gov.cn/article/i/dxfw/cj/201511/20151101161198.shtml.

[136] Michael Kohn, "Mongolia's Central Bank Plans to Double Currency Swap with China," Bloomberg, March 29, 2014, http://www.bloomberg.com/news/articles/2014-03-20/mongolia-s-central-bank-plans-to-double-currency-swap-with-china.

[137] "China, Mongolia Meet on Cross-border Trade Zone," Xinhua, March 27, 2015, http://news.xinhuanet.com/english/2015-03/27/c_134103416.htm.

[138] "Inner Mongolia Works for Northward Opening Up," *China Daily*, July 22, 2014, http://www.chinadaily.com.cn/m/innermongolia/2014-07/22/content_17896370.htm.

[139] "Sun Weiren."

for Beijing to use with regard to Moscow. Heralding progress under the BRI banner is more difficult and less necessary with a country that had already entered into agreements to cooperate on infrastructure development, especially in the energy domain, before BRI was launched than it is with countries for which the initiative offers new opportunities. Russia's initial reaction to BRI was cautious. It was not until May 2015 that Presidents Putin and Xi signed an agreement pledging to find possible areas for cooperation between Russia's Eurasian integration plan (the Eurasian Economic Union) and China's BRI.[140] Both countries agreed to identify a list of infrastructure projects and to increase bilateral trade by establishing an economic partnership that would eventually become a free trade area.[141] Several Sino-Russian energy infrastructure projects have been in the works for over a decade.[142] In May 2014, China National Petroleum Corporation and Gazprom signed the Power of Siberia gas deal, and in November 2014 the two companies signed an MOU on the Altai pipeline (or Power of Siberia 2, connecting Russia's West Siberian gas fields to Xinjiang). These projects, however, have faced hurdles due to lower global energy prices and increasing economic pressure in both countries.[143] In March 2016 the Silk Road Fund took a 9.9% stake, worth $12 billion, in the Yamal liquefied natural gas project, with production scheduled to begin in 2017.[144] In May 2015, Xi and Putin also signed several agreements on building transportation infrastructure, including two railway lines in the Republic of Tyva (one from the Elegest coal mine to Kuragin and another from Kyzyl to western China) and a project related to the Vanino port in the Khabarovsk region,

---

[140] Irina Kobrinskaya, "Is Russia Coming to Terms with China's 'Silk Road'?" Program on New Approaches to Research and Security in Eurasia, Policy Memo, no. 439, September 2016, http://www.ponarseurasia.org/memo/russia-comes-terms-chinas-silk-road.

[141] Alexander Gabuev, "China's One Belt, One Road Initiative and the Sino-Russian Entente," interview by Greg Shtraks, National Bureau of Asian Research, August 9, 2016, http://www.nbr.org/research/activity.aspx?id=707; and "Putin Eyes EEU-China FTA amid Regional Consensus on Silk Road Cooperation," China Radio International, June 23, 2016, http://english.cri.cn/12394/2016/06/23/4081s931802.htm.

[142] Edward C. Chow and Zachary D. Cuyler, "New Russian Gas Export Projects: From Pipe Dreams to Pipelines," CSIS, Commentary, July 22, 2015, https://www.csis.org/analysis/new-russian-gas-export-projects---pipe-dreams-pipelines.

[143] Olesya Astakhova and Chen Aizhu, "Exclusive: Russia Likely to Scale Down China Gas Supply Plans," Reuters, January 15, 2016, http://www.reuters.com/article/us-russia-china-gas-exclusive-idUSKCN0UT1LG; and Michael Lelyveld, "China-Russia Project Stalls as Energy Prices Plunge," Radio Free Asia, January 25, 2016, http://www.rfa.org/english/commentaries/energy_watch/china-russia-01252016152633.html.

[144] Neil Buckley, "Sino-Russian Gas Deal: Smoke without Fire," *Financial Times*, May 11, 2016.

situated at the end of the Baikal-Amur railway.[145] Finally, China expressed interest in investing in the Moscow-Kazan high-speed railway project, and the China Railway Corporation signed an agreement with Russian Railways in June 2016 to cooperate on the project's development as part of a future high-speed line between Moscow and Beijing.[146]

China–Indochina Peninsula economic corridor. During a December 2014 meeting on the Greater Mekong Subregion economic cooperation, Premier Li argued in favor of the benefits that BRI and deeper relations with China could bring to the five countries of the Indochina Peninsula (Cambodia, Laos, Myanmar, Thailand, and Vietnam) and committed $1 billion to connectivity projects in the region.[147] Yet progress on infrastructure building has not been as quick and smooth as Beijing had hoped despite some encouraging initial agreements. After the termination of the MOU for the Sino-Myanmar railway project in 2014, and given political discord with Vietnam over South China Sea issues, China centered its efforts on Laos and Thailand. Although concerns related to environmental impact and interest rates attached to the Chinese loans have caused delays with those countries as well, China skillfully worked its way around recurring obstacles, and cross-border economic cooperation zones have been created along the Sino-Lao border.[148] This flexible approach toward Thailand and Laos is meant to demonstrate goodwill that could entice Vietnam and Myanmar to reconsider their reluctance to cooperate.[149]

China–Central Asia–West Asia economic corridor. China has long been a major investor in Central Asia's infrastructure building and natural resource extraction, and its overall engagement with the five republics within that

---

[145] "China's CRCC Agrees Railway, Port Projects in Russia," Reuters, May 10, 2015, http://www.reuters.com/article/china-russia-railway-idUSL3N0Y205F20150511; and "Chinese Company Signs Tyva Railway Agreement," *Railway Gazette*, May 25, 2015, http://www.railwaygazette.com/news/infrastructure/single-view/view/chinese-company-signs-tyva-railway-agreement.html.

[146] Paul Sonne, "China to Design New Russian High-Speed Railway," *Wall Street Journal*, June 19, 2015, http://www.wsj.com/articles/china-to-design-new-russian-high-speed-railway-1434729400; and David Briginshaw, "Russian and Chinese Railways Agree Joint Strategy," *International Railway Journal*, June 27, 2016, http://www.railjournal.com/index.php/asia/russian-and-chinese-railways-agree-joint-strategy.html.

[147] Zhao Yanrong and Qin Jize, "China Commits $1bn to Greater Mekong Subregion," *China Daily*, December 20, 2014, http://www.chinadaily.com.cn/world/2014livisitkst/2014-12/20/content_19133622.htm.

[148] For more on China's persistence in overcoming obstacles in Thailand and Laos, see Simon Webb, "China, Laos Say Rail Project to Go Ahead, Pending Environment Study," Reuters, July 9, 2016, http://www.reuters.com/article/us-laos-china-railway-idUSKCN1091AO; and Sijia Jiang, "Not Taking No for an Answer, China Railway Group Says Hi-Speed Project in Thailand 'Still On,'" *South China Morning Post*, April 7, 2016, http://www.scmp.com/business/companies/article/1934243/not-taking-no-answer-china-railway-group-says-high-speed-project.

[149] Yun Sun, "China's Strategic Focus on Mainland Southeast Asia," CSIS, cogitASIA, December 22, 2015, http://cogitasia.com/chinas-strategic-focus-on-mainland-southeast-asia.

region has been growing substantially over the last two decades. But Beijing intends to go a step further in achieving greater coordination among those states within the BRI framework, and Central Asian leaders did not wait for more details to be revealed to react positively to the idea of building the new Silk Road Economic Belt.[150] Xi received their immediate support in September 2013 during his tour of Central Asia, which produced a series of contracts with Kazakhstan ($30 billion), Uzbekistan ($15 billion), and Turkmenistan ($16 billion), as well as promises for China to provide loans and aid to Turkmenistan ($8 billion) and Tajikistan ($1 billion).[151] China also signed energy deals to develop Turkmenistan's Galkynysh natural gas reserves and to acquire an 8.33% stake in Kashagan, Kazakhstan's largest oil deposit.[152] During his visit to Kyrgyzstan, Xi expressed China's interest in investing in the construction of a civil air hub at Kyrgyzstan's Manas airport. Only a few days after U.S. forces ceased providing logistical support to NATO's International Security Assistance Force and left the airport base, China announced a $1 billion investment in its makeover, as well as another $300 million of funding for the country's second airport in the southern city of Osh.[153]

Railway connectivity has also made progress, even if the projects now underway had already been discussed a few years before any mention of BRI. The Xi'an-Almaty international cargo train traveling along the Kazakhstan-Uzbekistan-Kyrgyzstan-Turkmenistan route has become one of the fastest ways for freight to move between China and its Central Asian neighbors: the travel time is only 6 days, compared with 26 days by road, reducing transportation costs by 30%.[154] Following a December 2014

---

[150] Virginia Marantidou and Ralph A. Cossa, "China and Russia's Great Game in Central Asia," *National Interest*, Buzz, October 1, 2014, http://nationalinterest.org/blog/the-buzz/china-russias-great-game-central-asia-11385.

[151] "Xi's Central Asia Trip Aimed at Common Development, All-Win Cooperation," Xinhua, September 15, 2013, http://news.xinhuanet.com/english/china/2013-09/15/c_125389057.htm. The contract with Turkmenistan includes funding for the world's longest natural gas pipeline, running from Turkmenistan to China through Uzbekistan, Tajikistan, and Kyrgyzstan.

[152] See Marat Gurt, "China Asserts Clout in Central Asia with Huge Turkmen Gas Project," Reuters, September 4, 2013, http://www.reuters.com/article/us-gas-turkmenistan-galkynysh-idUSBRE9830MN20130904; and Mariya Gordeyeva, "China Buys into Giant Kazakh Oilfield for $5 Billion," Reuters, September 7, 2013, http://www.reuters.com/article/us-oil-kashagan-china-idUSBRE98606620130907.

[153] "China Interested in Hub Creation at Kyrgyz Manas International Airport," Trend, September 12, 2013, http://en.trend.az/casia/kyrgyzstan/2189036.html; and Chris Rickleton, "China Leads Russia in Contest for Kyrgyzstan's Airports," EurasiaNet, July 8, 2014, http://www.eurasianet.org/node/68911.

[154] "Xi'an-Almaty Cargo Train Begins Operation," Xinhua, November 28, 2013, http://news.xinhuanet.com/english/china/2013-11/28/c_132925690.htm; and Alexander Kim, "China and the Silk Road: Marching Westward," Jamestown Foundation, Eurasia Daily Monitor, March 3, 2014, https://jamestown.org/program/china-and-the-silk-road-marching-westward/#sthash.VwlLwGUd.dpuf.

agreement between China, Kyrgyzstan, Afghanistan, and Iran, preliminary work started in Xinjiang in early January 2016 on a rail line linking Kashgar to Herat.[155] Although negotiations stalled between Beijing and Bishkek over the technical and financial aspects of constructing the Kyrgyz leg, the two parties finally came to an agreement in late December 2016 and included the new railway in the Silk Road Economic Belt framework.[156] In June 2016, Xi and then Uzbekistan president Islam Karimov remotely presided over the inauguration of the Qamchiq tunnel on the Angren-Pap railway line—currently the largest project undertaken by a Chinese company in Uzbekistan—which bypasses Tajikistan to reach the Ferghana Valley.[157] Xi hailed the realization of such a complex project as a "major achievement of the China-Uzbekistan joint-construction of the 'Belt and Road' initiative."[158] Kazakhstan's president Nazarbayev, for his part, in May 2015 announced a joint plan with China to build a railway from the Khorgos dry port on the Chinese border to the Caspian Sea port of Aktau.[159] Meanwhile, the Khorgos Gateway dry port, set to become a key logistical hub on the new Silk Road, began operating in August 2015, while the Khorgos–Eastern Gate Special Economic Zone will benefit from a $600 million, five-year investment from Jiangsu Province signed in September 2015.[160]

In order to reach Europe, the China–Central Asia–West Asia economic corridor leaves Central Asia to go through the South Caucasus region, locked between the Caspian and Black Seas. During Vice Premier Zhang Gaoli's visit to the region in June 2016, Georgia, Armenia, and Azerbaijan all officially

---

[155] Cui Jia, "Work to Start on Rail Link with Iran," *China Daily*, January 15, 2016, http://www.chinadaily.com.cn/china/2016-01/15/content_23096031.htm.

[156] Fozil Mashrab, "Bishkek Puts Brakes on China-Kyrgyzstan-Uzbekistan Railway," Jamestown Foundation, Eurasia Daily Monitor, November 3, 2015, https://jamestown.org/program/bishkek-puts-brakes-on-china-kyrgyzstan-uzbekistan-railway; and "Construction of Railway China-Kyrgyzstan-Uzbekistan to Begin in 2016," *Uzbekistan Today*, December 23, 2015, https://ut.uz/en/business/construction_of_railway_chinakyrgyzstanuzbekistan_to_begin_in_2016.

[157] "Two Presidents Open Angren-Pap Railway," *Railway Gazette*, July 7, 2016, http://www.railwaygazette.com/news/infrastructure/single-view/view/two-presidents-open-angren-pap-railway.html.

[158] "Xi Jinping and President Islam Karimov of Uzbekistan Jointly Attend Video Link Activity for the Opening of Angren-Pap Railway Tunnel," Ministry of Foreign Affairs (PRC), June 23, 2016, http://www.fmprc.gov.cn/mfa_eng/topics_665678/xjpdsrwyblwzbkstjxgsfwbcxshzzcygyslshdschy/t1375398.shtml.

[159] John C.K. Daly, "China and Kazakhstan to Construct a Trans-Kazakhstan Railway Line from Khorgos to Aktau," Jamestown Foundation, Eurasia Daily Monitor, May 20, 2015, https://jamestown.org/program/china-and-kazakhstan-to-construct-a-trans-kazakhstan-railway-line-from-khorgos-to-aktau.

[160] Summer Zhen, "China's Silk Road Strategy Takes Shape in Khorgos," *South China Morning Post*, October 18, 2015, http://www.scmp.com/business/china-business/article/1869193/chinas-silk-road-strategy-takes-shape-khorgos.

declared their support for BRI and their willingness to participate in the initiative in cooperation with Beijing.[161] A few days after Georgia hosted the October 2015 Tbilisi Silk Road Forum, which some observers saw as a clear endorsement of China's BRI policy, then prime minister Irakli Garibashvili publicly described Georgia as Europe's natural gateway to Asia and underlined his goal for a prosperous country that "leverages its geographic location as a vital crossroads connecting East and West, and North and South."[162] He had previously presented this vision of Georgia as a regional hub for exchanges to his Chinese counterpart and to Chinese businessmen during his visit to China in September 2015. Both countries agreed to launch FTA negotiations, which were concluded a year later, and signed a bilateral currency swap agreement. In addition, State Power Investment Corporation showed interest in investing in the Anaklia deepwater port and developing an industrial park on the site, Huawei expressed interest in building safety infrastructure and Internet systems, and Dongfang Electric pledged to contribute $180–$200 million for the construction of a thermal power plant in Georgia's western Tkibuli region.[163] In February 2016, China experienced its first setback as Georgia's new government chose a U.S. consortium over China Power Investment Corporation to build the Anaklia port and industrial site.[164] Nonetheless, the Baku-Tbilisi-Kars railway seems to be making progress, with a first test train having traveled to Georgia in January 2015 and another to Turkey in July 2015.[165] A new deadline for completion of this project has been set for 2017.[166]

Finally, the first regular freight train linking China to the Middle East arrived in Tehran in February 2016 after fourteen days of travel from Yiwu

---

[161] "Chinese Vice Premier's Four-Nation Tour Harvests Broader Consensus on Belt Initiative," Xinhua, June 9, 2016, http://news.xinhuanet.com/english/2016-06/08/c_135422738.htm.

[162] Raffaello Pantucci and Sarah Lain, "Tbilisi Silk Road Forum: Next Steps for Georgia and the Silk Road," Royal United Services Institute, Workshop Report, August 2016, 1, https://rusi.org/sites/default/files/201608_wr_tbilisi_silk_road_forum.pdf; and Irakli Garibashvili, "Georgia Can Help Build a Silk Road of Trade from Brighton to Beijing," *Telegraph*, October 28, 2015, http://www.telegraph.co.uk/news/worldnews/europe/georgia/11959643/Georgia-can-help-build-a-Silk-Road-of-trade-from-Brighton-to-Beijing.html.

[163] "Georgia-China, 13 Things Georgian PM Did in China Last Week," *Caucasus Business Week*, September 14, 2015.

[164] Monica Ellena, "Georgia: China Experiences Black Sea Setback," EurasiaNet, February 15, 2016, http://www.eurasianet.org/node/77321.

[165] "First Test Train Operates on Baku-Tbilisi-Kars Railway," Agenda, January 28, 2015, http://agenda.ge/news/28897/eng; and Tamar Svanidze, "Baku-Tbilisi-Kars Train Tested in Turkey," *Georgia Today*, July 30, 2015, http://georgiatoday.ge/news/791/Baku-Tbilisi-Kars-Train-Tested-In-Turkey.

[166] Vasili Rukhadze, "Completion of Baku-Tbilisi-Kars Railway Project Postponed Again," Jamestown Foundation, Eurasia Daily Monitor, March 2, 2016, https://jamestown.org/program/completion-of-baku-tbilisi-kars-railway-project-postponed-again.

via Kazakhstan, Kyrgyzstan, Uzbekistan, and Turkmenistan.[167] Iran has pledged to support BRI, and during Xi's visit to Tehran in January 2016—the first by an international leader after the removal of trade sanctions—he hailed China and Iran as "natural partners" in implementing BRI. Along with signing seventeen bilateral agreements on cooperation in infrastructure and investment, Xi offered Chinese assistance in financing and building a high-speed railway between Tehran and Mashhad.[168] If completed, this project would be a key portion of a more ambitious plan, proposed in November 2015 by China Railway Corporation, to link China to Iran via Central Asia by high-speed rail.[169] Like many other countries on the Eurasian continent, Iran sees itself as a crucial node on the new Silk Road and is apparently willing to make the best use of China's BRI for its own purposes. The Iranian government can already see the potential for its own energy exports to China. Through its ambassador in Beijing, Iran has announced its desire to use the initiative's framework to extend into China an existing natural gas pipeline that runs to its border with Pakistan.[170]

Beijing did not officially provide a roadmap for the completion of the economic corridors, either in terms of the timeline or in terms of the relative importance of each project. It appears that the hierarchy of priorities is evolving, as China takes advantage of opportunities wherever they occur.

Information and Telecommunication Infrastructure: A Nascent "Digital Silk Road"

Along with transportation infrastructure, BRI also includes plans to improve telecommunication infrastructure across Eurasia. Because cables can be laid easily along rail lines, the future Eurasian fiber-optic backbone will benefit from transportation networks that will be built along the new Silk Road. For landlocked countries across the continent, this could mean greater access to international data networks, at a cost averaging 10% that

---

[167] Najmeh Bozorgmehr, "First Freight Trains from China Arrive in Tehran," *Financial Times*, May 9, 2016, https://www.ft.com/content/e964a78e-0bd8-11e6-9456-444ab5211a2f.

[168] "China to Help Iran Build High-Speed Rail as Part of 'One Belt, One Road' Strategy," *South China Morning Post*, January 24, 2016, http://www.scmp.com/news/china/diplomacy-defence/article/1904757/china-help-iran-build-high-speed-rail-part-one-belt-one.

[169] Zheng Yanpeng, "New Rail Route Proposed from Urumqi to Iran," *China Daily*, November 21, 2015, http://www.chinadaily.com.cn/china/2015-11/21/content_22506412.htm.

[170] "Iran, China Embark on 'New Silk Road,'" *Financial Tribune*, January 26, 2016, https://financialtribune.com/articles/economy-business-and-markets/35000/iran-china-embark-on-new-silk-road; and Teddy Ng, "Iran Backs Pipeline to China under 'One Belt One Road' Initiative: Ambassador," *South China Morning Post*, April 23, 2015, http://www.scmp.com/news/china/policies-politics/article/1774422/iran-wants-help-energy-pipeline-expansion-part-chinas.

of satellite communications and with bandwidth significantly enhanced by fiber-optic technology.

A number of projects are already underway. In 2006 the telecom giant ZTE was commissioned by Afghanistan to establish the country's first fiber-optic cable network, while Huawei obtained a series of contracts, including one in Turkmenistan to construct fiber-optic communications lines and another in Kyrgyzstan to increase the bandwidth of existing lines.[171] China and Russia have also partnered in building major terrestrial telecommunication links across the Eurasian continent, including the world's longest terrestrial cable link, the Trans-Europe Asia, in addition to the Europe-Russia-Mongolia-China network, the Trans-Eurasian Information Super Highway, and the Diverse Route for European and Asian Markets. The last of these projects is an ambitious Eurasian fiber-optic communication landline that was announced by Russia's MegaFon in October 2013 and will be built with equipment supplied by China's Huawei.

Several new projects are now aimed at building telecommunication networks between Asia and Europe under the BRI banner, and the Chinese government is also trying to forge international cooperation in this domain. While visiting Brussels in July 2015, Lu Wei, the head of China's Cyberspace Administration, called for a joint project with the EU to build a "digital Silk Road, a Silk Road in Cyberspace," and insisted on the commonalities between China's "Internet plus" Strategy and the EU's digital agenda.[172] A few months after that visit, the EU and China issued a declaration on the development of 5G mobile networks, showing that both parties expect to harmonize their standards and develop common research in this domain.[173]

Beyond institutional cooperation, the Chinese government intends to further develop international cooperation by pushing its own information and communications technology companies to join the BRI efforts by stoking investment in network infrastructure and speeding up the construction of

---

[171] "First Fiber Optic Network in Afghanistan," Wadsam, December 2, 2012, http://wadsam.com/afghan-business-news/first-fiber-optic-network-in-afghanistan-798; and Deirdre Tynan, "Central Asia: Are Chinese Telecoms Acting as the Ears for Central Asian Authoritarians?" EurasiaNet, February 15, 2012, http://www.eurasianet.org/node/65008.

[172] "Europe 2020 Strategy," European Commission, https://ec.europa.eu/digital-single-market/en/europe-2020-strategy; and Liu Jia and Gao Shuang, "China, EU to Promote Digital Silk Road," *China Daily*, July 7, 2015.

[173] "The EU and China Signed a Key Partnership on 5G, Our Tomorrow's Communication Networks," European Commission, September 28, 2015, http://europa.eu/rapid/press-release_IP-15-5715_en.htm.

a digital Silk Road.¹⁷⁴ In May 2016, China Telecom Global signed a contract with Kazakhtelecom, inaugurating the two companies' direct cooperation on a Europe-Asia telecommunication link, while China's CITIC Telecom International CPC (a subsidiary of the state-owned investment company CITIC) acquired the Dutch company LinxTelecom.¹⁷⁵ With this contract, CITIC Telecom International CPC acquired extensive telecommunication infrastructure in fourteen countries across Central and Eastern Europe, Western Europe, and Central Asia; a 470 km fiber-optic network in the Baltic Sea; and a data center in Tallinn. The contract was publicly hailed as a way to "capture opportunities arising from China's 'One Belt, One Road' cooperation initiative." "With this new competitive advantage," stated its CEO Stephen Ho, "we will continue to support the 'One Belt, One Road' Initiative through ongoing investment and development of telecommunication infrastructure and premium ICT services."¹⁷⁶

Parallel with these efforts to build fiber-optic cables, China is pushing for the completion of a "space-based Silk Road." A June 2016 white paper announced the objective to expand the BeiDou Navigation Satellite System services to most countries covered by BRI by 2018, before global coverage is completed by 2020.¹⁷⁷ International cooperation under BRI is officially described as one of the priority objectives for BeiDou, which not only offers global satellite navigation services but also intends to demonstrate its usefulness in "transportation, tourism, maritime application, disaster reduction and relief, and agriculture" and in "serving the world and benefiting mankind."¹⁷⁸ BeiDou has already started to offer its services to countries such as Pakistan, Thailand, and the UAE, as well as regional organizations such as ASEAN and the Arab League, and China has signed

---

[174] Zhao Huanxin, "Digital Silk Road Linked to 'Net Plus,'" *China Daily*, July 20, 2015, http://usa.chinadaily.com.cn/epaper/2015-07/20/content_21335526.htm.

[175] Paul Mah, "China Telecom Signs with Kazakh Firm for New Link to Europe," Data Center Dynamics, May 3, 2016, http://www.datacenterdynamics.com/core-edge/china-telecom-signs-with-kazakh-firm-for-new-silk-road-to-europe/96115.fullarticle; and "CITIC Telecom CPC Acquires Telecommunication Assets of Linx Telecommunications," CITIC Telecom International CCP, Press Release, April 28, 2016, http://www.citictel.com/upload/news/797168769385.pdf.

[176] "CITIC Telecom CPC Acquires Telecommunication Assets of Linx Telecommunications."

[177] Jiang Jie, "Nation Considers Space-Based 'Silk Road of Satellites' to Provide Data Services," *Global Times*, May 31, 2015, http://www.globaltimes.cn/content/924600.shtml.

[178] State Council Information Office (PRC), "China's BeiDou Navigation Satellite System" (Beijing, June 2016), available at http://news.xinhuanet.com/english/china/2016-06/16/c_135441516.htm.

an MOU on global navigation satellite system cooperation with Saudi Arabia and the Arab League.[179]

Xi Jinping himself has showed a strong interest in telecommunication technologies that could be used for expanding BRI coverage. Inmarsat, a leader in providing mobile satellite services, was the only British company he visited during his state visit to London in October 2015. Subsequently, Inmarsat signed an MOU with China Transport Telecommunication Information Center to implement a strategic partnership worth more than 2 billion pounds in order to deliver Inmarsat's 5G satellite service, Global Xpress, throughout the BRI region.[180] Inmarsat and BeiDou have already started to integrate their services: fishing boats in Fujian, for example, are equipped with Chinese-made devices that deploy both BeiDou and Inmarsat services for navigation and communication. Based on this previous experience, Inmarsat could work with its Chinese partners to integrate its satellite communication services with BeiDou in BRI regions.[181]

Conclusion

What is the Belt and Road Initiative? What is its geographic scope? What is its timeline? How many countries belong to BRI? Are countries that signed MOUs with China the only ones officially included? How many projects are underway? Are infrastructure projects that were negotiated before 2013 also included? Chinese officials and scholars alike have not given clear answers to any of these questions. Instead, they insist that BRI is open and inclusive and that every country that wants to join is welcome (see **Table 1** for an overview of BRI). From a Western perspective, this can be frustrating, and some analysts have been tempted to reject BRI altogether as an empty slogan. Surely, if Beijing were serious about the initiative, the government would have stated a clear goal, formulated a detailed plan to achieve it, and started to exert its will to execute this plan.

---

[179] "Progress in the BeiDou Navigation Satellites System and Application of Multi-Frequency and Multi-Constellation GNSS," PRC, Working Paper, August 31, 2016, http://www.icao.int/Meetings/a39/Documents/WP/wp_333_en.pdf.

[180] "Chinese State Visit: Up to £40 Billion Deals Agreed," UK Trade and Investment, October 23, 2015, https://www.gov.uk/government/news/chinese-state-visit-up-to-40-billion-deals-agreed; and "Inmarsat Plc Agrees Strategic Partnership with China," *China Daily*, October 23, 2015, http://www.china.org.cn/international/2015-10/23/content_36870652.htm.

[181] Zhang Jiawei and Huang Yong, "China's Belt and Road Initiative Catches World's Imagination: Inmarsat CEO," Xinhua, January 6, 2016, http://news.xinhuanet.com/english/2016-01/06/c_134980780.htm.

TABLE 1   The Belt and Road Initiative in one chart

Timeline	• 2013–16: Mobilization • 2016–21: Planning • 2021–49: Implementation
Geographic scope	60–65 countries 19 Chinese provinces • *Silk Road Economic Belt:* Shaanxi, Gansu, Qinghai, Sichuan, Yunnan, Ningxia, Xinjiang, Inner Mongolia, Guangxi, Henan, Chongqing, Heilongjiang, Jilin, and Liaoning • *21st Century Maritime Silk Road:* Jiangsu, Zhejiang, Fujian, Guangdong, and Hainan 6 economic corridors *Silk Road Economic Belt* • New Eurasian land bridge • China-Pakistan economic corridor • China-Mongolia-Russia economic corridor • China–Central Asia–West Asia economic corridor *21st Century Maritime Silk Road* • China–Indochina Peninsula economic corridor • Bangladesh-China-India-Myanmar economic corridor
Principles	• **Five Principles of Peaceful Coexistence** (mutual respect for each other's sovereignty and territorial integrity, mutual nonaggression, mutual noninterference in each other's internal affairs, equality and cooperation for mutual benefit, and peaceful coexistence) • **Openness** (not limited to the ancient Silk Road area but open to all countries) • **Harmonious and inclusive** (respect for the paths and modes of development chosen by different countries, support for dialogue among civilizations) • **Market rules** (allowing governments to perform their due functions) • **Mutual benefit** (win-win cooperation)
Framework	**Vision and Actions on Jointly Building the Silk Road Economic Belt and 21st Century Maritime Silk Road:** "Win-win cooperation that promotes common development and prosperity and a road towards peace and friendship by enhancing mutual understanding and trust, and strengthening all-round exchanges"

Table 1 continued

Priorities for cooperation	Five links: • Policy coordination • Infrastructure connectivity • Unimpeded trade • Financial integration • People-to-people exchanges
Mechanisms	• **Existing bilateral and multilateral cooperation mechanisms:** APEC, ASEAN +1, Asia Cooperation Dialogue, Asia-Europe Meeting, Central Asia Regional Economic Cooperation, China–Arab States Cooperation Forum, Conference on Interaction and Confidence-Building Measures in Asia, Greater Mekong Subregion, and Shanghai Cooperation Organisation. • **International forums:** Boao Forum for Asia, China-ASEAN Expo, and Euro-Asia Economic Forum

SOURCE: "Silk Road Economic Belt Construction: Vision and Path," Chongyang Institute for Financial Studies, Renmin University, Research Paper, no. 4, June 28, 2014; and NDRC, Ministry of Foreign Affairs, and Ministry of Commerce (PRC), "Vision and Actions on Jointly Building Silk Road Economic Belt and 21st-Century Maritime Silk Road," March 28, 2015, http://en.ndrc.gov.cn/newsrelease/201503/t20150330_669367.html.

Instead, what we see is a loose collection of activities that look dispersed, irrelevant, or even foolish, leaving some observers feeling underwhelmed by the initiative's concrete results.[182]

Notwithstanding such skepticism, a careful study of Xi Jinping's speeches and the central government's official documents reveals the broad contours of a coherent, purposeful undertaking. If BRI had been marketed by a Western advertising firm, it might have been given a more forward-looking label like "China-Asia Connectivity 2050." Regardless of the name, it is a long-term project that aims at creating a web of connections between China and the Eurasian continent that are both hard and soft—from transportation, telecommunication, and energy infrastructure to financial integration and political coordination. Over three years after its launch, BRI has started to take shape: 6 main economic corridors will constitute its

---

[182] Jiafeng Chen, "Camel Bells and Smoky Deserts," *Harvard Political Review*, March 13, 2016, http://harvardpolitics.com/world/camel-bells-and-smoky-deserts.

backbone, 56 MOUs and 11 FTAs with BRI countries have been signed,[183] new financial institutions have been created, and China has identified hundreds of projects for possible bilateral cooperation, some of which have already sprung up from the ground.

But BRI appears to be much more than just the sum of its parts. As François Jullien superbly explains in his book *A Treatise on Efficacy: Between Western and Chinese Thinking*, a Chinese strategist does not impose his plan on the world. Instead, he seeks to discern the propensity of things, assesses the potential inherent in the situation, and lets himself be carried along with it.[184] Xi articulated a broad vision for China in reaction to a combination of factors that will be described in the next chapter. The rest of the country was then mobilized to participate in a nationwide effort to help achieve this vision. Regardless of their own opinions and assessments regarding BRI's merits, and regardless of their possible personal skepticism about its financial returns, economic benefits, or political gains, Chinese diplomats, businessmen, state-owned enterprises, scholars, and journalists have all embraced the initiative and now praise and seek to contribute to it in their own domains. The entire country is now striving toward the same goal given from the top. Such a mobilization of various instruments of national power, both hard and soft, linking internal and external dimensions to achieve an overarching vision makes BRI look like neither an engineering project nor a development aid program but rather a grand strategy. In the words of Peking University professor Zhai Kun, the Silk Road Economic Belt and the 21st Century Maritime Silk Road initiatives are President Xi's "mega-strategy."[185]

The accumulation of evidence about BRI's concrete manifestations still leaves unanswered questions regarding the precise objectives that this strategy is meant to serve. Why did Xi decide to launch such a far-reaching initiative, which has already summoned a tremendous amount of national human and financial resources? What are BRI's drivers? What are its publicly acknowledged and unspoken motives? And what are its goals? The next chapter will attempt to address these critical questions.

---

[183] Author's discussions with scholars from Jiaotong University's International Energy Research Center, Shanghai, December 2016.

[184] François Jullien, *A Treatise on Efficacy: Between Western and Chinese Thinking*, trans. Janet Lloyd (Honolulu: University of Hawaii Press, 2004).

[185] Zhai Kun, "The Xi Jinping Doctrine of Chinese Diplomacy," China-U.S. Focus, March 25, 2014, http://www.chinausfocus.com/political-social-development/the-xi-jinping-doctrine-of-chinese-diplomacy.

Chapter 3

Drivers of the Belt and Road Initiative

In less than three years, the Belt and Road Initiative (BRI) has become the defining concept of China's foreign policy and is now omnipresent in official rhetoric. It has established a general direction for the country's efforts to build an interconnected, integrated Eurasian continent before 2050. Judging by the importance that the leadership has given the concept, and the quantity of financial, diplomatic, and intellectual resources that have been devoted to it, arguing that BRI is just an empty shell or vacuous political slogan has become increasingly difficult. Its paramount importance for the core leadership is also hard to deny. What is so crucial about the initiative that the vital energies of the entire country have been mobilized to give it the best chances of succeeding? Why is Beijing so eager to invest billions of dollars in Eurasia's infrastructure connectivity? What are the drivers behind BRI and what are its goals?

A first partial answer to these questions can be found in Xi Jinping's speeches. In several instances, he has argued that it is only natural that China, after having itself benefited from its integration into the international system, has now started to make its own contribution to global development by providing "more public goods to the international community." China will do so, Xi has repeatedly claimed, not to pursue its own purposes (as a "one-man show") or to establish an exclusive sphere of influence, but rather to produce mutually beneficial outcomes and prosperity for all.[1] The March 2015 "Vision and Actions" document portrays BRI in the same generous light—it is "a great undertaking that will benefit peoples around the world" and also an answer to "the weak recovery of the global economy and a complex international and regional situation."[2]

---

[1] Taylor Soper, "Full Text: China President Xi Gives Policy Speech in Seattle, Wants to Fight Cybercrime with the U.S.," GeekWire, September 22, 2015, http://www.geekwire.com/2015/full-text-china-president-xi-gives-policy-speech-in-seattle-pledges-to-fight-cybercrime-with-u-s; and "Wang Yi: 'Belt and Road' Is 'Symphony' Jointly Performed by All Countries," Ministry of Foreign Affairs of the People's Republic of China (PRC), February 2, 2015, http://www.fmprc.gov.cn/mfa_eng/zxxx_662805/t1234406.shtml.

[2] National Development and Reform Commission (NDRC), Ministry of Foreign Affairs, and Ministry of Commerce (PRC) "Vision and Actions on Jointly Building Silk Road Economic Belt and 21st-Century Maritime Silk Road," March 28, 2015.

BRI emerged after two major events, one economic and the other strategic, and has rapidly become Xi's signature concept. Not long after Xi rose to the position of vice president of the People's Republic of China (PRC) in March 2008, China began to feel the aftershocks of the global financial crisis. Shortly after he became vice chairman of the Central Military Commission in fall 2010, the Obama administration announced its intention to "rebalance" to the Asia-Pacific. These two events had a profound impact on the Chinese elites' ongoing assessment of their country's economic development prospects and external strategic environment. In the wake of the financial crisis, the global economy—including China—entered a period of low growth without any prospect of short-term recovery. In 2011 the United States started to push for the establishment of the Trans-Pacific Partnership, a regional free trade agreement that was seen in Beijing as a way to expand U.S. access in Asia while marginalizing and isolating China. At the same time, the Chinese leadership perceived mounting security challenges in the country's immediate environment, developments that Beijing blamed on the Obama administration's rebalancing strategy and its attempts to strengthen regional military alliances and incite U.S. allies to stir trouble on maritime issues. Given the extreme complexity of this environment, Chinese authorities concluded that relying on a "conventional approach" to achieve China's rise was no longer sufficient. In the words of Jiang Zhida, a fellow at the China Institute of International Studies, Beijing had to "think strategically to turn challenges into opportunities" and to "create favorable conditions" for China's unimpeded rise.[3] BRI can best be understood as an attempt to set the direction for China to achieve its ambitions as a preponderant regional power, in the context of mounting challenges in both the economic and strategic domains.

The next two sections of this chapter will look at BRI's drivers. The first will focus on economic rationales for BRI and show how the initiative is thought of as a way to boost China's economy, eliminate some of its excess industrial capacity, stimulate the global expansion of its state-owned enterprises (SOE), and help with the gradual internationalization of its currency. The second part of the chapter will focus on strategic drivers, which, although not officially acknowledged, are a fundamental rationale behind BRI. Specifically, Beijing seeks to alleviate terrorist threats, secure energy resources, strengthen its regional influence, and counter the U.S. presence in Asia.

---

[3] Jiang Zhida, "'Yidai Yilu': Yi 'kongjian' huan 'shijian' de fazhan zhanlüe" ["Belt and Road": The Development Strategy That Turns "Space" into "Time"], *Heping yu Fazhan* 4 (2015).

Economic Rationales

Even before the global financial crisis of 2008–9, China's leaders had begun to worry that their long-standing development model—with its heavy emphasis on investment, exports, and SOEs—had outlived its usefulness and that a new approach was needed, one that would give a greater role to domestic consumption and private initiative.[4] Despite this awareness, the regime's response to the slump in global demand that followed the onset of the financial crisis was to unleash a massive stimulus program, with yet more state-directed investment in infrastructure and basic industries.[5] Although this program served its immediate purpose of boosting growth, back to an impressive rate of 10.6% in 2010, it only delayed the day of reckoning. By the time Xi Jinping assumed the top posts in the Chinese Communist Party (CCP) and government at the end of 2012, growth rates had fallen again to well below pre-crisis levels and appeared to be on a steep downward trajectory.[6] Despite the strong rebound in 2010, growth rates never returned to the 2007 level (14.2%) and fell to below 8% from 2012 onward.[7]

Xi's response to this troubling reality took two forms: on the one hand, at the Third Plenum of the 18th Party Congress in November 2013, he announced a package of wide-ranging reforms designed to elevate the market to "play a decisive role in allocating national resources" and emphasizing the need to "encourage, support and guide" the "non-publicly owned economy." At the same time, however, the CCP Central Committee reaffirmed "the leading role of the state-owned economy" in its plans for future development.[8] It is against this backdrop that BRI was launched at the end of 2013.

The official narrative surrounding BRI describes it as a generous gift to humankind, with China not seeking unilateral gains but rather working

---

[4] In early 2007, then prime minister Wen Jiabao said that the Chinese economy had to face major issues—"unstable, unbalanced, uncoordinated and unsustainable problems." See "Premier: China Confident in Maintaining Economic Growth," Xinhua, March 16, 2007, http://news.xinhuanet.com/english/2007-03/16/content_5856569.htm.

[5] Nicholas R. Lardy, *Sustaining China's Economic Growth after the Global Financial Crisis* (Washington, D.C.: Peterson Institute for International Economics, 2012), 5–41.

[6] Dwight H. Perkins, "China's Growth Slowdown and Its Implications," National Bureau of Asian Research (NBR), NBR Analysis Brief, November 4, 2013, http://nbr.org/publications/analysis/pdf/brief/110413_Perkins_ChinaSlowdown.pdf.

[7] World Bank, World Development Indicators Databank, http://databank.worldbank.org/data/reports.aspx?source=2&series=NY.GDP.MKTP.KD.ZG&country=CHN.

[8] See "Decision of the Central Committee of the Communist Party of China on Some Major Issues Concerning Comprehensively Deepening the Reform, Adopted at the Third Plenary Session of the 18th Central Committee of the Communist Party of China on November 12, 2013," available at http://www.china.org.cn/china/third_plenary_session/2014-01/16/content_31212602.htm.

for common prosperity and shared benefits. A closer look at Chinese publications provides a different perspective on Beijing's motivations. Xi's vision of Eurasian integration appears much more China-centered and principally designed to serve national interests. As described, for example, by the director of the Central Party School's Institute of International Studies, BRI is meant to achieve several objectives, including promoting better-balanced domestic development, opening up China's inland provinces to the outside world, expanding export markets for Chinese goods, and increasing available channels for energy imports. The initiative is described as further broadening China's "strategic hinterland and international space" and creating a secure and stable peripheral environment for the country's continued development and rise. The focus here is clearly on China and its interests rather than those of its neighbors.[9]

According to Chinese analysts, the countries along the belt and road, taken together, have enormous economic potential. With a total population of 4.4 billion and a combined GDP of $21 trillion—accounting for 63% and 29% of world totals, respectively—the region covered by BRI stands out as the dynamic core of the world economy.[10] Before the global financial crisis, Chinese analysts had already started to think about ways to revitalize the ancient Silk Road, but they saw the economic gap between the Eurasian heartland and its two more prosperous peripheries, Europe to the west and Asia to the east, as a significant obstacle.[11] Nonetheless, Eurasia's overall economic situation was considered to be improving. In the previous decade, China's trade with countries along the belt and road had recorded between

---

[9] This view is shared by analysts from the China Institutes of Contemporary International Relations (CICIR), the think tank affiliated with China's Ministry of State Security. Author's interviews, Beijing, November 2015. See also Han Baojiang, "Sichouzhi Lu Jingji Dai zaofu yantu geguo renmin de da shiye" [Silk Road Economic Belt to Bring Great Benefits to People of All Countries], *Renmin Ribao*, July 3, 2014, http://theory.people.com.cn/n/2014/0703/c40531-25232236.html.

[10] Chen Fengying, "Xi Jinping 'Yidai Yilu' gouxiang zhanlüe yiyi shenyuan" [Strategic Far-Reaching Significance of Xi Jinping's "Belt and Road" Concept], China Radio International, October 10, 2014, http://gb.cri.cn/42071/2014/10/10/882s4720906.htm. Chen Fengying is a fellow with CICIR. See also "Belt and Road Initiatives Get Kick Start," Information Office of the CCP International Department, China Insight, December 27, 2014, http://english.cccws.org.cn/archiver/cccwsen/UpFile/Files/Default/20141231095436722769.pdf.

[11] See, for example, Zhu Xianping and Zou Xiangyang, "Zhongguo-Zhongya Xin Sichouzhi Lu Fazhan Dai gouxiang" [China-Central Asia New Silk Road Economic Development Belt Concept], *Dongbeiya Luntan*, September 2006; Xia Liping, "Dangdai Ya'ou Dalu kua quyu hezuo qushi jiqi yingxiu" [Cooperation Trends and Influence in Contemporary Eurasia], *Eluosi Zhongya Dong'ou Yanjiu* 6 (2005): 63–65; Zheng Rujian, "Chongzhen Sichouzhi Lu: Zhongya wuguo dui Xin Ya'ou Dalu Qiao de yunzuo" [Silk Road Revival: Central Asia's Five States and the New Eurasian Land Bridge's Operations], *Zhongguo Ruankexue* 1 (1995): 54–57; Cui Guanjie, "Xin Ya'ou Daluqiao yanxian: Woguo you yige kaifang jingjidai" [Along the New Eurasian Land Bridge: China's Other Opened Economic Belt], *Zhongguo Ruankexue* 1 (1995): 29–34; and Yang Shu and Wang Shusen, "Sichuzhilu Jingjidai: Zhanlüe gouxiang jiqi tiaozhan" [Silk Road Economic Belt: Strategic Concept and Challenges], *Lanzhou Daxue Xuebao* 1 (2014): 24–25.

10% and 20% average annual growth, compared with only 3% growth in China's overall foreign trade during the same period.[12] Given the region's economic potential, Chinese analysts speculated that BRI could unlock promising new markets across Eurasia, even as demand from the developed world slackened.[13]

Boosting the Chinese Economy: A New Stimulus Package?

Economic growth is essential to the continued legitimacy of China's one-party state and to the country's great-power ambitions.[14] After the 1989 Tiananmen Square incident, steady improvements in the standard of living became a crucial part of Deng Xiaoping's tacit social contract with the Chinese people in return for their continued acceptance of the CCP's monopoly on political power.[15] High growth rates are also believed to be necessary to avoid massive unemployment and potential social unrest, which could weaken the country and therefore the regime. In 2007 the CCP amended its constitution to inscribe the objective of transforming China into a "moderately prosperous society" by 2021 when the party celebrates its hundredth anniversary.[16] This broad goal was given a more concrete definition by Hu Jintao in his opening speech to the 18th Party Congress in 2012, at a time when the Chinese economy had already started to feel the aftershocks of the global financial crisis: by 2020, China would double its 2010 GDP and per capita income for both urban and rural residents. This goal was reiterated by Xi in his first public speech as CCP general secretary

---

[12] Wang Wen (remarks at a conference organized by the Center for Strategic and International Studies, Washington, D.C., April 18, 2016); and Wang Yiwei, *Yidai Yilu: Zhongguo jueqi gei shijie dailai shenme* [Belt and Road: What China's Rise Will Offer to the World] (Beijing: Xin Shijie Chubanshe, 2016), 18.

[13] See, for example, Feng Zongxian, "Ouya diqu jingji fazhan xingshi fenxi he zhanwang" [Eurasia's Economic Development Trends, Analysis and Outlook], in *2013 OuYa Jingji Luntan fazhan baogao* [2013 Euro-Asia Economic Forum Development Report] (Xi'an: Xi'an Jiaotong Daxue Chubanshe, 2013), 55–63; and Gan Junxian, "Sichouzhi Lu fuxing jihua yu Zhongguo waijiao" [Planning for a Revival of the Silk Road and China's Diplomacy], *Dongbei Luntan* 19, no. 5 (2010): 65–73.

[14] Nadège Rolland, "China's National Power: A Colossus with Iron or Clay Feet?" in *Strategic Asia 2015–16: Foundations of National Power in the Asia-Pacific*, ed. Ashley J. Tellis, Alison Szalwinski, and Michael Wills (Seattle: NBR, 2015), 23–54.

[15] As the demonstrations were gaining momentum in Tiananmen Square in 1989, Deng said that "two hundred dead could bring 20 years of peace to China." Kris Cheng, "200 Dead Could Bring 20 Years of Peace, Ex-China Leader Deng Said Ahead of Tiananmen Massacre," *Hong Kong Free Press*, December 30, 2016, https://www.hongkongfp.com/2016/12/30/200-dead-could-bring-20-years-of-peace-ex-china-leader-deng-said-ahead-of-tiananmen-massacre.

[16] An English translation of the CCP's constitution is available from Xinhua at http://news.xinhuanet.com/english/2007-10/25/content_6944738.htm.

in November 2012, as he visited a "road to revival" exhibition with his fellow Politburo comrades.[17]

The massive $586 billion stimulus package launched in 2008 in response to the global financial crisis cushioned the blow to the Chinese economy, but its beneficial effects were short-lived. By 2011, the days of double-digit growth were clearly over, and China was left with a "stimulus package hangover."[18] The leadership now had to face the prospect of a protracted economic slowdown, a situation that Xi described in 2014 as the country's "new normal."[19]

The transformation of China's economic development model—from credit-fueled investment and export-driven growth to higher domestic consumption—is a conundrum for the Xi administration, which has chosen to prioritize achieving quantitative GDP targets over the difficult business of economic restructuring.[20] In this context, BRI enables the Chinese leadership to revert to what it knows best and breathes new life into the old model. Beijing is once again investing heavily in construction and infrastructure projects, only this time outside the already saturated territory of China. The hope seems to be that this new "stimulus package in disguise" will enable the country to sustain the GDP growth rates deemed necessary for social stability—just as was the case after the 2008 crisis—and achieve the 2021 goal of a moderately prosperous society. In the longer run, infrastructure development may also open new markets and help create new foreign demand for Chinese products.[21] Chinese economic commentators

---

[17] "Chengqian qihou jiwang kailai jixu chaozhe Zhonghua minzu weida fuxing mubiao fenyong qianjin" [Bridging the Past and the Future: Dauntlessly Forging Ahead toward the Goal of the Great Rejuvenation of the Chinese People], Xinhua, November 29, 2012, http://news.xinhuanet.com/politics/2012-11/29/c_113852724.htm.

[18] Zhao Hai (remarks at the U.S. Institute of Peace, Washington, D.C., December 1, 2016), http://www.usip.org/events/will-cpec-be-force-peace-or-conflict.

[19] "Xi Says China Must Adapt to 'New Normal' of Slower Growth," Bloomberg, May 11, 2014, http://www.bloomberg.com/news/articles/2014-05-11/xi-says-china-must-adapt-to-new-normal-of-slower-growth; and "Xi's 'New Normal' Theory," Xinhua, November 9, 2014, http://news.xinhuanet.com/english/china/2014-11/09/c_133776839.htm.

[20] For a thorough discussion of the stakes and risks of this transformation of China's economic model, see the transcript of the U.S.-China Economic and Security Review Commission's hearing on China's 13th Five-Year Plan, April 27, 2016, available at http://www.uscc.gov/Hearings/hearing-china's-13th-five-year-plan. In 2015, Xi reiterated a pledge to lift the GDP by 6.5% by 2020. See Mark Magnier, "China Lowers Expectations for Growth," Wall Street Journal, November 3, 2015, http://www.wsj.com/articles/chinas-president-xi-jinping-says-economy-to-grow-by-at-least-6-5-1446566259; and Jane Cai and Victoria Ruan, "China's Politburo Turns to 'Tried and Tested' Playbook to Spur Growth through Investment, Property," South China Morning Post, May 1, 2015, http://www.scmp.com/news/china/economy/article/1783142/china-hints-further-easing-monetary-policy-economy-loses-steam.

[21] Li Qiaoyi, "Making It Work," Global Times, March 10, 2015, http://www.globaltimes.cn/content/911258.shtml; and Wang Jingjing, "'One Belt, One Road' Likely to Raise China's GDP," China Daily, March 25, 2015, http://usa.chinadaily.com.cn/business/2015-03/25/content_19908927.htm.

and analysts appear optimistic about BRI's prospects for stimulating GDP growth. Officials at the National Development and Reform Commission (NDRC) agree with Justin Yifu Lin, former World Bank official and Peking University professor, that BRI's infrastructure investments are a crucial economic growth engine and will "create big market demand" for China's excess production.[22] More concretely, a report published in 2015 by Beijing-based Minsheng Securities estimated that BRI could contribute as much as 0.25% to China's growth rate.[23]

Overcapacity

The 2008 stimulus package delayed the Chinese economy's day of reckoning but also aggravated its structural imbalances. While the influx of government investment in state-owned heavy industries sustained aggregate economic growth, it also added yet more capacity in already overbuilt sectors such as steel, aluminum, and cement, flooding global markets with Chinese products. Even though the CCP's annual Central Economic Work Conference listed addressing overcapacity as a priority every year from 2007 to 2015, fundamental changes have yet to take place.[24] Tackling overcapacity is now "more urgent than ever," according to European Chamber of Commerce in China president Joerg Wuttke, and the "cost of maintaining the status quo is far too high."[25] Yet dealing with overcapacity is a politically sensitive issue for Chinese officials, with consequences they would prefer to avoid.[26] Indeed, managing the problem of overcapacity would require a major overhaul of China's model of state capitalism, with potentially worrisome implications for the CCP's hold on political power. Heavy industries require large workforces, and cutting their activity would generate mass layoffs and increase the risk of

---

[22] Author's interviews with officials from the NDRC, Beijing, December 2016. See also "Zhuanjia jiedu xin changdai xia Yidai Yilu: Wei Zhongguo jingji dailai zhongyao zengzhang dongli" [Expert Interprets Belt and Road under New Normal: An Important Engine for China's Economic Growth], Xinhua, March 7, 2015, http://finance.sina.com.cn/china/hgjj/20150307/225521669818.shtml.

[23] "Quanshang: 'Yidai Yilu' huo ladong GDP zengzhang 0.25 ge baifendian" [Broker: "Belt and Road" May Bring 0.25% of GDP Growth], Ta Kung Pao, March 25, 2015, http://finance.takungpao.com.hk/hgjj/q/2015/0325/2955088.html.

[24] European Chamber of Commerce in China, "Overcapacity in China: An Impediment to the Party's Reform Agenda," February 2016, http://www.iberchina.org/files/2016/Overcapacity_in_China.pdf; and Rui Fan, "China's Excess Capacity: Drivers and Implications," Law Offices of Stewart and Stewart, June 2015, http://www.stewartlaw.com/Content/Documents/China%27s%20Excess%20 Capacity%20-%20Drivers%20and%20Implications.pdf.

[25] European Chamber of Commerce in China, "Overcapacity in China."

[26] Tom Mitchell and Yuan Yang, "China Rails against Global 'Hype' on Overcapacity," Financial Times, June 6, 2016, https://www.ft.com/content/9ee9f1ca-2bca-11e6-a18d-a96ab29e3c95.

social instability. In the face of China's continuing economic slowdown, the government announced a cut of 1.8 million jobs at SOEs in February 2016—1.3 million in coal and 500,000 in steel out of a total workforce of 12 million in both industries[27]—but the priority given to sustaining growth and maintaining employment still supersedes the need to implement structural reforms.

So what should China do with its excess capacity? A number of foreign commentators have suggested that Chinese planners might see BRI as an answer to the country's overcapacity problem, although most also point out that demand from BRI countries is clearly not sufficient to absorb all of China's excess production.[28] Still, even if it does not resolve the issue, some analysts believe that the initiative could help Beijing buy time to enact further domestic reform and rebalancing.[29]

Chinese officials publicly deny that BRI has anything to do with overcapacity and prefer to use the term "international industrial cooperation." They portray China's proposed projects as magnanimous gifts to underdeveloped countries in desperate need of basic transportation networks or energy supplies to which China brings its experience in infrastructure construction and urban development.[30] They insist that what China is doing is "fundamentally different from the transfer of excess capacity practiced in the past by developed countries"[31] and is not meant to dump outdated or low-quality products on its poorer neighbors, who are "not stupid" and would never agree to such treatment.[32] Yet, despite these denials, exporting excess production to neighboring countries appears to

---

[27] Kevin Yao and Meng Meng, "China Expects to Lay Off 1.8 Million Workers in Coal, Steel Sectors," Reuters, February 29, 2016, http://www.reuters.com/article/us-china-economy-employment-idUSKCN0W205X.

[28] See, for example, Simeon Djankov and Sean Miner, eds., "China's Belt and Road Initiative: Motives, Scope, and Challenges," Peterson Institute for International Economics, Briefing, March 2016, 11, https://piie.com/system/files/documents/piieb16-2_1.pdf; David Dollar, "China's Rise as a Regional and Global Power: The AIIB and the 'One Belt, One Road,'" *Horizons*, no. 4 (2015): 162–72, https://www.brookings.edu/wp-content/uploads/2016/06/China-rise-as-regional-and-global-power.pdf; and Brenda Goh and Koh Gui Qing, "China's 'One Belt, One Road' Looks to Take Construction Binge Offshore," Reuters, September 6, 2015, http://www.reuters.com/article/china-economy-silkroad-idUSL5N10H1XR20150906.

[29] "Fitch Interview: China Steel Production Capacity to Peak in 2016," Reuters, November 19, 2015, http://af.reuters.com/article/metalsNews/idAFFit94038920151119; and Eric Ng, "'One Belt' Infrastructure Investments Seen as Helping to Use Up Some Industrial Over-capacity," *South China Morning Post*, November 2, 2015, http://www.scmp.com/business/article/1874895/one-belt-infrastructure-investments-seen-helping-use-some-industrial-over.

[30] Li Ziguo (remarks at U.S.-China Young Leaders Dialogue, Yinchuan, December 2016).

[31] Huo Jianguo, "China Exporting Industrial Benefits, Not Overcapacity," *Global Times*, March 17, 2016, http://www.globaltimes.cn/content/974284.shtml.

[32] Remarks by a senior director of the International Liaison Department at a closed-door roundtable, Washington, D.C., November 15, 2016.

currently be the Chinese authorities' preferred solution to the overcapacity problem. As Huang Libin, an official with the Ministry of Industry and Information Technology, commented, "for us there is overcapacity, but for the countries along the 'One Road One Belt' route, or for other BRIC nations, they don't have enough and if we shift it out, it will be a win-win situation."[33] He Yafei, vice minister of the Overseas Chinese Affairs Office of the State Council, suggested that China's excess capacity challenge could be turned into an opportunity for growth and create a new "thrust in the metamorphosis of China's economic development" if combined with a renewed push for Chinese companies to "go out" into global markets.[34]

A Fresh Boost to Chinese Firms' "Going Global" Strategy

The role of overseas investment was highlighted by Premier Li Keqiang at a meeting on participation by SOEs in BRI held in June 2016. According to Li, boosting such investment is essential to moderating China's economic slowdown, maintaining medium- to high-speed growth, and attaining medium- to high-level development.[35] Not surprisingly, Chinese SOEs have been enthusiastic about BRI, which they see as creating favorable conditions for investment abroad.[36]

Seen in this context, the initiative is a continuation of the "going global" strategy formulated in 2000 by then premier Zhu Rongji to encourage Chinese companies to invest abroad, enhance their international competitiveness, and become China's "national champions."[37] Then, as now, Chinese companies are responding to signals from the top. In the decade prior to China's accession to the World Trade Organization (WTO), SOEs went through a process of breaking up into multiple entities in order to demonstrate the nation's willingness to accept market competition. Today, by contrast, the government favors the consolidation

---

[33] David Stanway, "Going Abroad the Solution to China's Overcapacity Woes—Ministry Official," Reuters, July 22, 2015, http://www.reuters.com/article/china-industry-overcapacity-idUSL3N10230E20150722. The BRIC nations are Brazil, Russia, India, and China.

[34] He Yafei, "China's Overcapacity Crisis Can Spur Growth through Overseas Expansion," *South China Morning Post*, January 7, 2014, http://www.scmp.com/comment/insight-opinion/article/1399681/chinas-overcapacity-crisis-can-spur-growth-through-overseas.

[35] Norman Sze and Flora Wu, "'One Belt, One Road': The Internationalization of China's SOEs," Deloitte, Perspective, vol. 5, 2016, https://www2.deloitte.com/content/dam/Deloitte/cn/Documents/about-deloitte/dttp/deloitte-cn-dttp-vol5-chapter2-en.pdf.

[36] Author's interviews with officials from the China Chamber of Commerce of Metals Minerals and Chemicals Importers and Exporters and China National Petroleum Corporation (CNPC), Beijing, December 2016. The China Chamber of Commerce of Metals Minerals and Chemicals Importers and Exporters has 6,300 members, who produce one-third of the PRC's total export volume.

[37] Author's interviews with officials from the NDRC, Beijing, December 2016.

of state-sector conglomerates. SOEs are the preferred instruments of the top leadership's national economic and social policies: they help support social stability by offering jobs and social services, carry the Chinese flag to international markets, enhance China's technological base, and foster indigenous innovation.[38] For all these reasons, Xi has described the SOEs as having a "dominant role in important sectors and crucial areas that affect national security and the commanding heights of the economy."[39] Xi has clear ambitions for a reinvigorated state sector, which reflect his views on top-down economic development under which SOEs respond to the party's will and operate according to a political rather than a purely market logic.[40] BRI is meant to promote their business activities abroad and help them expand their international clout, but it also uses SOEs as the political leadership's strong arm to gain leverage and influence in host countries. Even if, as a high-ranking representative from the China National Petroleum Corporation (CNPC) suggests, "the emperor is in Beijing but generals who are on the battlefield ultimately make the decisions," Chinese state firms do not have much say when the central leadership gives them instructions. Indeed, the same CNPC cadre acknowledged that sometimes profit must be sacrificed for the sake of national security, and profitable projects must compensate for those that are losing money.[41] The return on investment may not even be entirely monetary, as a Ministry of Commerce official explains, but can sometimes be measured in increased "friendship" (in other words, in Chinese influence) secured in host countries.[42]

The second wave of Chinese SOEs going global under BRI will not, as in the past, compete against each other for international contracts. In order to avoid duplication and to better compete for market share against their foreign challengers, several firms operating in sectors that are key to

---

[38] Andrew Batson, "Villains or Victims? The Role of SOEs in China's Economy," Dragonomics Research and Advisory, China Economic Quarterly, June 2016; Barry Naughton, "State Enterprise Reform: Missing in Action," Dragonomics Research and Advisory, China Economic Quarterly, June 2016; Michael Komesaroff, "Return of the Line Ministries," Dragonomics Research and Advisory, China Economic Quarterly, June 2016; and Wendy Leutert, "Challenges Ahead in China's Reform of State-Owned Enterprises," *Asia Policy*, no. 21 (2016): 83–99.

[39] Barry Naughton, "Two Trains Running: Supply-Side Reform, SOE Reform and the Authoritative Personage," Hoover Institution, China Leadership Monitor, no. 50, Summer 2016, 7, http://www.hoover.org/sites/default/files/research/docs/clm50bn.pdf.

[40] Xi Jinping, "Guanyu 'Zhonggong Zhongyang guanyu quanmian shenhua gaige ruogan zhongda wenti de jueding' de shuoming" [A Note on the "CCP Central Committee Decision on Several Major Issues Concerning Comprehensively Deepening Reforms"], *People's Daily*, November 16, 2013, http://paper.people.com.cn/rmrbhwb/html/2013-11/16/content_1325399.htm. See also Leutert, "Challenges Ahead in China's Reform of State-Owned Enterprises"; and Batson, "Villains or Victims?"

[41] Author's interviews with CNPC officials, Beijing, December 2016.

[42] Author's interviews with a representative from the Ministry of Commerce, Yinchuan, December 2016.

the realization of BRI have recently been merged. The State-Owned Assets Supervision and Administration Commission reiterated in March 2016 the objective of reforming the state sector by making companies "bigger and better" through mergers and acquisitions.[43] This pattern is evident in the case of the container shipping operator China COSCO Shipping Corporation (formerly China Ocean Shipping Group Company and China Shipping Group), the tanker shipping and logistics business China Merchants Group (which purchased Sinotrans and CSC Holdings Co.), the mining giant China Minmetals Corporation (which incorporated the China Metallurgical Group), and the power company China State Power Investment Corporation (formerly China Power Investment Corporation and State Nuclear Power Technology Corporation).[44]

China's great strides in the high-speed rail sector offer a particularly striking example of the mutual reinforcement and increased synergies between the objectives of the central government and those of the SOEs. The merger of China South Railway and China North Railway into China Railway Rolling Stock Corporation was announced in 2015 as China's international "high-speed railway diplomacy" and BRI were both gathering momentum. Throughout 2014 and 2015, both Li Keqiang and Xi Jinping trumpeted the merits of Chinese high-speed rail technology during each of their official visits to Europe and Asia. High-speed rail quickly became a symbol not only of China's global industrial competitiveness but also of the diplomatic message that is at the heart of BRI: connection, interaction, and cooperation with China can lead to development in countries where Western countries and international institutions have previously failed.[45] But in the end, the initiative mostly serves China's interests. With the support of political authorities and ready access to policy bank credits, the SOEs can expand their overseas activities and contribute to China's growth as they generate income and jobs for Chinese workers. Meanwhile, the political leadership uses the prospect of infrastructure projects to widen the scope of bilateral cooperation and deepen China's influence in BRI countries. As a recent study of China's high-speed railway diplomacy observes, "agreements for deepening cooperation in military affairs, culture, research and education, or other areas, are often negotiated simultaneously

---

[43] "China Tells Foreign Firms to Brace for Bigger Competitors," Bloomberg, March 15, 2016, https://www.bloomberg.com/news/articles/2016-03-15/china-congress-to-foreign-firms-brace-for-bigger-competitors.

[44] Leutert, "Challenges Ahead in China's Reform of State-Owned Enterprises."

[45] "Top Spokesman—Premier Li Promotes China's High-Speed Rail," State Council of the PRC, December 25, 2015, http://english.gov.cn/premier/news/2015/12/29/content_281475262862422.htm.

with—or in the aftermath of—the railway deals," ultimately contributing greatly to China's growing global presence and influence.[46]

In addition to benefiting companies that specialize in transportation infrastructure and logistics, BRI will also stimulate the global expansion of Chinese conglomerates with expertise in critical infrastructure, including electrical power and information and communication technology (ICT).[47] Thus, for example, the central government is actively pushing the China State Grid Corporation to expand its activities into third-country markets. The company has mastered the ultra-high-voltage technology needed to transmit power across large distances within China, and this technology could prove critically important for supplying power in BRI countries. Deploying power grids across the Eurasian continent would offer China a large share of the global market and enable it to shape international standards.[48] Similarly, the "digital Silk Road" cannot be built without the active engagement of Chinese ICT firms, which the central government is likewise encouraging.[49] ZTE and Huawei are already major contributors to research on international fifth-generation, or 5G, standards for mobile networks and are looking for new opportunities to expand their markets. As a result of the partnership that China and the European Union agreed to in September 2015, Chinese companies will likely help set the standards for the new generation of global mobile communications, as well as electronic commerce, banking, and logistics.[50]

The Internationalization of the Renminbi

As Chinese SOEs become more internationalized, so does the renminbi. In the wake of the global financial crisis, the Chinese government, worried by China's increased vulnerability to external shocks and volatility—especially from the U.S. dollar—started to think about

---

[46] Agatha Kratz and Dragan Pavlićević, "China's High-Speed Rail Diplomacy: Riding a Gravy Train?" King's College London, Lau China Institute, Working Paper Series, no. 1, 2016, http://www.kcl.ac.uk/sspp/sga/lci/documents/working-papers/Lau-China-Institute-Working-Papers-1.pdf.

[47] Willy Wo-Lap Lam, "'One Belt, One Road' Enhances Xi Jinping's Control Over the Economy," Jamestown Foundation, China Brief, March 15, 2015, https://jamestown.org/program/one-belt-one-road-enhances-xi-jinpings-control-over-the-economy; and Li, "Making It Work."

[48] "Power Play: China's Ultra-High Voltage Technology and Global Standards," Paulson Institute, Paulson Paper on Standards, April 2015, http://www.paulsoninstitute.org/wp-content/uploads/2015/04/PPS_UHV_English.pdf.

[49] Zhao Huanxin, "Web Companies Asked to Support 'Digital Silk Road,'" *China Daily*, July 18, 2015, http://usa.chinadaily.com.cn/business/2015-07/18/content_21318972.htm.

[50] "The EU and China Signed a Key Partnership on 5G, Our Tomorrow's Communication Networks," European Commission, Press Release, September 28, 2015, http://europa.eu/rapid/press-release_IP-15-5715_en.htm.

ways to strengthen the renminbi's position and develop it as a global trade and investment currency.⁵¹ The International Monetary Fund added the renminbi to its "special drawing rights" basket in October 2016, describing this step as a "milestone in the integration of the Chinese economy into the global financial system."⁵² But a considerable gap still exists between ambition and reality, especially because, as in many other domains, the Chinese authorities are reluctant to relinquish control over their monetary policy. There is increasing tension between "preserving stability and allowing the freedom and flexibility required of a global currency," but for the time being China will likely maintain its hybrid approach of free float mixed with recurrent state intervention.⁵³

In this context, the People's Bank of China seems to favor the gradual internationalization of the renminbi through the creation of a global network of offshore renminbi clearing banks, currency-swap agreements, and integrated electronic infrastructure.⁵⁴ BRI can help serve as a stimulus for all these developments by creating opportunities for greater use of the renminbi in international transactions, especially those related to energy development and investment in infrastructure.⁵⁵ As changes in trade patterns inevitably affect the use of currencies in international settlements, Chinese companies' increasing activity in Eurasian markets can help narrow the gap between China's trade and the renminbi's global position. In 2016, China's proportion of global exports rose to 13.8%, while the renminbi's share of world payments (1.7%) lagged significantly behind the U.S. dollar (64.0%)

---

[51] For a comprehensive discussion about the increased international role of the renminbi and its challenges, see Eswar Prasad, "The Renminbi's Ascendance in International Finance," in *Policy Challenges in a Diverging Global Economy*, ed. Reuven Glick and Mark M. Spiegel (San Francisco: Federal Reserve Bank of San Francisco, 2015), 157–206, http://prasad.dyson.cornell.edu/doc/FRBSF-AEPC2015Final.pdf; and Arthur Kroeber, "China's Global Currency: Lever for Financial Reform," Brookings-Tsinghua Center for Public Policy, Monograph Series, no. 3, February 2013, https://www.brookings.edu/wp-content/uploads/2016/06/china-global-currency-financial-reform-kroeber.pdf.

[52] "IMF Adds Chinese Renminbi to Special Drawing Rights Basket," International Monetary Fund, September 30, 2016, http://www.imf.org/en/News/Articles/2016/09/29/AM16-NA093016IMF-Adds-Chinese-Renminbi-to-Special-Drawing-Rights-Basket.

[53] Gabriel Wildau and Tom Mitchell, "China: Renminbi Stalls on Road to Being a Global Currency," *Financial Times*, December 11, 2016, https://www.ft.com/content/e480fd92-bc6a-11e6-8b45-b8b81dd5d080.

[54] Gregory Chin, "Globalizing the RMB? Beijing Appoints Three New Clearing Banks in London, Frankfurt, and Seoul," Asian Development Bank Institute, Asia Pathways, July 29, 2014, http://www.asiapathways-adbi.org/2014/07/globalizing-the-rmb-beijing-appoints-three-new-clearing-banks-in-london-frankfurt-and-seoul.

[55] Yang Mei, Guo Fang, and Yao Dongqin, "Xinsilu zhanlüe de jingji zhidian" [The New Silk Road Strategy's Economic Fulcrum], *Zhongguo Jingji Zhoukan*, July 2014, http://paper.people.com.cn/zgjjzk/html/2014-07/07/content_1450774.htm.

and even the Canadian dollar (1.96%).[56] Experts believe that this gap will begin to close thanks to the progress of China's new Cross-Border Interbank Payment System (CIPS) and the opening of new offshore clearing centers, which have the potential to transform the Asian financial landscape in the coming decade.[57]

In addition to the overseas branches of China's major state-owned commercial banks, there are currently nineteen renminbi clearing centers worldwide, but very few are located in countries covered by BRI. Hong Kong, which processes 71% of offshore renminbi payments, is the largest one.[58] China seems to favor bilateral swap agreements for BRI countries but also would like to create cross-border payment systems parallel to the ones currently operated by the international financial giants the Society for Worldwide Interbank Financial Telecommunication (SWIFT) and Visa.[59] These would facilitate the completion of transactions without using dollars or going through institutions under U.S. surveillance or control.

Launched in October 2015, CIPS is both a funds transfer system and a communication channel for financial institutions that does not use an offshore clearing center.[60] It has been designed so that international renminbi transactions can be made independently of SWIFT, thus reducing China's reliance on Western payment systems and financial markets.[61] For its

---

[56] China's share of global exports is the highest that any country has enjoyed since the United States in 1968. See Elias Glenn and Pete Sweeney, "China Seizes Biggest Share of Global Exports in Almost 50 Years," Reuters, April 22, 2016, http://www.reuters.com/article/us-china-exports-idUSKCN0XJ097. In 2013 the renminbi ranked as the tenth most used currency in global settlements, with a share of 0.87%. See Kenneth Rapoza, "Canada's Dollar Beats China's Currency in World Trade but Not for Long," Forbes, July 21, 2016, http://www.forbes.com/sites/kenrapoza/2016/07/21/canadas-dollar-beats-chinas-currency-in-world-trade-but-not-for-long/#107bb1991692.

[57] "RMB Tracker," Society for Worldwide Interbank Financial Telecommunication, July 2016, https://www.swift.com/node/33851; and Standard Chartered and Thomson Reuters, "Renminbi Roadmap," Asia Securities Industry and Financial Markets Association, May 2014, https://www.sc.com/en/resources/global-en/pdf/Research/RMB-Roadmap-SC-branded.pdf.

[58] The list of offshore renminbi clearing centers at the time of writing includes Argentina, Australia, Canada, Chile, Frankfurt, Hong Kong, London, Luxembourg, Macao, Malaysia, Paris, Qatar, Russia, Singapore, South Africa, South Korea, Switzerland, Taiwan, and Thailand. Duan Ting, "RMB's Unstoppable Climb to the Global Stage," China Daily, September 9, 2016, http://www.chinadailyasia.com/focus/2016-09/09/content_15492913_2.html.

[59] As seen in chapter 2, China signed a series of renminbi bilateral swap agreements, including with Singapore, Malaysia, Indonesia, Thailand, Kazakhstan, Uzbekistan, Nepal, Pakistan, Sri Lanka, the United Arab Emirates, Qatar, Belarus, Russia, Ukraine, and Turkey. See "China's 'One Belt, One Road'—Opportunities for Chinese and Foreign Businesses," HSBC, July 31, 2015, https://globalconnections.hsbc.com/hong-kong/en/articles/chinas-one-belt-one-road-opportunities-chinese-and-foreign-businesses.

[60] Paul Golden, "China's International Payment System Gathers Steam," Euromoney, November 12, 2015, http://www.euromoney.com/Article/3505807/Chinas-international-payment-system-gathers-steam.html.

[61] Eswar S. Prasad, Gaining Currency: The Rise of the Renminbi (New York: Oxford University Press, 2017), 115–16.

part, state-controlled UnionPay, which was created in 2002 and is under the purview of the People's Bank of China and the State Council, provides a system for interbank and cross-border transactions and already delivers services to the majority of BRI countries.[62]

The latest phase in the development of China's international payment systems is tailored specifically to the needs of BRI transactions. State-owned China Merchants Port Holdings, which specializes in transportation, logistics, and harbor services, is a leading example of this new model. Together with IZP Technologies, a provider of big data services founded in 2008, China Merchants Port Holdings launched a new entity in March 2016. The Silk Road E-Merchants Information Technologies is a foreign-trade service company that designs digital platforms for customs clearance and electronic cross-border trade and payments. In association with the NDRC, IZP has created a big data center dedicated to BRI, which aims to "collect global port trade, finance, GIS [geographical information system] information, domestic and foreign statistics and industry business data as well as domestic and foreign internet data, data of mainstream news media and social media and other mass data, and analyze, mine and apply them."[63] IZP also operates digital platforms for electronic commerce, such as Haixuan and Globebuy, as well as the online payment platform Globebill, which mostly serves corporate clients that have cross-border businesses and transactions with China.[64]

IZP's CEO, former Huawei employee Luo Feng, unabashedly presents Globebill as the "new Visa system along the Silk Road" and articulates a clear objective: "The U.S. dollar dominates the dual-currency card market now but in 10 years, it will be Renminbi plus one."[65] For this purpose, IZP has established several "Silk Road stations" (in Italy, Kyrgyzstan, Sri Lanka, Djibouti, Belarus, and Lithuania, among other countries) that can "stimulate more Chinese goods to be exported to Belt and Road countries."[66] In 2015, IZP signed agreements with Russia's Trade and Economic Committee,

---

[62] "UnionPay Expands along the 'Belt and Road,'" Xinhua, February 9, 2015, http://news.xinhuanet.com/english/china/2015-02/09/c_133981413.htm.

[63] "Data Engine of OBOR Strategy: Overall Framework of 'the Belt and Road (OBOR)' Big Data," IZP Technologies, http://www.izptec.com/en/index.php?m=content&c=index&a=lists&catid=1.

[64] Song Mengxing and Wang Sujuan, "Globebill Indeed Goes Global with Range of Currencies," China Watch, December 26, 2014, http://chinawatch.washingtonpost.com/2014/12/globebill-indeed-goes-global-with-range-of-currencies.

[65] Dai Tian, "Big Data Conglomerate Dreams Big on Silk Road," China Daily, July 29, 2015, http://www.chinadaily.com.cn/business/fourmoninternet/2015-07/29/content_21432401.htm.

[66] "Silk Road Station: Aircraft Carrier in World Trade along One Belt One Road!" IZP Technologies, http://www.izptec.com/en/index.php?m=content&c=index&a=lists&catid=11.

as well as with Lithuania's central bank, enabling trade clearing services that allow direct transactions between renminbi and local currencies without going through U.S.-dollar exchanges.[67] Finally, IZP operates in conjunction with China Merchants Port Holdings in several countries, including Sri Lanka, Belarus, and Djibouti. In Sri Lanka, IZP has a stake in Mattala Rajapaksa International Airport, 16 kilometers away from China Merchants–controlled Hambantota port and industrial zone. In Djibouti, it controls the Silk Road International Bank (created in December 2016) along with Silk Road E-Merchants Information Technologies and Djibouti's Ministry of Finance. China Merchants has also owned a 23% stake in the port of Djibouti since 2012.[68] The Silk Road International Bank's official goals are to become the biggest bank card issuer in East Africa, as well as to provide financial solutions for bilateral trade between China and Africa and promote Chinese investment in the region.

Implications

From an economic perspective, BRI can be seen as the third phase of China's reform and opening-up policy, a rationalization and an outward expansion of various earlier efforts.[69] The PRC's entry into the WTO in 2001 raised hopes that Beijing would gradually give up its planned economy and fully embrace the market. However, these expectations for the Chinese economy to be transformed under a more market-oriented, consumption-led growth model will not be realized through BRI. To the contrary, BRI is an attempt to patch China's most pressing economic problems without fundamentally altering its development model, a situation French economist Michel Aglietta summarized as "the market, as far as possible; the State, as much as necessary."[70] BRI will not bring economic liberalization to China;

---

[67] "IZP Group Signs Strategic Agreement with Trade and Economic Committee of Russian Federation," PR Newswire, September 25, 2015, http://www.prnewswire.com/news-releases/izp-group-signs-strategic-agreement-with-trade-and-economic-committee-of-russian-federation-300147696.html; and "China's Payment Operator IZP Technologies to Develop Services in Lithuania," People's Daily, June 23, 2015, http://en.people.cn/business/n/2015/0623/c90778-8909795.html.

[68] "Jibuti Silu Guoji Yinhang zhengshi chengli zhuli 'Yidai Yilu' jinrong jichu sheshi jianshe" [Djibouti Silk Road International Bank Officially Launched to Help with "Belt and Road" Financial Infrastructure], News163, November 17, 2016, http://news.163.com/16/1117/09/C62IUU80000187V8.html; and "Silk Road International Bank Opens First Africa Office in Djibouti," Capital Ethiopia, January 9, 2017, http://capitalethiopia.com/2017/01/09/silk-road-international-bank-opens-first-africa-office-djibouti/#.WKN2kE2QxhE.

[69] The first phase began in 1978; the second phase started in 1992 with accelerated openness to foreign capital and increased manufacturing capacity.

[70] Michel Aglietta, "La nouvelle époque de la réforme chinoise: Progrès et obstacles" [China's Reforms New Era: Progress and Obstacles] (presentation at Conférence du Printemps de l'Economie, Paris, April 11, 2016), https://www.youtube.com/watch?v=BXhYxzdJM8c.

it will, to the contrary, help perpetuate the Chinese system of state control. The CCP wants to achieve the target it set for the country by 2021—to transform China from being "the world's manufacturer" into a moderately prosperous economy and society—without setting in motion reforms that would either require the party to relinquish its political control over the economy or create serious social and political consequences for its legitimacy. To reach this goal, Chinese authorities believe that they must sustain GDP growth at around 6.5% until 2021, prolong the process of winding down excess capacity so as not to provoke industrial (and social) disruption, restructure and consolidate SOEs, and promote the renminbi's internationalization. BRI is a means to achieve all these ends. How the initiative will play out and whether it can succeed in the long run as Beijing hopes are important questions. But they lie beyond the scope of this study.

Given China's political, economic, and social characteristics, some Chinese analysts believe that BRI is not really a matter of choice. As Tsinghua University professor He Maochun observes, "One Belt, One Road is an upgraded version of the reform and opening up, an upgraded version of China's international trade, and an upgraded version of China's 'going out,'" and it is the only path for China to achieve its rise.[71] By committing itself to the realization of BRI, China is following an economic trajectory that ultimately does not converge with the liberal model but instead perpetuates socialism with Chinese characteristics.

Strategic Rationales

For all the reasons detailed above, economic factors might be important enough in themselves to provide China's leaders with sufficient motivation to launch BRI. Indeed, in their interactions with foreigners, Chinese officials tend to downplay or even discard any discussion of the initiative in noneconomic terms. But there is much more to BRI than that. A closer look at Chinese sources reveals another set of factors that go to the heart of what the leadership wants to achieve. While the official rhetoric emphasizes enhancing connectivity and unlocking Eurasia's economic potential, strategic considerations provide the second key driver for BRI. The projects that the initiative comprises are meant to address nontraditional security threats and to secure China's periphery in order to counter what Chinese

---

[71] He Maochun, "'Yidai Yilu' shi Zhongguo xiang shang de biyou zhilu" ["Belt and Road" Is the Only Road China Must Follow to Rise], Tsinghua University (unpublished manuscript), http://www.ccwe.tsinghua.edu.cn/upload_files/file/20160105/1451965408815080054.pdf.

strategic thinkers regard as their country's greatest existential challenge: U.S. hegemony.

Enhancing Security by Providing Development

Economic development ultimately helps promote key strategic goals for China by enhancing internal social stability and national unity.[72] Reducing the development gap between coastal and inner provinces is necessary to preserve social stability, especially in the western province of Xinjiang, where the central government, for fear of local "splittist" tendencies, has tightened its control in recent years. This goal was at the heart of the Great Western Development campaign launched in 1999–2000, and it is one of the major motivations for the linking of Xinjiang with the cross-border regional infrastructure and economic projects envisaged by BRI.[73] During the 2015 National People's Congress, the party secretary of Xinjiang's Kashgar explained, for example, that BRI brought "an important historic opportunity to safeguard social stability and lasting political order."[74]

Of course, things are not so simple. Amnesty International's regional director for East Asia argues that the assumption that "substantially raising living standards among ethnic communities will extinguish potential ethno-nationalist aspirations" is mistaken, especially if "target groups have no say in the design and implementation of these policies and continue to face everyday discrimination and no meaningful political representation."[75] Restrictions on religious practices, curbs on culture and language, political repression, and unequal distribution of economic opportunities and benefits between Han immigrants and local populations are certainly better explanations for the violence that has erupted in China's western provinces since 2008 than a lack of local transportation infrastructure.[76]

---

[72] Sun Zhiyuan, "'Yidai Yilu' zhanlüe gouxiang de sanzhong neihan" [The Three Contents of the "Belt and Road" Strategy Concept], *Zhongguo Jingji Shibao*, August 12, 2014.

[73] Author's interviews with NDRC, Yinchuan, December 2016.

[74] Liu Zhiqiang, Li Yi, Zheng Yi, and Wang Yunna, "Zhimian xin changtai: Yidai Yilu kaifang gongying tuo xinju" [Facing the New Normal: Belt and Road Expanding Opening-Up and Win-Win to New Domains], *Renmin Ribao*, March 13, 2015, http://cpc.people.com.cn/n/2015/0313/c83083-26687854.html.

[75] "Are Ethnic Tensions on the Rise in China?" ChinaFile, February 13, 2014, https://www.chinafile.com/conversation/are-ethnic-tensions-rise-china.

[76] Consider, for example, the work of economics professor Ilham Tohti, who was sentenced to life in prison in September 2014 after being convicted of "separatism." See Andrew Jacobs, "Uighur Intellectual Who Won't Back Down in China," *New York Times*, August 20, 2010, http://www.nytimes.com/2010/08/21/world/asia/21china.html; and Edward Wong, "China Sentences Uighur Scholar to Life," *New York Times*, September 23, 2014, https://www.nytimes.com/2014/09/24/world/asia/china-court-sentences-uighur-scholar-to-life-in-separatism-case.html.

Nevertheless, the Chinese leadership clearly hopes that promoting development and reducing poverty will help diminish unrest and discourage radicalization and terrorist recruitment, both within China's borders and beyond. Beijing believes that BRI, by bringing infrastructure connectivity and economic development to neighboring countries, will help reduce the likelihood of terrorism or insurgencies that might spill over into Xinjiang: "increased economic exchanges and trade, enhanced living standards in Central Asia, and cultural exchanges to strengthen trust between people will eliminate the basis for fundamentalism and terrorism."[77] More generally, it hopes that economic development will alleviate the threat from the "three evil forces" (terrorism, separatism, and extremism) and "cut off the external linkages that exist with western China's separatist forces."[78]

Securing Energy Resources

In 2014, Xi Jinping made the case that security is a "holistic concept" encompassing domestic and international aspects, traditional and nontraditional threats, and domestic and overseas interests.[79] Economics and security are interrelated and inseparable. Energy and resources stand at the nexus of both domains: securing access to raw materials is essential for sustained manufacturing and industrial production and hence for the continued growth of China's wealth and power. In this context, Chinese political economist Liu Yingqiu writes that BRI has "a particularly important strategic significance."[80]

A 2014 report by the Development Research Center of the State Council, published after two years of research, examined various options for securing China's energy future. It identified three major factors that will shape the nation's prospects in this vital arena: technological

---

[77] Gan Junxian, "'Sichouzhi Lu' fuxing jihua yu Zhongguo waijiao" [Planning for a Revival of the "Silk Road" and China's Diplomacy], *Dongbeiya Luntan* 19, no. 5 (2010).

[78] Jiang, "'Yidai Yilu': Yi 'kongjian' huan 'shijian' de fazhan zhanlüe." See also Zhao Minghao, "'March Westward' and a New Look on China's Grand Strategy," *Mediterranean Quarterly* 26, no. 1 (2015): 97–116; and Zhao Minghao, "China's New Silk Road Initiative," Istituto Affari Internazionali, Working Paper, October 2015.

[79] "Jianchi zongti guojia anquan guan, zou Zhongguo tese guojia anquan daolu" [Adhere to the Holistic National Security Concept, Take the Road to National Security with Chinese Characteristics], Xinhua, April 15, 2014, http://news.xinhuanet.com/politics/2014-04/15/c_1110253910.htm. For an analysis of the implications of Xi's new concept, see Timothy Heath, "The 'Holistic Security Concept': The Securitization of Policy and Increasing Risk of Militarized Crisis," Jamestown Foundation, China Brief, June 19, 2015, https://jamestown.org/program/the-holistic-security-concept-the-securitization-of-policy-and-increasing-risk-of-militarized-crisis.

[80] Liu Yingqiu, "Zhongguo jingji da zhuanxing yu xin zhidian" [China's Economic Transformation and the New Fulcrum], *Guojia Xingzheng Xueyuan Xuebao*, September 1, 2014, http://theory.people.com.cn/n/2014/0901/c217905-25581213.html.

innovation, shifts in global supply and demand patterns, and the risks associated with geopolitical developments. The next twenty years will not see any fundamental change in global demand for oil and gas: it will remain high, with China and India as the main drivers of growth. Chinese dependence on oil and gas imports will also continue to grow: the report estimates that China's petroleum consumption will reach 600 million tons in 2020 and 800 million tons in 2030, three-quarters of which will need to be imported. To address this considerable dependence, the report recommends that China redistribute its current energy portfolio (coal, oil, gas, nuclear, and renewables), develop new technologies that will help provide clean and efficient energy, and prioritize energy-security measures such as increasing the size of its strategic petroleum reserves, accelerating diversification of oil imports, reducing dependence on imports that transit through the Malacca Strait, and securing energy transportation routes.[81] The vast and growing quantities of oil and natural gas necessary to sustain China's current economic development travel from the Middle East, East Africa, and maritime Southeast Asia along sea lines of communication and through the Malacca Strait chokepoint that the country has virtually no capacity to defend. Chinese strategists have been worried about this so-called Malacca dilemma for over a decade.[82] In the last five years, fears of a possible U.S. naval blockade in the event of an armed conflict, discussed in Washington as part of the debate over the air-sea battle concept, have renewed discussion in Beijing about strengthening the capacity of the People's Liberation Army (PLA) Navy, as well as diversifying oil and gas imports and developing alternative transportation routes.[83]

Overland pipelines, which are an essential feature of BRI, may not fully compensate for the potential interruption of shipments by sea. But they could ease some of China's strategic vulnerability by providing at least a portion of the country's essential needs in the event of a conflict with the United States and its allies. In a paper written in 2015, Han Jingkuan, vice president of CNPC's China Petroleum Planning and

---

[81] Li Wei, "Zhongguo weilai nengyuan fazhan zhanlüe fenxi" [Analysis of China's Future Energy Development Strategy], *Renmin Ribao*, February 12, 2014, http://politics.people.com.cn/n/2014/0212/c1001-24329909.html.

[82] Liu Jiangping and Feng Xianhui, "Zouchuqu: Kuayue 600 nian de duihua" [Going Out: A Dialogue across 600 Years], *Liaowang*, 2005, 14–19.

[83] Liang Fang, a professor at China's National Defense University, writes, for example, that air-sea battle and offshore control could enable the United States to "blockade energy and raw supplies imports and industrial exports so as to cut off the lifeblood of China's economy." See "Jinri 'Haishang Sichouzhi Lu' tongdao fengxian you duoda?" [How Big Are the Risks on the "Maritime Silk Road" Today?], *Guofang Cankao*, February 11, 2015, http://www.81.cn/jwgd/2015-02/11/content_6351319.htm.

Engineering Institute, describes how by 2030 countries along the belt and road—especially Russia and the Central Asian states, which he identifies as "key areas" for China's "national energy security supply base"—would be able to provide large chunks of China's crude oil and natural gas imports. He estimates that China will need to import 600 million tons of crude oil and 300 billion cubic meters of natural gas annually and that in 20 to 30 years energy imports from the different continental corridors envisaged by BRI (China–Central Asia–Russia–West Asia, China–Russian Siberia, and China-Myanmar-Bangladesh-India-Pakistan-Iran) will provide up to 143 million tons of crude oil and 206 billion cubic meters of natural gas—a significant portion of China's projected energy needs.[84]

Russia, Kazakhstan, Uzbekistan, Turkmenistan, Azerbaijan, Iran, and other energy-producing countries along the Silk Road Economic Belt have been dubbed by Chinese experts as the "21st century strategic energy and resource base." In June 2014 the Central Leading Group for Financial and Economic Affairs convened a meeting specifically dedicated to energy security, during which Xi called for renewed efforts to promote energy cooperation with countries along the Silk Road Economic Belt.[85] The priority given by the top leadership to enhanced energy cooperation is underpinned by the assumption that such cooperation is a textbook win-win situation: energy-producing countries are happy to export to the promising Chinese market, while China secures access to diversified sources of supply. Such cooperation is therefore considered a showcase for China's "amicable, mutually beneficial, and inclusive" foreign policy. Chinese experts argue that access to new sources of supply would also give Beijing more leverage in determining prices in global energy markets.[86]

Energy security has been a core concern for Chinese strategic planners over the years. BRI will facilitate Beijing's plans to diversify its supplies and help draw the regional pipelines map in a way that favors Chinese interests.

---

[84] Han Jingkuan, "Zhuazhu guojia jianshe 'Yidai Yilu' zhongyao zhanlüe jiyu" [Seizing the Opportunity of the "Belt and Road" Strategy's National Construction], *Shiyou Guancha*, July 11, 2015, http://bpmti.cnpc.com.cn/bpmti/gdlb/201505/21454ab32e9b4792951511d426016c63/files/65470af3cf3e4d2682f7a707a7ba1a71.pdf.

[85] Yang Mei, Guo Fang, and Yao Dongqin, "Xinsilu zhanlüe de jingji zhidian" [The New Silk Road Strategy's Economic Fulcrum], *Zhongguo Jingji Zhoukan*, July 2014, http://paper.people.com.cn/zgjjzk/html/2014-07/07/content_1450774.htm.

[86] Shi Ze and Yang Chenxi, "The Diplomacy of Promoting Cooperation on Energy Resources under the Belt and Road Initiative," in "The 'Belt and Road' Monograph," China Energy Fund Committee, 2016, 51–52; and author's interviews with an energy expert at the Chinese Academy of Social Sciences, Beijing, November 2015.

Strengthening China's "Neighborhood Diplomacy"

During the first year after his nomination as CCP general secretary in November 2012, Xi redefined China's economic and diplomatic directions for the decade ahead. In many respects, his approach is not dissimilar to that of his predecessor. Indeed, many of Xi's decisions and initiatives are arguably a continuation of Hu Jintao's approach, but with a twist, particularly in the foreign policy domain. In retrospect, 2013 appears as the year when the country's diplomacy started to undergo a subtle but significant shift—from a cautious stance in line with Deng Xiaoping's 1991 admonition to "keep a low profile" to a more proactive stance embodied by the slogan "striving for achievement" that Xi articulated in October 2013 during the Peripheral Diplomatic Work Forum.[87] The forum—the first meeting of its kind since the establishment of the PRC—followed a series of important Politburo study sessions dedicated to China's foreign policy,[88] as well as a dense stream of high-profile regional visits by Xi and Li Keqiang, including to Kazakhstan and Indonesia, where the Chinese president first aired the Belt and Road concept.[89]

To the Politburo Standing Committee and Central Committee members, state counselors, and Chinese ambassadors attending the forum, Xi stressed the strategic importance of neighborhood diplomacy for China's successful rise. Nurturing good relations with neighbors would seem to be a natural starting point for any country's diplomacy, but before Xi's accession to power, Beijing's hierarchy of diplomatic priorities had always given pride of place to relationships with "major powers." The unusual, high-visibility forum signaled that diplomatic relations with the region would now be elevated in importance, a message reinforced one year later at the Central Foreign Affairs Work Conference held in Beijing in November 2014.[90]

---

[87] "Xi Jinping zai Zhoubian Waijiao Gongzuo Zuotanhui shang fabiao zhongyao jianghua" [Xi Jinping Delivers an Important Speech at the Forum on Peripheral Diplomatic Work], Xinhua, October 25, 2013, http://news.xinhuanet.com/politics/2013-10/25/c_117878897.htm; and Xuetong Yan, "From Keeping a Low Profile to Striving for Achievement," *Chinese Journal of International Politics* 7, no. 2 (2014): 153–84.

[88] Timothy Heath, "Diplomacy Work Forum: Xi Steps Up Efforts to Shape a China-Centered Regional Order," Jamestown Foundation, China Brief, November 7, 2013.

[89] Zhao Minghao, "Cong yuanshou waijiao kan zhoubian waijiao da zhuanxing" [High-Profile Diplomacy Illustrates the Great Transformation of China's Peripheral Diplomacy], *Liaowang*, September 16, 2014, http://news.xinhuanet.com/politics/2014-09/16/c_1112492464.htm.

[90] Michael D. Swaine offers comprehensive reports of Chinese interpretations of both events. See Michael D. Swaine, "Chinese Views and Commentary on Periphery Diplomacy," Hoover Institution, China Leadership Monitor, no. 44, Summer 2014; and Michael D. Swaine "Xi Jinping's Address to the Central Conference on Work Relating to Foreign Affairs: Assessing and Advancing Major Power Diplomacy with Chinese Characteristics," Hoover Institution, China Leadership Monitor, no. 46, Winter 2015.

This shift toward a more proactive diplomacy centered on China's neighbors reflects the leadership's growing concern about the continuing U.S. presence in the region as well as Washington's alleged role in ratcheting up tensions in the East and South China Seas. As China's relations with Japan, the Philippines, and Vietnam deteriorated over maritime disputes and as concerns grew over Beijing's increased assertiveness, the Obama administration decided in 2011 to show its commitment and resolve by inaugurating a rebalance of its diplomatic, economic, and military efforts to the Asia-Pacific. The move caused alarm in Beijing, as it was perceived as an accelerated effort, directed from Washington, meant to challenge China's interests in the region. Chinese experts debated how the country should respond. One prominent view was that because the United States will never endorse China's rise, Beijing's only option is to try to reduce potential resistance from countries on its periphery and gain their support for its own objectives.[91] China cannot push the United States out of the region altogether, but it also cannot stand idly by while Washington seeks to contain its rise.[92] To prevent this, China must refocus and increase its own regional influence: as Xi himself put it, in order to "be at ease and able to manage our own matters free from anxiety," we must build "peace and security at our doorstep," discouraging neighbors from succumbing to the lure of the United States.[93] Aware of regional countries' misgivings about its growing might, China must play to its strengths as the world's second-largest economy and use its increasing wealth to gain influence with its neighbors.

This idea is at the core of BRI. Economic cooperation is not just a way to boost development or to bring financial returns. It is also a tool to be used for political and strategic gain—a method that Renmin University's Shi Yinhong has labeled "strategic economy."[94] When Xi tells China's neighbors

---

[91] Yan Xuetong, "Zhengti de 'zhoubian' bi Meiguo geng zhongyao" [The Overall "Periphery" Is More Important Than the U.S.], *Huanqiu Shibao*, January 13, 2015, http://opinion.huanqiu.com/1152/2015-01/5392162.html.

[92] Wu Zhicheng and Xing Haibing, "Strategic Planning for Its Neighboring Diplomacy," *Contemporary International Relations* 25, no. 2 (2015): 62–65; Yan, "Zhengti de 'zhoubian' bi Meiguo geng zhongyao"; Guo Shuyong, "'Zhoubian shi youhao,' dang yi quyu zhili youxian" ["Periphery Is Primary," Time for Regional Governance to Be Prioritized], *Huanqiu Shibao*, February 11, 2015, http://opinion.huanqiu.com/1152/2015-02/5651079.html; and Zhang Qingmin, "Lijie Shibada yilai de Zhongguo waijiao" [Understanding China's Diplomacy since the 18th Party Congress], *Waijiao Pinglun*, no. 2 (2014), http://paper.usc.cuhk.edu.hk/webmanager/wkfiles/2012/201408_13_paper.pdf.

[93] Zhao, "Cong yuanshou waijiao kan zhoubian waijiao da zhuanxing."

[94] Shi Yinhong, "The Latest Transfer in China's Foreign Strategy: From 'Military Strategy' to 'Economic Strategy,'" *Contemporary International Relations* 25, no. 2 (2015); and Shi Yinhong, "China's Complicated Foreign Policy," European Council on Foreign Relations, Commentary, March 31, 2015, http://www.ecfr.eu/article/commentary_chinas_complicated_foreign_policy311562.

that they should take advantage of the economic opportunities offered by its development and by BRI, this is what he has in mind. Countries that are friendly to China, support its interests, or at a minimum do not challenge it on sensitive issues will receive economic and security benefits from Beijing; conversely, countries that oppose China, or infringe on its security and sovereignty, will be denied access to these rewards and might even be actively punished.[95]

Pivoting Westward to Counter the U.S. Pivot to Asia

Broader strategic considerations also underlie the Belt and Road vision. Since at least the end of the Cold War, Chinese planners have viewed the United States as an oppressive global hegemon determined to prevent the rise of any potential challenger. Together with its command of the world's oceans, the United States' forward military presence and enduring alliance system have long been seen as posing the most direct and serious challenge to China's security: from Japan to the South China Sea to India and Afghanistan, this presence creates a "C-shaped encirclement ring" that squeezes China's "strategic space."[96] Beijing's newfound assertiveness in the East and South China Seas since 2010 illustrates the leadership's desire to push outward and extend the contours of this strategic space. Not surprisingly, when Washington declared its intention to rebalance to the Asia-Pacific in

---

[95] See, for example, Li Chengyang, "Zhongguo zai zhoubian diqu de moupian buju" [China's Plans in the Peripheral Areas], *Shijie Zhishi*, 2014; Wang Sheng and Luo Xiao, "Changes in the International Order and China's Regional Diplomacy," *Xiandai Guoji Guanxi*, February 2, 2013, http://www.cicir.ac.cn/chinese/Article_5007.html; and Xue Li, "'Yidai Yilu' beijing xia de Zhongguo zhoubian waijiao fanglüe" [China's Peripheral Diplomatic Strategy in the Context of "Belt and Road"], *Financial Times* (Chinese edition), January 11, 2016, http://m.ftchinese.com/story/001065641.

[96] The concept of C-shaped encirclement was put forward by PLA Air Force colonel Dai Xu in his 2010 book *C-Xing Baowei: Neiyou waihuan xia de Zhongguo tuwei* [C-Shaped Encirclement: China's Breakthrough under Domestic Problems and Foreign Aggression] (Shanghai: Wenhui Press, 2010). Jiang Lingfei, a professor at China's National Defense University, describes for his part a "U-shaped turbulence zone" around China and prescribes stabilizing China's continental and maritime periphery as a priority to ensure its national security. Jiang Lingfei, "Guoji dabian ju xia de daguo zhanlüe xuanze" [Strategic Choices of Major Powers in a Situation of Global Changes], *Dangdai Shijie*, January 2010, 17–21. Chinese analysts tend to agree that China faces omnidirectional strategic pressures from the United States but diverge over whether to give priority to the consolidation of continental or maritime power. Debates between proponents of a wider naval buildup, such as Zhang Wenmu and Ni Lexiong, and advocates of land power consolidation, such as Ye Zicheng, were particularly lively during the past decade. Discussions reflecting concerns about U.S. pressure on China's strategic space can be found, among other places, in Wang Wei, "Zhongguo nengfou chongpo 'ezhi liantiao'?" [Can China Break the "Island Chain Containment"?], *Lingdao Yishu*, 2005, 59–64; Yu Zhengliang and Que Tianshu, "Tixi zhuanxing he Zhongguo de zhanlüe kongjian" [System Transformation and China's Strategic Space], *Shijie Jingji yu Zhengzhi* 10 (2006): 29–35; Zhang Jian, "Meiguo yatai waijiao gongshi jiya Zhongguo zhanlüe kongjian" [U.S. Diplomatic Campaign Squeezes China's Strategic Space], *Zhongguo Shehui Kexue Bao*, December 13, 2011; and Dai Xu, "Meiguo weidu zhi xia, Zhongguo xin de zhanlüe kongjian zai nali?" [Under American Containment, Where Is China's New Strategic Space?], *Huanqiu Shibao*, December 19, 2012, http://www.caogen.com/blog/infor_detail.aspx?id=153&articleId=43957.

2011, Chinese observers concluded that a new and more intense phase in Sino-U.S. competition was at hand. China needed to find ways to respond. The solution, as leading expert Wang Jisi argued in late 2012, was to "march westward," avoiding a direct confrontation with the United States and its maritime allies by directing China's own strategic energies toward its interior frontiers.[97] Wang, who at that time was dean of the School of International Studies at Peking University and close to Hu Jintao, recommended that China increase its economic and trade cooperation to all "West Asian nations" along three major land routes (southern, central, and northern) and an additional maritime route passing through the Indian Ocean. He envisioned the establishment of a cooperation and development fund, as well as an increase of China's investment in diplomatic resources, calling "marching westwards" a "strategic necessity for China's involvement in great power cooperation, the improvement of the international environment and the strengthening of China's competitive abilities." Finally, Wang also listed possible obstacles and advised national leaders to "avoid risks, balance all sides, increase efforts in research and development and be part of an overall strategic plan."[98]

In retrospect, Wang's article looks like a prophetic advance draft for the BRI strategy. Contrary to what is usually believed, however, the leadership's renewed interest in Eurasia was not sparked by his article. Rather, it was the other way around.[99] The ideas laid out in Wang's 2012 article were not entirely new. Several noted Chinese experts have argued for some time that, in response to an increased U.S. push in East Asia, China should seek to preserve a favorable balance of power by enhancing its position in continental Eurasia.[100] As early as 2001, PLA general Liu Yazhou, one of China's most prominent strategic writers, asserted that advancing westward was "a historical necessity for the Chinese nation, and it is also our destiny."[101] General Liu proposed selecting "appropriate locations in the border regions" to set up Shenzhen-like trading hubs that would serve as the basis for a

---

[97] Wang Jisi, "'Marching Westwards': The Rebalancing of China's Geostrategy," Center for International and Strategic Studies, Peking University, Report, October 7, 2012.

[98] Ibid.

[99] Author's interviews with representatives from CICIR and Renmin University, Beijing, November 2015.

[100] For example, see Tang Yongsheng, "Jiji tuijin xixiang zhanlüe" [Actively Promoting Westward Strategy], *Xiandai Guoji Guanxi* 11 (2010); Ye Zicheng, "Zhongguo de heping fazhan: Luquan de huifu yu fazhan" [China's Peaceful Development and the Return to Land Power], *Shijie Jingji Yu Zhengzhi* 2 (2007); and Li Xiaohua, "Ouya Dalu diyuan zhengzhi xin geju yu Zhongguo de xuanze" [New Geopolitical Setting in Eurasia and China's Choice], *Xiandai Guoji Guanxi* 4 (1999).

[101] Liu Yazhou, "Da guoce" [The Grand National Strategy], 2001, http://www.aisixiang.com/data/2884.html. An English translation of this essential text can be found in *Chinese Law and Government* 40, no. 2 (2007): 13–36.

future Central Asian "common market." He also advocated the opening up of a "Europe-Asia land bridge to form a greater Euro-Asian symbiotic economic belt and use the countless economic links and common interests with countries to the West in order to dismantle the U.S. encirclement of China." A more unified Eurasian core would provide "the anchor of our western strategy and break U.S. attempts to drive wedges" between China and its western neighbors.[102]

General Liu emphasized again the critical importance of China's greater western region in a short article written in August 2010. He described Central Asia as a "rich piece of cake given to today's Chinese people by heaven" and underlined its crucial importance in light of China's energy security vulnerability. As Liu pointed out, the maritime "arteries bringing in China's oil are all under the eyes not only of the American navy but also, for that matter, the Indian navy as well." Central Asia should thus be regarded "as territory to be recovered in our advance, not as a border region."[103] It is worth noting that Liu is believed to be among several military officers who periodically brief Xi on national security strategy and appears to belong in the Chinese president's closest circle.[104]

BRI does not signal a radical shift in strategic focus toward China's continental backyard and away from its maritime claims in the East and South China Seas. Both the Silk Road Economic Belt and the 21st Century Maritime Silk Road serve the same objective of pushing back against perceived U.S. attempts to pressure and contain China's strategic space, whether on land or at sea, but attempt to do so in ways that minimize the risk of military conflict. BRI is therefore much more than a development initiative. It is not merely a series of engineering projects but a strategic concept meant to break through U.S. attempts to "strangle China."[105] In the words of PLA Air Force general Qiao Liang, the Belt and Road strategic construct is "truly the strategy of the shrewd." If China had chosen a direct collision course with the United States, the cost would have been too high; instead, a strategy of expansion toward the west preserves China's national

---

[102] Liu, "Da guoce."

[103] "Kongjun Zhongjiang Liu Yazhou zhuan 'Xibu lun' zongtan xijin zhanlüe" [Air Force Lieutenant General Liu Yazhou Writes 'Western Theory,' Talks of Strategy to March Westward], *Wenweipo*, August 10, 2010, http://info.wenweipo.com/?action-viewnews-itemid-32266.

[104] Willy Wo-Lap Lam, "The Generals' Growing Clout in Diplomacy," Jamestown Foundation, China Brief, April 3, 2015.

[105] Huo Jianguo, "'Yidai Yilu' shi zhanlüe gouxiang, bushi 'gongcheng xiangmu'" ["Belt and Road" Is a Strategic Concept, Not an "Engineering Project"], *People's Daily*, March 19, 2015, http://finance.people.com.cn/money/n/2015/0319/c42877-26719589.html.

interests and avoids confrontation, while offsetting U.S. pressure on China.[106] As another high-ranking PLA officer observed, it is no longer necessary for a country to protect its national interests by resorting to military conquest and territorial expansion. The Belt and Road vision helps transform the traditional mindset grounded in geopolitical competition into one focusing on "geopolitical cooperation."[107]

Conclusion

The Belt and Road Initiative is meant to address both China's economic situation and its security environment in order to realize Xi's "China dream"—that is, his vision for the great rejuvenation of the nation. It is the organizing concept of Xi's vision for China as a rising global power that has unique national characteristics. Even if it is officially framed as a product of China's benevolence and a friendly offer to neighboring countries to jump "aboard the Chinese development train,"[108] BRI is in fact conceived in strategic terms, mostly as a response to existential challenges posed by the United States. The concept sets the general long-term direction for China and seeks to mobilize and coordinate the use of all available national resources (political, economic, diplomatic, military, and ideological) to pursue internal (economic development) and external (diplomacy and national security) objectives in an integrated way.

As such, BRI is a "grand strategy" that is meant to serve China's unimpeded rise to great-power status.[109] Its architects hope that the increasingly dense and intricate web of regional economic interconnections created by the initiative will eventually help alleviate any remaining "contradictions" between China and its neighbors. As more countries benefit from Beijing's largesse, they will come to realize that common

---

[106] Qiao Liang, "Quanqiu shiye xia de da zhanlüe gouxiang" [The Grand Strategy Concept under the Global Vision], in *Gaibian shijie jingji dili de "Yidai Yilu"* ["Belt and Road" Transforming the World's Economy, Geography], ed. Liu Wei (Shanghai: Shanghai Jiaotong University Press, 2015), 51–65.

[107] Senior Colonel Xu Hui's 2015 television interviews are available at https://www.youtube.com/watch?v=dmZ6Xbm9rsE.

[108] "Welcome Aboard China's Train of Development," Xinhua, August 22, 2014, http://news.xinhuanet.com/english/china/2014-08/22/c_133576739.htm.

[109] Xu Xiaojie, "'Sichouzhi Lu' zhanlüe gouxiang de tezheng yanjiu" [A Study of the Characteristics of the "Silk Road" Strategic Concept], *Eluosi Yanjiu*, no. 6 (2014), available at http://www.aisixiang.com/data/96454.html; Du Debin and Ma Yahua, "Yidai Yilu: Zhonghua minzu fuxing de dizhi da zhanlüe" [Belt and Road: The Grand Geostrategy for China's National Rejuvenation], *Dili Yanjiu* 34, no. 6 (2015): 1005–14; and Xue Li, "Yidai Yilu zhanlüe shi daguo yangmou" [Belt and Road Strategy Is a Plan for Great Power-ness], *Financial Times* [Chinese edition], December 14, 2015, http://www.ftchinese.com/story/001065182.

development is more urgent and important than opposing China's interests or challenging its views. Pulled ever more closely into China's economic orbit, BRI countries—which may eventually include a large portion of the Eurasian continent, encompassing much of Europe and the Middle East—will find it increasingly difficult to stand up to Beijing. As China gains political influence over its neighborhood, it will be able to push back against U.S. dominance and reclaim its own regional strategic space.[110]

---

[110] Tang Yongsheng, "Exploit Strategic Geopolitical Advantages and Positively Influence the Regional Order," *Contemporary International Relations* 23, no. 6 (2013).

Chapter 4

A Vision for China as a Risen Power

As shown in chapter 3, the Belt and Road Initiative (BRI) is the Chinese leadership's attempt to respond to mounting challenges in both the economic and strategic domains. From Beijing's perspective, it is a defensive reaction against a perceived increase in external pressure on China. But BRI can also be seen as a proactive effort to shape the region, and maybe the world, in accordance with Beijing's worldview and broader strategic objectives. Its potential transformative effects have been subtly but repeatedly emphasized, including by Chinese government officials and public intellectuals who anticipate that "in the near future the world wealth distribution will focus around the Silk Road Economic Belt and the shift of the world's wealth will be followed by changes of the global strategic landscape."[1]

What are the changes that Beijing would like to see emerge in Eurasia's strategic landscape as a consequence of BRI? What vision is the initiative intended to serve? How does Beijing foresee its own role in a Eurasian continent that, if BRI succeeds, will have become more closely integrated with China? Official and authoritative sources have yet to openly formulate answers to these questions. This may be because Beijing's vision is not yet fully fleshed out, but perhaps also because Chinese officials fear that a straightforward announcement of their ambitions would provoke negative reactions and even active counter-responses. As one officer with the People's Liberation Army notes, "if you tell people, 'I come with political and ideological intentions,' who will accept you?"[2]

Even though the political leadership remains guarded about its real intentions, it is possible to delineate the essential features of an emerging vision by examining the ongoing discussions among Chinese intellectuals and scholars. Over the past decade, the outlines of debates about China's identity as a rising power have indeed appeared in the public sphere, like shadows of a play that is taking place behind the Politburo curtain. Ideas that

---

[1] "Silk Road Economic Belt Construction: Vision and Path," Renmin University, Chongyang Institute for Financial Studies, June 28, 2014, 8.
[2] Qiao Liang, "Zhongguo lujun de fazhan fangxiang zhengque ma? Heli ma?" [Is the PLA Army's Development Direction Correct? Reasonable?], *PLA Daily*, May 7, 2015, http://military.china.com/important/11132797/20150507/19650325_all.html.

have become mainstream under Xi Jinping can be traced back to discussions that were initiated during the Hu Jintao era. Looking back to the turn of the century, it is possible to discern a subtle but steady progression in the thinking of public intellectuals about China's identity and role as a great power—from a largely introverted developing country, still "crossing the river by feeling the stones" as it engages cautiously with the outside world, to a more proactive player seemingly ready to shape its regional environment according to its own desires.

Elements of this newfound ambition are now visible in concepts associated with BRI, most notably the ideas of a "community of common destiny" and the "Silk Road spirit." As innocuous as they might appear, these concepts give important indications of Beijing's view of the regional order that BRI could call into existence, in terms of both the distribution of power and the norms that would govern a future Eurasian community. The intangible narrative that is being woven around the concrete BRI infrastructure projects is a work in progress, but it is an essential component of China's vision for itself and for the region. As Ambassador Wu Jianmin wrote in 2015, BRI is the "most significant and far-reaching initiative that China has ever put forward."[3] It is therefore worth taking some time to speculate about its potential impact on the Eurasian regional order.

This chapter will begin by examining China's dream of re-emergence as well as the debates that have informed the leadership's views about China's identity as a risen power. After an overview of these debates, the following two sections will explore the still largely unspoken meaning of a community of common destiny and the Silk Road spirit. The last section will take a leap into the future, speculating about what a new Sinocentric Eurasian order might look like if BRI succeeds and Beijing is able to fulfill its ambitions.

Dreaming of Re-emergence

"The role we play in international affairs is determined by the extent of our economic growth. If our country becomes more developed and prosperous, we will be in a position to play a great role in international affairs," declared Deng Xiaoping in 1980.[4] Ever since the foundation of the

---

[3] Wu Jianmin, "'One Belt, One Road,' Far Reaching Initiative," China-U.S. Focus, March 26, 2015, http://www.chinausfocus.com/finance-economy/one-belt-and-one-road-far-reaching-initiative.

[4] Deng Xiaoping, "The Present Situation and the Tasks before Us," in *Selected Works of Deng Xiaoping*, vol. 3 (Beijing: Foreign Language Press, 1994), 159.

People's Republic of China (PRC), Chinese leaders have demonstrated an admirable consistency in the goals they set for their country, even if they have chosen very different means to achieve them: Marxist revolution for Mao Zedong and reform and opening-up for Deng. In addition to defending national sovereignty and territorial integrity, Xi Jinping, like Mao, Deng, Jiang Zemin, and Hu Jintao before him, aims at building a strong and prosperous nation that can regain its rightful place as a great power on the international stage.

Having survived the successive traumas of the Tiananmen Square incident and the collapse of the Soviet Union, the Chinese Communist Party (CCP) leadership at the end of the Cold War kept its focus on retaining domestic power and achieving China's international rise. As Gilbert Rozman observes, "of all the contenders in the quest for national identity in the 1990s, the notion of China as a great power (*daguo*) has gained a clear-cut victory."[5] And as predicted by Deng in 1980, as China's "comprehensive national power" increased, so too did its clout on the international scene.[6]

Where Does China Stand? The "Dream of the Great Rejuvenation of the Nation"

China's rise, its role in the world, and its prospects for leadership have been among the most hotly debated topics in the last 40 years, not least among Chinese thinkers and scholars themselves. The internal debate over China's identity as a great power and its broader domestic and international security imperatives was particularly intense during Hu Jintao's first five-year term (2002–7), a period marked by a gradually growing confidence about the upward trajectory of the nation's power. As the political elite sought to define a new vision and develop an accompanying grand strategy that would better fit the changing realities of the international system, their deliberations were aided by the work of academics and policy analysts who discussed at length China's foreign policy, the nature of its power, and the most desirable strategy for achieving a smooth power transition. The options and ideas that emerged during this period informed Xi's own thoughts and plans as he was groomed to succeed Hu.[7]

---

[5] Gilbert Rozman, "China's Quest for Great Power Identity," *Orbis* 43, no. 3 (1999): 383–402.

[6] "Comprehensive National Power" comprises a mix of material (economic, military, technological) and nonmaterial (political, cultural, ideational) elements. For a detailed study of this concept, see Michael Pillsbury, *China Debates the Future Security Environment* (Washington, D.C.: National Defense University Press, 2000), 203–58.

[7] Xi became a member of the Politburo Standing Committee in 2007, vice president of the PRC in 2008, and vice chairman of the Central Military Commission in 2010.

Among the issues debated by these experts during the first decade of the new century was whether China should give priority to strengthening its position as a continental power or to developing its maritime and naval capabilities. BRI has sidestepped this question by pursuing both directions.[8] The years prior to Xi's accession were also marked by debates over whether Deng's foreign policy principle of "hiding our capabilities and biding our time" should be replaced by something more proactive or assertive in order to defend China's redefined "core interests."[9] Analysts drew lessons from previous power transitions.[10] Finally, Chinese scholars discussed the emergence of a "Chinese school of international relations theory," whose primary vocation would be to help define the conditions under which China could achieve its rise without provoking counterbalancing or sparking conflict.[11]

As David Shambaugh points out, it is remarkable that very "few, if any, other major or aspiring powers engage in such a self-reflective discourse."[12] With the support of public intellectuals, China's leaders sought to assess their country's relative power in a changing international environment and to formulate a concept that would encapsulate their evolving worldview.[13] Zheng Bijian's notion of "peaceful rise," introduced in November 2003,

---

[8] The "maritime school," represented by Zhang Wenmu and Ni Lexiong, disagreed with the "continental school," represented by Ye Zicheng—a debate followed closely by U.S. Naval War College professors Andrew Erickson, Lyle Goldstein, James Holmes, and Toshi Yoshihara. See, for example, James R. Holmes and Toshi Yoshihara, "The Influence of Mahan upon China's Maritime Strategy," *Comparative Strategy* 24, no. 1 (2005): 23–51; and Andrew S. Erickson, Lyle J. Goldstein, and Carnes Lord, eds., *China Goes to Sea: Maritime Transformation in Comparative Historical Perspective* (Annapolis: U.S. Naval Institute Press, 2009). For Chinese articles, see in particular Ye Zicheng, "Zhongguo de heping fazhan: Luquan de huigui yu fazhan" [China's Peaceful Development and the Return to Land Power and Development], *Shijie Jingji yu Zhengzh*, no. 2 (2007); Ni Lexiong, "Cong luquan dao haiquan de lishi biran: Jian yu Ye Zicheng jiaoshou shangque" [The Historical Necessary Shift from Land Power to Sea Power: A Response to Professor Ye Zicheng], *Shijie Jingji yu Zhengzhi*, no. 11 (2007); and Zhang Wenmu, *Lun Zhongguo haiquan* [On China's Sea Power] (Beijing: Haiyang Chubanshe, 2009).

[9] Camilla T.N. Sørensen, "The Significance of Xi Jinping's 'Chinese Dream' for Chinese Foreign Policy: From 'Tao Guang Yang Hui' to 'Fen Fa You Wei,'" *Journal of China and International Relations* 3, no. 1 (2015): 53–73.

[10] Jingdong Yuan, "Remapping Asia's Geopolitical Landscape: China's Rise, U.S. Pivot, and Security Challenges for a Region in Power Transition," in *China's Rise and Changing Order in East Asia*, ed. David Arase (New York: Palgrave Macmillan, 2016), 49–62. See also the popular 2007 CCTV series about the "rise of great powers" and the "lessons of powerful nations," which can be viewed at http://www.cctv.com/program/cultureexpress/20070601/104110.shtml.

[11] Qin Yaqing, "Guoji guanxi lilun Zhongguo pai shengcheng de keneng he biran" [Possibility and Necessity of a Chinese School of International Relations Theory], *Shijie Jingji yu Zhengzhi*, no. 3 (2006): 7–13; and Nele Noesselt, "Is There a 'Chinese School' of IR?" German Institute of Global and Area Studies (GIGA), Working Paper, no. 188, March 2012.

[12] David Shambaugh, "China's Identity as a Major Power" (unpublished manuscript), https://www2.gwu.edu/~sigur/assets/docs/major_powers_091407/Shambaugh_on_China.pdf.

[13] William A. Callahan, "China's Strategic Futures: Debating the Post-American World Order," *Asian Survey* 52, no. 4 (2012): 617–40.

gave way to "peaceful development," before finally being replaced by "harmonious world," a catchphrase introduced by Hu in a 2005 speech to the United Nations.[14] Discussions continued over the following seven years, with the proponents of a low-profile, prudent, and gradualist approach tending to lose ground as the debate progressed.[15]

The CCP leadership's sense of optimism and its anticipation of impending glory were palpable in 2008 as Beijing prepared to host the Olympic Games. These feelings of confidence were reinforced by the fallout from the global financial crisis. In the eyes of Chinese analysts, the crisis exposed the institutional and social flaws of the Western development model and provided a "historic opportunity to promote changes in the international structure." With the global center of gravity increasingly shifting toward Asia, the possibility of a multipolar world was close at hand—a world in which China's role and voice would inevitably be greater.[16] Although China favored multipolarity at the global level, it quite clearly preferred unipolarity—its own preponderance—at the regional level.[17] By the same token, Chinese leaders wanted the international system to be redefined so as to reflect the latest changes in the structure of power, giving more influence to non-Western emerging nations and, of course, to China itself. As political economist Xu Xiujun explained in a 2012 essay, "the old system is no longer justifiable in terms of these new actors' interests and beliefs."[18]

In the aftermath of the financial crisis, China's dream of taking back its leading position in Asia seemed to be more in reach than at any time

---

[14] Robert L. Suettinger, "The Rise and Descent of 'Peaceful Rise,'" Hoover Institution, China Leadership Monitor, no. 12, Fall 2004, http://media.hoover.org/sites/default/files/documents/clm12_rs.pdf; Bonnie S. Glaser and Evan S. Medeiros, "The Changing Ecology of Foreign Policy-Making in China: The Ascension and Demise of the theory of 'Peaceful Rise,'" *China Quarterly*, no. 190 (2007): 291–310; and Hu Jintao, "Build towards a Harmonious World of Lasting Peace and Common Prosperity" (statement at the UN Summit, New York, September 15, 2005), http://www.un.org/webcast/summit2005/statements15/china050915eng.pdf.

[15] Read the very informative China Institutes of Contemporary International Relations roundtable report "Current Situation in China's Surrounding Areas and Its Strategy," *Xiandai Guoji Guanxi*, no. 10 (2013), which reflects the subtly discordant notes among Chinese foreign policy thinkers. On the same topic, see "China's Neighbourhood Policy," European Council on Foreign Relations (ECFR) and Asia Centre, China Analysis, February 2014, http://www.ecfr.eu/page/-/China_Analysis_China_s_Neighbourhood_Policy_February2014.pdf.

[16] *Lanpishu: Guoji xingshi he Zhongguo waijiao* [Blue Book: International Situation and China's Foreign Policy] (Beijing: Shishi Zhishi Chubanshe, 2012).

[17] Amitav Acharya, "Can Asia Lead? Power Ambitions and Global Governance in the Twenty-First Century," *International Affairs* 84, no. 4 (2011): 851–69.

[18] Xu Xiujun, "Xinxing jingjiti yu quanqiu jingji zhili jiegou zhuanxing" [Emerging Economies and the Structural Transformation of Global Economic Governance], *Shijie Jingji yu Zhengzhi*, no. 10 (2012): 49–79. Xu is deputy director of the International Political Economy Center at the Chinese Academy of Social Sciences (CASS).

since the founding of the PRC. This was Xi's message when, days after his designation as general secretary of the CCP in November 2012, he took his newly appointed colleagues in the Politburo Standing Committee on a tour of the National Museum. In front of the "Road to Revival" exhibit, which portrayed China's suffering at the hands of foreign powers in the "century of humiliation" and its glorious recovery under CCP rule, Xi pledged to realize the "Chinese dream of the great rejuvenation of the nation."[19] Henceforth, China would "strive for achievement" rather than continuing to "hide and bide."[20]

Xi's "China dream" is subtly different from that of his predecessors: it changes the narrative regarding the century of humiliation and portrays China not as a developing country or a victim of colonialist oppression but rather as a great power with growing ambitions and aspirations, ready to reassume its rightful place in the driver's seat.[21] According to one Chinese scholar at Beijing University, the current leadership "has a very strong sense of mission, a focus on efficiency and hard work, no shortage of risk-awareness, and little fear of dangers or difficulties." The nation's political elites "tend to act proactively and seek steady progress on diplomatic fronts, with higher voices and rational use of Chinese power, in order to effectively safeguard Chinese interests and maximize China's contribution."[22] Xi recognized in 2014 that, thanks to the West's waning dominance in world affairs, China had now "entered a crucial stage of achieving the great renewal of the Chinese nation." Although mindful of the risks and challenges associated with a complex period of global economic readjustment, he stressed the new opportunities offered by China's increasing power.[23]

Xi's sense of purpose and his determination to seize the moment have been echoed by various prominent military and civilian intellectuals. General Peng Guangqian, for example, stated in 2014 that "nothing can hold back China's advancement and the nation's rejuvenation."[24] According to General

---

[19] "Xi Pledges 'Great Renewal of Chinese Nation,'" Xinhua, November 29, 2012, http://news.xinhuanet.com/english/china/2012-11/29/c_132008231.htm.

[20] Yan Xuetong, "From Keeping a Low Profile to Striving for Achievement," *Chinese Journal of International Politics* 7, no. 2 (2014): 153–84.

[21] Sørensen, "The Significance of Xi Jinping's 'Chinese Dream' for Chinese Foreign Policy," 64.

[22] Zhai Kun, "The Xi Jinping Doctrine of Chinese Diplomacy," China-U.S. Focus, March 25, 2014, http://www.chinausfocus.com/political-social-development/the-xi-jinping-doctrine-of-chinese-diplomacy.

[23] Chen Xiangyang, "A Diplomatic Manifesto to Secure the China Dream," China-U.S. Focus, December 31, 2014, http://www.chinausfocus.com/foreign-policy/a-diplomatic-manifesto-to-secure-the-chinese-dream.

[24] Peng Guangqian, "Can China and the U.S. Transcend Thucydides' Trap?" China-U.S. Focus, January 9, 2014, http://www.chinausfocus.com/foreign-policy/can-china-and-the-us-transcend-thucydides-trap.

Qiao Liang, in 2008 "the bell chimed" for the end of the U.S.-led order.[25] In a similarly emphatic way, Zhang Weiwei, dean of Fudan University's China Institute, describes China as being on track to surpass the United States: China's "institutional arrangements seem to be working better than the American ones now....The world is changing; China is progressing, the U.S. is backsliding."[26] In this new context, the world "will have to adapt and adjust to China's rise." But China will also have to take a leading role in Asian affairs, contributing "more to public goods because this fits its own interests, but also because it fits with its status as a great power."[27] While Europeans and Americans debated the future of the West at the annual Munich Security Conference in February 2017,[28] Xi was addressing a national security work forum in Beijing. There, he called for China to "guide the international community's efforts to create a more just and reasonable international new order" and "to guide the international community in maintaining international security."[29] Xi's aspiration for China to take a more proactive stance in shaping the international system was unmistakable.

Whereas the rise of China may be assessed using material measures of national power, William Callahan writes that the rejuvenation of the Chinese nation is a "moral narrative that seeks to correct what is seen as the historical injustice of the century of national humiliation and return China to its rightful place at the center of the world," looking back to "the heyday of imperial China as a model."[30] Xi's China dream is about "revival" or "renewal," which means regaining China's past place as a great power. Indeed, Li Xiguang, the president of Tsinghua University's International Center for Communication Studies, reminds us that China has already risen to regional predominance four times in history—during the Han, Tang, Yuan, and Qing dynasties. Each rise "occurred in an oval-shaped area" consisting of Central Asia, South Asia, Southeast Asia, and the Middle East. This is the region that Western geopoliticians have identified as the Eurasian "heartland," an area

---

[25] Qiao, "Zhongguo lujun de fazhan fangxiang zhengque ma? Heli ma?"

[26] Zhang Weiwei, *The China Horizon: Glory and Dream of a Civilizational State* (Hackensack: World Century Press, 2016), xiv, 3.

[27] Jiang Lingfei, "Guoji dabian juxia de daguo zhanlüe xuanze" [Strategic Choices of Large Powers in Changing International Situation], *Dangdai Shijie*, January 2010, 17–21. Jiang Lingfei is a professor at China National Defense University.

[28] See the panel "The Future of the West: Downfall or Comeback?" at the 2017 Munich Security Conference, which can be viewed at https://www.youtube.com/watch?v=tjVZ4r6X75s.

[29] "Xi Jinping shouti 'liangge yindao' you shenyi" [Xi Jinping's New 'Two Guidelines' Have a Profound Meaning], Central Party School, February 21, 2017, http://www.ccln.gov.cn/hotnews/230779.shtml.

[30] William A. Callahan, "China 2035: From the China Dream to the World Dream," *Global Affairs* 2, no. 3 (2016): 247–58.

whose control will supposedly enable world domination. Not coincidentally, this vast expanse corresponds to the current geographic scope of BRI.[31] It is fitting that BRI's main focus is on the continental swaths of land surrounding China, because, as two Chinese geographers put it, "only vast lands can cradle great powers. Eurasia has always been the stage for the rise of new international orders: Vienna, Versailles, Yalta."[32] Beijing envisions that a new, Chinese-led international order will likewise arise in Eurasia. BRI is thus the main instrument of the grand strategy that will help China regain its "great power-ness," returning it to the dominant position from which it was unjustly removed and from which it has been absent for far too long.[33]

What Kind of Great Power Will China Be?

Despite the diversity of views expressed during the decade-long debates prior to Xi's accession to the top leadership, the great majority of the discussion among experts has been "animated by a prominent proclamation about the unique qualities of a Chinese great power"—in other words, by a strong sense of Chinese exceptionalism.[34] As Zhang Feng, a fellow at Australian National University notes, exceptionalism does not determine policy, but it has become "an essential part of the worldview of the Chinese government and many intellectuals."[35] This worldview rejects the supposed superiority and universality of the Western concepts of individual freedom and human rights. Instead, intellectuals and scholars searching for ways to define China's own path revisit the nation's history and its traditional political and strategic culture for inspiration. For the past decade, a growing corpus of "neo-literature" (e.g., neo-Tianxia, neo-Confucianist) has emerged, drawing parallels between previous periods in Chinese history and contemporary world politics and borrowing from ancient Chinese thought to develop

---

[31] Li Xiguang, "'Yidai Yilu' gaibian shijie jingji dili buju chengwei zuida jingjiti" ["Belt and Road" Will Change the World Economic Geography Layout and Become the Largest Economic System], *Caijing*, November 7, 2015, http://economy.caijing.com.cn/20151107/4005419.shtml.

[32] Du Debin and Ma Yahua, "'Yidai Yilu': Zhonghua minzu fuxing de diyuan da zhanlüe" ["Belt and Road": The Grand Geostrategy for China's National Rejuvenation], *Dili Yanjiu* 34, no. 6 (2015): 1006.

[33] Xue Li, "Yidai Yilu zhanlüe shi daguo yangmou" [Belt and Road Strategy Is an Overt Plot for Great Power-ness], *Financial Times* (Chinese edition), December 14, 2015, http://www.ftchinese.com/story/001065182?full=y; and Li Xing, "Sichouzhilu jingjidai: Zhicheng 'Zhongguo meng' de zhanlüe, haishi celüe?" [Silk Road Economic Belt: Strategy or Tactics to Support the "China Dream"?], *Dongbeiya Luntan* 2, no. 118 (2015): 85–92.

[34] Zhang Feng "The Rise of Chinese Exceptionalism in International Relations," *European Journal of International Relations* 19, no. 2 (2011): 305–28.

[35] Ibid.

new concepts applicable to China's 21st-century rise.[36] These writings seek to demonstrate that China will be a great power, entirely different from, and morally superior to, recent Western historical examples. According to Amitav Acharya, Chinese scholarship on international relations reflects "an attempt to legitimize the rise of China as a fundamentally positive force in international relations."[37]

Table 1 provides an overview of Chinese perceptions of the key differences between Western and Chinese worldviews. Strikingly, China's identity as a risen power is being defined in perfect opposition to the Western model. In contrast with a West described as exploitative and aggressive, China is portrayed by Chinese scholars as inherently benevolent and peaceful. The missionary character of the West, which seeks to spread its values (freedom, democracy, and human rights) and institutions, imposing them by force if necessary, is opposed to China's magnanimous inclusion and accommodation of political systems and cultures different from its own. The wars and military conquest imposed by the West as a result of its inclination toward ideological proselytism will not occur in a Chinese system that favors "harmony with differences" and rests on the rule of virtue and "humane authority." As William Callahan explains, "the problem with Western imperialism is not imperialism itself but only its Western form; the solution is not universal equality or justice but Tianxia's Chinese-led benevolent empire." What Chinese authors are constructing is "a new interpretation of Confucianism's hierarchical system that values order over freedom, ethics over law, and elite governance over democracy and human rights."[38]

Not only will China be the preponderant regional power, it also will be a "driving force in the reconstruction of the global economic governance system," which "needs to be reformed and adjusted." BRI is "a

---

[36] See, among other sources, Zhao Tingyang, *Tianxia Tixi: Shijie zhidu zhexue daolun* [The Tianxia System: An Introduction to the Philosophy of a World Institution] (Nanjing: Jiangsu Jiaoyu Chubanshe, 2005); Zhao Tingyang, "Rethinking Empire from a Chinese Concept 'All-under-Heaven' (Tian-xia)," *Social Identities* 12, no. 1 (2006): 29–41; Zhao Tingyang, "Tianxia gainian yu shijie zhidu" [The Tianxia Concept and the World System], in *Zhongguo Xuezhi Kan Shijie: Guoji Zhixu Chuan*, ed. Qin Yaqing [Chinese Scholars View the World: International Order] (Beijing: New World Press, 2006), 3–35; Qin Yaqing, "Theoretical Problematic of International Relationship Theory and Construction of a Chinese School," *Social Sciences in China* (2005): 62–72; Qin Yaqing, "Yanjiu sheji yu xueshi chuangxin" [Research Program and the Innovative Renewal of the (IR) Discipline], *Shijie Jingji yu Zhengzhi* (2008): 75–80; and Yan Xuetong, *Ancient Chinese Thought, Modern Chinese Power* (Princeton: Princeton University Press, 2011). A study of similar works can also be found in William A. Callahan and Elena Barabantseva, eds., *China Orders the World: Normative Soft Power and Foreign Policy* (Baltimore: Johns Hopkins University Press, 2012).

[37] Acharya, "Can Asia Lead?"

[38] Callahan, "China's Strategic Futures," 631.

TABLE 1 Chinese vs. Western worldviews (as seen through Chinese eyes)

West	China
Democracy leads to stability and peace	Development leads to stability and peace
Universal values: freedom, democracy, human rights	Value-free (as long as China's interests are not challenged or its political system is not criticized)
Democracy and liberalism	Each country should choose its own socio-political system and development path
Internal political diversity/external uniformity (democracies)	Internal political uniformity/external diversity (multipolarity)
Individual	State
Missionary, militaristic	Benevolent, peaceful
Anarchic order	Hierarchical order/Sinocentric
Rules-based governance	Rule of virtue

SOURCE: The author thanks Gan Junxian, assistant professor of political science at Zhejiang University, for laying out the differences between Chinese and Western worldviews. Author's interviews, Beijing, December 2016. See also Khong Yuen-Foong, "The American Tributary System," *Journal of International Politics* 6, no. 1 (2013): 1–47.

response to this need."[39] In the view of Chinese theorists, what is called "globalization" should more accurately be referred to as "Westernization or Americanization"; it is a process that has enabled the West to dominate the world politically and economically. BRI is an attempt to challenge that domination, says General Peng Guangqian. It "does not limit the nature of a given country's political system, is not underlined by ideology, does not create tiny circles of friends, does not set up trade protectionism, does not set up economic blockades, does not exercise control of other countries' economic lifelines or change other countries' political system." In contrast to the existing international political and economic order, which is defined by "its inequality, its forcefulness and its exclusiveness," and in which "military, financial and language superiority" are used for "selfish, predatory [and] mercenary" purposes, the Belt and Road strategic concept "upholds the

---

[39] "Gouzhu Zhongguo jingji fazhan xin zhanlüe" [Building a New Strategy for China's Economic Development], *China Youth Daily*, August 22, 2016, http://www.sasac.gov.cn/n86302/n86361/n86396/c2415776/content.html.

Silk Road spirit of openness and tolerance where all countries, big or small, strong or weak, rich or poor, are equal."[40]

The intellectual discussions described above are not confined solely to the academic and theoretical realms but instead inform and contribute directly to the leadership's thinking about foreign policy. To take one prominent example, Fu Ying, director of the Foreign Affairs Committee of the National People's Congress, has argued on a number of occasions that the current world order needs to adjust and adapt to the new distribution of global power. The "old concepts" that underpinned the U.S.-led world order (such as the rejection of nondemocratic governments and the building of military alliances that create exclusive blocs) have lost their relevance. What is needed now is "new thinking to build a new global framework, or, we may use the term global order." According to Fu, BRI is a mechanism that will transform "the existing international system and will help its gradual evolution into a fairer and more inclusive structure."[41] It would be difficult to be blunter about expressing China's dissatisfaction with the legitimacy and effectiveness of the current global governance system.

The Chinese leadership, however, does not stop at an increasingly critical and dismissive view of the U.S.-led order but now offers BRI as the key to creating an alternative order. In many ways, the initiative is a laboratory in which the prototype for a Chinese-led order, or as Li Xing puts it, a "new platform for global governance," is being developed.[42]

The concrete details about what this order would look like have yet to emerge. But Chinese leaders and scholars are clearly giving the topic serious thought and working to develop a coherent vision.[43] From the discussions that have occurred over the past decade, one thing appears certain: a Chinese-led order will not bear much resemblance to the current one.

What would the implementation of BRI mean for the region and the world? As vacuous as they might sound to Western ears, the terms attached to BRI—"inclusiveness," a "community of common destiny," and the "Silk Road spirit"—are infused with a set of references that are not at

---

[40] Peng Guangqian, "'Yidai Yilu' zhanlüe gouxiang yu guoji zhixu zhonggou" ["Belt and Road" Strategic Concept and the Reconstruction of the International Order], *Renmin Ribao*, January 9, 2015, http://world.people.com.cn/n/2015/0109/c157278-26358575.html.

[41] Fu Ying, "China's Growth and the Debates on Order" (speech at the University of Chicago, Chicago, May 19, 2015), available at http://www.chinausfocus.com/foreign-policy/chinas-growth-and-the-debates-on-order; and Fu Ying, "Putting the Order(s) Shift in Perspective" (speech at the 52nd Munich Security Conference, Munich, February 13, 2016), https://www.securityconference.de/en/activities/munich-security-conference/msc-2016/speeches/speech-by-fu-ying.

[42] Li, "Sichouzhilu jingjidai: Zhicheng 'Zhongguo meng' de zhanlüe, haishi celüe?"

[43] Nadine Godehardt, "No End of History: A Chinese Alternative Concept of International Order?" Stiftung Wissenschaft und Politik, Research Paper, January 2016.

all meaningless. The next sections will look in turn at the concepts of a community of common destiny and the Silk Road spirit in an attempt to illuminate their possible meaning and content.

A Community of Common Destiny: Sinocentric Order in the 21st Century

BRI intends to accelerate the integration of much of Eurasia around China through political coordination, infrastructure connectivity, unimpeded trade, financial integration, and people-to-people exchanges. The Chinese leadership has clearly stated that the initiative is not intended to build a new regional and supranational institution that would be an Asian equivalent of the European Union but rather to create an Asian "community of common destiny."[44] This amorphous communitarian concept suggests that the Chinese authorities envisage regional interactions taking place within a sort of network-based community rather than a rigid institutional framework. Contrary to treaty-based models of integration, the new Silk Road's community of common destiny has not been defined geographically; there is no definite list of member countries, no central institutional mechanism, no secretariat. Equally important, the principles and norms that will regulate and frame the interactions between its members have not been clearly stated. The prospects for building such a community without shared institutions and norms might seem so meager at first glance that it is tempting to dismiss this goal as another of Beijing's grandiloquent, yet empty, slogans. But even if they are not fully spelled out, official slogans convey deeper meanings; the "community of common destiny" is no exception.

Hu Jintao used the term community of common destiny (*minyun gongtongti*) in his 17th National Party Congress report in 2007 to describe the special relationship between the mainland and Taiwan, implying that two politically different entities could have reasonably good relations despite their dissimilarities.[45] Xi Jinping first used the term at the April 2013 Boao Forum as he underlined to the (mostly Asian) participants the need for

---

[44] National Development and Reform Commission (NDRC), Ministry of Foreign Affairs, and Ministry of Commerce of the People's Republic of China (PRC), "Vision and Actions on Jointly Building Silk Road Economic Belt and 21st-Century Maritime Silk Road," March 2015.

[45] Christopher R. Hughes, "When Big Powers Pivot, the Little States Roll: Southeast Asia between China and Japan," *Asan Forum*, December 1, 2014, http://www.theasanforum.org/when-big-powers-pivot-the-little-states-roll-southeast-asia-between-china-and-japan. The term is also sometimes translated in English as "community of shared destiny."

common development: "As members of the same global village, we should foster a sense of community of common destiny, follow the trend of the times, keep to the right direction, stick together in time of difficulty and ensure that development in Asia and the rest of the world reaches new highs."[46] Over the following two years, Xi used the term more than 60 times, including in several of his major foreign policy speeches—for example, when addressing the Indonesian parliament on October 2, 2013, when he announced the Maritime Silk Road, and a few weeks later, in front of a domestic audience, during the Conference on Diplomatic Work with Neighboring Countries.[47] Xi described bilateral and regional relationships based on amity (*qin*), sincerity (*cheng*), mutual benefit (*hui*), and inclusiveness (*rong*), one-word expressions that sound like modern replicas of Confucian principles.[48]

Interestingly, Xi also used the term community of common destiny in the context of two major events related to security: during the first meeting of the newly created National Security Commission in April 2014 and at the summit of the Conference on Interaction and Confidence Building Measures in Asia (CICA) in May 2014. During the former, Xi noted the connection between national security and economic development and underlined that internal and external security were equally important to China. He also noted that China needed to "pay attention to its own security, but also to common security, create a community of common destiny, promote mutual benefit and advance together toward the objective of common security."[49] One month later, during the CICA summit, Xi asserted: "We all live in the same Asian family. With our interests and security so closely intertwined, we will swim or sink together and we are increasingly becoming a community of common destiny."[50]

The context in which the concept has been used therefore provides several important indications about its meaning. First, it is inclusive,

---

[46] Xi Jinping, "Working Together toward a Better Future for Asia and the World" (keynote speech at the Boao Forum for Asia, Boao, April 7, 2013), http://www.china.org.cn/business/Boao_Forum_2013/2013-04/10/content_28501562.htm.

[47] Zeng Lingliang, "Conceptual Analysis of China's Belt and Road Initiative: A Road towards a Regional Community of Common Destiny," *Chinese Journal of International Law* 15, no. 3 (2016): 517–41; and Xi Jinping, "Let the Sense of Community of Common Destiny Take Deep Root in Neighbouring Countries" (conference remarks, Beijing, October 25, 2013), http://www.fmprc.gov.cn/mfa_eng/wjb_663304/wjbz_663308/activities_663312/t1093870.shtml.

[48] Geremie R. Barmé, ed., *The China Story 2014 Yearbook: Shared Destiny* (Canberra: ANU Press, 2015).

[49] "Xi Jinping waijiao xin zhanlüe: 'Mingyun gongtongti' zhutui guoji geju xin zhixu" [Xi Jinping's New Diplomatic Strategy: "Community of Common Destiny" to Boost a New International Order], *Renmin Ribao*, July 23, 2014, http://politics.people.com.cn/n/2014/0723/c1001-25328439.html.

[50] Xi Jinping, "New Asian Security Concept for New Progress in Security Cooperation" (remarks at the 4th Summit of the Conference on Interaction and Confidence Building Measures in Asia, Shanghai, May 21, 2014), http://www.fmprc.gov.cn/mfa_eng/zxxx_662805/t1159951.shtml.

suggesting the possibility of countries working together despite major sociopolitical or cultural differences. Second, it applies mostly to Asia and China's neighbors.[51] Third, the concept has both an economic and a security component (matching the two main drivers for BRI). Its objectives are to consolidate both "common development" and "common security," reflecting Xi's general view that "development is the foundation for security, and security is a condition for development."[52]

In sum, while the community of common destiny that BRI will help create is not a formal institutional structure, it could still eventually become a way for China to "form a bloc with those countries that more or less depend on its economy"[53] and to build a "new type of coalition" that is "not directed against a third party, but which, faced with security threats, can speak with the same voice and have a united response."[54] The community of common destiny transcends traditional regional boundaries and "eliminates the artificial divisions between the Middle East, West Asia, Central Asia, and East Asia." Thanks to what analysts describe as the "East-West double opening brought about by the Belt and Road strategic development, China will become a country at the center of Asia."[55] Because the community is "inclusive," it is theoretically open to any country, regardless of its political system or geographic proximity. Relations among the community's members are not bound by treaty nor by any specific set of written rules but are "jointly built through consultation to meet the interests of all."[56] Member countries are "not required to transfer their sovereignty nor to accept any military presence."[57] China, the biggest and most powerful participant in the community, provides leadership: it initiated the BRI project, portraying itself as the magnanimous provider of public goods; proposed a list of possible

---

[51] The neighborhood's geographic scope should be understood here in its broadest extension. Xi also used the term at a summit between China and the Community of Latin American and the Caribbean States in July 2014. See "Xi Jinping Attends China–Latin America and the Caribbean Summit and Delivers Keynote Speech," Ministry of Foreign Affairs (PRC), July 18, 2014, http://www.fmprc.gov.cn/mfa_eng/topics_665678/xjpzxcxjzgjldrdlchwdbxagtwnrlgbjxgsfwbcxzlldrhw/t1176650.shtml.

[52] See Timothy R. Heath, "The 'Holistic Security Concept': The Securitization of Policy and Increasing Risk of Militarized Crisis," RAND Corporation, RAND Blog, June 2015, http://www.rand.org/blog/2015/06/the-holistic-security-concept-the-securitization.html.

[53] Jin Kai, "Can China Build a Community of Common Destiny?" *Diplomat*, November 28, 2013.

[54] Wang Xiangsui, "Fazhan yu anquan: Yidai Yilu de liangyi" [Development and Security: Belt and Road's Two Wings], *Caijing*, April 6, 2015, http://finance.china.com.cn/news/zjsd/20150406/3041787.shtml.

[55] Li Xiguang, "Ruhe lijie 'Yidai Yilu'" [How to Understand "Belt and Road"] (speech at the CITIC Foundation's lecture series on the Chinese path, December 5, 2015).

[56] NDRC, Ministry of Foreign Affairs, and Ministry of Commerce (PRC), "Vision and Actions."

[57] Shi Yinhong, "'Yidai Yilu': Qiyuan shenshen" ["Belt and Road": Calling for Prudence], *Shijie Jingji yu Zhengzhi*, no. 7 (2015): 151–54.

areas for cooperation under the umbrella of BRI; and urged other countries to get "onboard China's train of development."[58] Beijing also offers material incentives in the form of investment, infrastructure projects, and general economic and security benefits to the members of the community. In return, it expects that they tacitly agree not to challenge China's core interests, criticize its posture, or seek to change its political system.[59]

Such a pattern of interaction, based on an implicit contract between a culturally and politically central China at the core and its Asian neighbors at the periphery, has a taste of "déjà vu." As Major General Qiao Liang noted when he recently addressed a National Defense University seminar on international security, the Belt and Road strategy "has a *tianxia* feeling."[60] Peter Chang, a senior lecturer at the University of Malaya's Institute of China Studies, also observes that in BRI "the markings of a modern metamorphoses of the ancient China tributary system are unmistakable, as Beijing reclaims the suzerain role, commanding deference and allegiance from the peripheral vassal states."[61]

Sinologist John Fairbank introduced the concept of the tributary (*tianxia*) system to describe the pattern of interaction between China and its neighbors down to the late nineteenth century.[62] The concept has been criticized by scholars who do not agree with Fairbank that Chinese emperors gave priority to rule by virtue and cultural attraction, as opposed to material factors such as economic and military power.[63] Wang Gungwu, for example, describes the Chinese empire as composed of a "hard core of *wei* (force)" surrounded by a "soft pulp of *de* (virtue)" and notes that China's superiority "was based on strength and was meaningless during periods of weakness and

---

[58] "Welcome Aboard China's Train of Development: President Xi," Xinhua, August 22, 2014, http://news.xinhuanet.com/english/china/2014-08/22/c_133576739.htm. See also David Arase, "China's Two Silk Roads: Implications for Southeast Asia," Institute of Southeast Asian Studies (ISEAS), ISEAS Perspective, no. 2, January 22, 2015.

[59] Author's discussions with a Chinese scholar, Beijing, December 2016.

[60] Qiao Liang, "'Yidai Yilu' yu daguo guanxi guanli" ["Belt and Road" and Great Power Relations Management], Sina, web log, June 12, 2015, http://blog.sina.com.cn/s/blog_5d98f6740102vshf.html.

[61] Peter Chang, "The Civilizational Fissures beneath China's OBOR," *Malaya Mail Online*, January 25, 2017, http://www.themalaymailonline.com/what-you-think/article/the-civilisational-fissures-beneath-chinas-obor-peter-chang.

[62] John King Fairbank, ed., *The Chinese World Order: Traditional China's Foreign Relations* (Cambridge: Harvard University Press, 1968).

[63] See, for example, Peter C. Perdue, "The Tenacious Tributary System," *Journal of Contemporary China* 24, no. 96 (2015): 1002–14; and Zhang Feng, "Rethinking the 'Tribute System': Broadening the Conceptual Horizon of Historical East Asian Politics," *Chinese Journal of International Politics* 2, no. 4 (2009): 545–74.

disorder."⁶⁴ Historian Takeshi Hamashita for his part has demonstrated that the tributary system not only performed a ritual and ceremonial function but also had a very concrete economic purpose and helped develop regional trade networks and commercial interactions.⁶⁵

Despite these differences in historical interpretation, several facts appear to be beyond dispute: until the nineteenth century, Asia was Sinocentric, depending heavily on China not only for culture but also for security and trade. The tributary system was the organizing principle for East Asia's external relations. Chinese rulers "largely viewed themselves governing not a nation, but a universal empire...whose authority...radiated, in theory, indefinitely outwards to civilize its non-Chinese, barbarian neighbors."⁶⁶ The "all under heaven" empire was defined according to five concentric and hierarchical zones—the three inner ones were directly ruled by the emperor, while the outer two were inhabited by barbarians. All five rings owed tribute to the emperor and observed the ceremonial rituals that were required by the Chinese court in exchange for imperial permission to engage in trade. Participants sought economic profit but also military protection, or at a minimum China's "credible commitment not to abuse its power in return for their acceptance of China's civilizational supremacy."⁶⁷ The Chinese emperors, for their part, expected their vassals to acknowledge their superiority not only for reasons of prestige and legitimacy but also as a way to ensure the stability of the empire's frontiers. These were populated by barbarian tribes—that is, "those without the blessings of the Chinese civilization," which were theoretically also part of the Chinese "empire without borders."⁶⁸

How is this concept relevant to modern-day international relations? Su-Yan Pan and Joe Tin-Yau Lo detect the "tributary mentality's" influence on contemporary China's vision of its rise, in particular its "Asian regionalism

---

⁶⁴ Wang Gungwu, "Early Ming Relations with Southeast Asia: A Background Essay," in Fairbank, *The Chinese World Order*, 49; and Wang Gungwu, "The Rhetoric of a Lesser Empire: Early Sung Relations with Its Neighbors," in *China Among Equals: The Middle Kingdom and Its Neighbors, 10th–14th Centuries*, ed. Morris Rossabi (Berkeley: University of California Press, 1983), 62.

⁶⁵ Takeshi Hamashita, *China, East Asia and the Global Economy: Regional and Historical Perspectives* (New York: Routledge, 2008).

⁶⁶ Julia Lovell, "Prologue: Beijing 2008—The Mixed Messages of Contemporary Chinese Nationalism," in *Beijing 2008: Preparing for Glory—Chinese Challenge in the "Chinese Century"*, ed. J.A. Mangan and Dong Jinxia (New York: Routledge, 2009), 8–28.

⁶⁷ Lai-Ha Chan, Pak K. Lee, and Gerald Chan, "China's Vision of Global Governance: A Resurrection of the 'Central Kingdom'?" in *China Joins the Global Governance: Cooperation and Contentions*, ed. Li Mingjiang (Plymouth: Lexington Books, 2012), 16.

⁶⁸ Marc Andre Matten, *Imagining a Postnational World: Hegemony and Space in Modern China* (Leiden: Brill, 2016), 32–62.

and community building, and its formidable diplomatic efforts at building a system of regional allies and friends."[69] Yuan Peng, vice president of the China Institutes of Contemporary International Relations, describes China as being at the core of the Asia-Pacific, surrounded by three concentric "rings"—(1) the fourteen countries with which it shares a land border, (2) its maritime neighbors of East Asia, Southeast Asia, South Asia, the Middle East, and the Pacific, and (3) an outer ring of countries far beyond—a view that resonates eerily with imperial China's five zones.[70] Fudan University professor Song Guoyu implicitly describes a Sinocentric regional order when he notes that, owing to BRI, "a regional economic circle with China as its center is accelerating its formation."[71] According to a professor at the Chinese Academy of Social Sciences (CASS), in this new Sinocentric regional order China is "not going to force others to be like [itself], like the United States does when it forces democracy on others. Today, countries are not equal, order is more important: each actor has to be at their right place, just as in ancient China's five concentric circles."[72]

A Sinocentric order would require the regional countries' implicit or explicit consent to China's primacy. There are competing views for Eurasia's integration, and Russia, among other countries, might not be willing to comply with Beijing.[73] In addition, there is the question of how regional countries will calculate the costs and benefits in economic, security, and political areas of a China-led order. Chinese scholars' candid description of what a community of common destiny would look like also raises the question of the norms and values that would allow the community to move forward. Beyond the broad concepts of inclusiveness and "win-win" that are presented as the fundamental features of the Silk Road spirit, there is no clear definition of what these principles might look like. Here too, however, it is possible to draw inferences from the writings of Chinese scholars and public intellectuals. The next section will analyze the meaning of the Silk Road spirt.

---

[69] Su-Yan Pan and Joe Tin-Yau Lo, "Re-Conceptualizing China's Rise as a Global Power: A Neo-Tributary Perspective," *Pacific Review* 17, no. 1 (2017): 7.

[70] Yuan Peng, "Thoughts on China's Great Periphery Strategy in the New Period," *Xiandai Guoji Guanxi*, no. 5 (2013).

[71] Song Guoyu, "Sichouzhilu jingjidai 'duichong' TPP" [Silk Road Economic Belt "Hedges Against" TPP] *Guoji Xianqu Daobao*, September 16, 2013, http://ihl.cankaoxiaoxi.com/2013/0916/272767.shtml.

[72] Author's discussions, Beijing, November 2015.

[73] See, for example, *Absorb and Conquer: An EU Approach to Russian and Chinese Integration in Eurasia* (London: ECFR, 2016), http://www.ecfr.eu/page/-/ECFR174_Absorb_and_Conquer.pdf.

The Silk Road Spirit: China's Normative Ambitions

As discussed in the first section of this chapter, Xi Jinping's China dream could not be complete with China's projected identity based solely on material strength; it requires an ideational dimension too. New models, preferably not Western-inspired and certainly not presenting any challenge to CCP rule, have been explored as possible substitutes for the failed Marxist-Leninist ideology. Concepts from ancient Chinese philosophy have thus been "excavated and reconfigured" to construct a new "frame of reference for a modern Chinese identity," which mixes historical narratives and repackaged traditions.[74] In particular, neo-Confucianism has made a remarkable return in China since 2005, initially mostly for domestic purposes.[75] But elites also believe that China can use its traditional culture as a way to "radiate outward" across Asia.[76] For Anne-Marie Brady, the selective use of Confucian values has a domestic and an external propaganda dimension: it reflects the need for the party to create a set of values that help deal with materialism and corruption within the country but also provide useful tools for China's soft-power push abroad.[77] Since Xi came to power, the leadership has decided to "change from passively reacting to changes to shaping the situation," and spreading China's worldviews and values is part of this broader objective.[78] In a Politburo study session in January 2014, Xi demanded that "the charm of Chinese culture" be shown to the world and that "modern Chinese values" be disseminated.[79] This call has been relayed by Li Xiguang, who stresses the necessity for China to build its "cultural power" and establish a "civilizational ring."[80] General Peng Guangqian for

---

[74] Nele Noesselt, "China and Socialist Countries: Role Change and Role Continuity," GIGA, Working Paper, no. 250, August 2014, https://www.giga-hamburg.de/en/system/files/publications/wp250_noesselt.pdf.

[75] Nadège Orban, "Contemporary China: Confucius Returns," S. Rajaratnam School of International Studies, Commentary, no. 124, November 19, 2007, https://www.rsis.edu.sg/wp-content/uploads/2014/07/CO07124.pdf.

[76] Men Honghua, "Quanqiuhua yu Zhongguo guojia rentong" [Globalization and China's National Identity], hexun.com, July 26, 2013, http://news.hexun.com/2013-07-26/156515566.html. Men is the director of the Institute of International Strategic Studies at the Central Party School of the Communist Party of China.

[77] Anne-Marie Brady, "State Confucianism, Chineseness, and Tradition in CCP Propaganda," in *China's Thought Management*, ed. Anne-Marie Brady (New York: Routledge, 2012), 57–75.

[78] Zhang Qingmin, "Lijie shibada yilai de Zhongguo waijiao" [Understanding China's Diplomacy since the 18th Party Congress], *Waijiao Pinglun*, no. 2 (2014), available at http://www.faobserver.com/NewsInfo.aspx?id=9875.

[79] "Xi: China to Promote Cultural Soft Power," Xinhua, January 1, 2014, http://news.xinhuanet.com/english/china/2014-01/01/c_125941955.htm.

[80] Li, "Ruhe lijie 'Yidai Yilu.'"

his part has no doubt that during the process of "reconstruction of the world civilization, the Chinese civilization will inevitably demonstrate its rightful role and establish its rightful position."[81]

But is the "beauty of Chinese culture" appealing enough to be exported abroad to help secure political influence? Which "modern Chinese values" does Xi have in mind that could provide the basis for shared beliefs and norms across the region? Whereas Chinese elites understand the necessity for China "to advocate a collection of Asian values that can be universally accepted and appreciated," they struggle to find anything that would fit this ideal description.[82] Scholars and policy analysts have been toying with concepts such as "pluralistic coexistence, independent participation, striving for development, value sharing," but also pushing for the adoption of neo-Confucian values such as "benevolence, good-neighborliness, harmony and justice."[83] In the normative domain, as in others, BRI gives the leadership an opportunity to test ideas and to delineate more precisely what the propaganda apparatus should emphasize in order to enhance China's soft power.[84]

First, the Silk Road narrative has not been chosen by chance. As Tim Winter explains, "reviving the idea of the silk roads, on both land and sea, gives vitality to histories of transnational, even transcontinental, trade and people-to-people encounters as a shared heritage."[85] This image has been used before—for example, during the opening ceremony of the 2008 Olympics in Beijing—as a symbol of China's "foreign policy mantra" to "make friends in every quarter, trade goods, learn from each other and enjoy respectful interaction."[86] The semi-mythical ancient Silk Road conjures up distant memories of amicable exchanges and shared prosperity and peace, a benevolent face that Beijing is eager to project abroad.[87] The values of "peace, mutual benefit and mutual learning, inclusiveness, and

---

[81] Peng, "'Yidai Yilu' zhanlüe gouxiang yu guoji zhixu zhonggou."

[82] Xue, "Yidai Yilu zhanlüe shi daguo yangmou."

[83] Ibid.; and Peng, "'Yidai Yilu' zhanlüe gouxiang yu guoji zhixu zhonggou."

[84] On China's soft power, see, among others, David Shambaugh, "China's Soft Power Push: The Search for Respect," *Foreign Affairs*, July/August 2015; and Osamu Sayama, "China's Approach to Soft Power: Seeking a Balance between Nationalism, Legitimacy and International Influence," Royal United Services Institute, Occasional Paper, March 2016.

[85] Tim Winter, "Heritage Diplomacy along the One Belt One Road," International Institute for Asian Studies, Newsletter, no. 74, Summer 2016, http://iias.asia/the-newsletter/article/heritage-diplomacy-along-one-belt-one-road.

[86] Geremie R. Barmé, "China's Flat Earth: History and 8 August 2008," *China Quarterly* 197 (2009): 64–86.

[87] Wang Yiwei, *The Belt and Road Initiative: What Will China Offer the World in Its Rise* (Beijing: New World Press, 2016), 29–38.

openness" are at the core of what official propaganda has now labeled the "Silk Road spirit." According to BRI's "Vision and Actions" document, this spirit has "been passed from generation to generation, promoted the progress of human civilization, and contributed greatly to the prosperity and development of the countries along the Silk Road."[88] In an April 2016 Politburo group study specifically dedicated to the history of the Silk Road, Xi reiterated these values as the core components of the Silk Road spirit, which supposedly grew out of the "friendly exchanges between the Chinese nation and other ethnic groups" and extended over many centuries along the Silk Road.[89]

More broadly, the norms that are conveyed by BRI belong to a general effort to discredit Western ideas and institutions while presenting China's model as an alternative—and implicitly superior—political and economic path.[90] A Xinhua editorial, for example, asserts the following:

> Today, there are different versions of new Silk Road initiatives in the central Asian passageway, such as the American "New Silk Road," Japan's "Silk Road Diplomacy" and China's "Silk Road Economic Belt." While some of them are based on belief in enduring peace and common prosperity for all countries, others seek domination by preaching confrontation and excluding other contenders....Any road that betrays the Silk Road spirit will not last long. Unlike the great sea routes to the New World discovered by the European navigators that prompted bloody conquest and colonization, the Silk Road was always a road of peace.[91]

At the core of the "Silk Road spirit" is the rejection of the promotion of democracy and human rights or, as the official rhetoric puts it, respect for the right of all countries to "independently choose their social systems and development path."[92] Li Xiguang rejects the U.S. "focus on alliance building, consolidation of democracies thanks to color revolutions, and objective of Eurasian fragmentation." According to Li, the United States has a binary view: "either you are a democracy and we deal with you, or you're not and you're excluded....The values we want to build on have nothing to do with Columbus's massacres. Along the Belt and Road, civilizations are diverse: we

---

[88] NDRC, Ministry of Foreign Affairs, and Ministry of Commerce (PRC), "Vision and Actions."

[89] "Xi Jinping zhuchi zhonggong zhongyang zhengzhi ju di sanshiyi ci jiti xuexi" [Xi Jinping Presided Over the 31st CPC Central Committee Politburo Group Study], Xinhua, April 30, 2016, http://news.xinhuanet.com/politics/2016-04/30/c_1118778656.htm.

[90] Mareike Ohlberg, "Boosting the Party's Voice," Mercator Institute for China Studies, China Monitor, July 21, 2016, http://www.merics.org/fileadmin/user_upload/downloads/China-Monitor/MERICS_China_Monitor_34_Eng_Indiological_War.pdf.

[91] "China Voice: Confrontation, Exclusiveness, Betray Silk Road Spirit," Xinhua, June 24, 2014, http://news.xinhuanet.com/english/china/2014-06/24/c_133434184.htm.

[92] Li, "Sichouzhilu jingjidai, zhicheng 'Zhongguo meng' de zhanlüe, haishi celüe?"

are tolerant, looking for win-win, and respect coexistence."[93] A senior official from the International Liaison Department explains:

> BRI has its own cultural connotation and roots: harmony, cooperation, synergies [*hexie, hezuo, huli*]. They are in our cultural genes, passed among generations for thousands of years. If you want to understand the content of BRI, you first have to know China's cultural traditions. The Silk Road is essentially about a common cultural and historical heritage....Only elites that have been there for a long time can make sound political decisions for their country. Imported concepts make things more difficult for local countries. The U.S. chose its own political system, it wasn't imposed from outside. For China, it is the same: after the empire collapsed, we tried several systems, went through reforms and the process was painful sometimes, but we finally found the one that suits us best.[94]

At a time of growing opposition to the negative effects of globalization, China's increasingly strident criticism of U.S-led liberalism, relayed through its propaganda machine, may resonate not only in the developing world but also in advanced industrial countries. At a November 2016 event in Washington, D.C., representatives from CASS, the Development Research Center of the State Council, and the China Energy Fund Committee unanimously appealed for a "new globalization phase" that would "benefit more people." Against a backdrop of possibly increasing U.S. protectionism, Li Xiangyang, the director of the CASS National Institute of International Strategy, explained BRI at this event as a "new paradigm in international trade liberalization" that is intended to "make up for the deficiencies of the current global system" and is dedicated to seeking "righteousness over profit." Downplaying the evident antagonism between the two approaches, Li described BRI as providing a "complementary view (like when you have the choice between tea or coffee)" that is not directly competing with the mainstream model but is simply "development-oriented as opposed to rule-oriented."[95]

As we look beyond the concrete list of investment and infrastructure construction projects, situate BRI in the broader context of China's regional and global aspirations, and carefully study the concepts associated with it, the initiative finally emerges in all of its dimensions. As we saw in the previous chapter, BRI is not just a series of practical and concrete plans for improving regional connectivity but is instead a considered response to perceived economic and strategic threats to China. The initiative is also a

---

[93] Li, "Ruhe lijie 'Yidai Yilu.'"

[94] Author's discussions with the CCP International Liaison Department's China Center for Contemporary World Studies, Beijing, December 2016.

[95] Li Xiangyang (presentation at the U.S.-China Belt and Road Forum, Washington, D.C., November 30, 2016). The agenda for the event is available at http://www.oborforum.org/index.php/agenda.

proactive effort to mold and shape Eurasia according to Beijing's ambitions for achieving regional preponderance, not only in material terms given the sheer size of China's economic, political, and military power but also in ideational and normative terms. The "soft" narrative that Beijing is trying to construct and weave around its "hardware" projects is still a work in progress, but it is clearly very different from the one propounded by supporters of the Western-led liberal order. Of course, as the next chapter will show, Chinese leaders face many obstacles on the way to realizing this dream. But supposing that everything goes according to plan and Beijing is able to achieve its vision, what will the regional order look like twenty years from now?

A Peek into a China-Led Eurasian Order

What follows is a speculative leap into Eurasia's future, an attempt to knit together the threads that the previous chapters have revealed in order to describe what kind of regional order Beijing would like to see emerge as a consequence of BRI. This exercise is speculative for several reasons. First, Xi Jinping and his Politburo comrades probably do not have a fully formed view of what they would prefer the region to look like by 2049, or even earlier. Even if they do have a master plan, there is no publicly available evidence of what it contains. Finally, of course, no one knows what the future will look like. History rarely proceeds in a straight line, and events do not emerge from a vacuum but rather are products of dialectical interactions among actors. Even if Beijing wishes the world to look a certain way, the world will not necessarily comply.

So let us fast-forward to 2035. Eurasia is now the cradle of more than 5 billion people (55% of the global population), including two-thirds of the global middle-class population.[96] More than 3.3 billion middle-class consumers order Chinese goods on Silk Road e-commerce platforms such as Alibaba's Tmall.com and Jindong's JD.com, using their UnionPay card to complete their transactions in renminbi. They also use Chinese currency to pay for hotels, restaurants, and train tickets as they travel across the region to discover the five hundred sites along the Silk Road that have been recorded in UNESCO's world heritage listing, eclipsing Italy in the "prestige stakes

---

[96] Mario Pezzini, "An Emerging Middle Class," in *OECD Yearbook 2012: Better Policies for Better Lives* (Paris: OECD Publishing, 2012), 64–65, available at http://oecdobserver.org/news/fullstory.php/aid/3681/An_emerging_middle_class.html. In the following section, Eurasia is described as the zone envisioned by BRI, comprising East, Southeast, South, Central, and West Asia; Russia; the South Caucasus; and Europe's eastern fringes.

of culture and civilization."⁹⁷ The region's tourism industry is booming and has become a significant factor in GDP growth. Places that used to be in the middle of nowhere have now become the center of a dynamic, economically thriving world. High-speed trains zoom across the continent, linking Beijing to Moscow in less than 30 hours and delivering Chinese goods to Western Europe in less than ten days, at rates competitive with the maritime shipping that still takes three times as long despite progress in unmanned navigation technologies.⁹⁸ Road signs on Eurasian highways are written in Chinese as well as in the local language, and from Vientiane to Prague, Mandarin has become one of the most commonly spoken foreign languages.⁹⁹ Industrial parks built, financed, and operated by Chinese state-owned corporations punctuate the region's landscape and provide jobs for both Chinese expatriates and local employees.

Eurasia is now covered by the Beidou positioning system, used for civil and military purposes, and by 5G mobile networks provided by Chinese state-owned telecommunication companies such as China Mobile and China Unicom. Unlike in North America and Western Europe, Eurasian people do not "google," have a Facebook or Twitter account, or watch the news on CNN or the BBC. Instead, they "baidu," use Weibo for their social connections, and watch China Global Television Network, whose programs are available in local languages. Children do not play "cowboys and Indians" but mimic the exploits of the Monkey King, one of their favorite heroes from the *Journey to the West* tale that has become a cartoon series regularly broadcast across the region. Their parents, meanwhile, relish watching Chinese television series and dramas and the Wanda Group's blockbuster films that are shown in local theaters. The fiber-optic cables crisscrossing the continent enable fast and reliable digital connections that are regulated and restricted behind a "great firewall" that now extends beyond China's cyberspace and covers the entire continent. The digital Silk Road, which is, according to the official narrative, a "peaceful, safe, open and cooperative online space," has nominally sealed off Eurasia from the rest of the global network.¹⁰⁰ This new Eurasian Internet is monitored by

---

⁹⁷ Winter, "Heritage Diplomacy along the One Belt One Road."

⁹⁸ Robert Wall and Costas Paris, "Ship Operators Explore Autonomous Sailing," *Wall Street Journal*, August 31, 2016, https://www.wsj.com/articles/ship-operators-explore-autonomous-sailing-1472635800.

⁹⁹ This scenario is similar to the Guangzhou-Paris highway depicted in the 2011 Russian dystopian movie *Mishen* [Target].

¹⁰⁰ "Lu Wei Delivers Keynote Speech to China–Arab States Expo Online Silk Road Forum," *China Daily*, September 10, 2015, http://www.chinadaily.com.cn/business/2015chinaarabforum/2015-09/10/content_21841735.htm.

automatic and human censors who control public cyberspace discussions, limit freedom of expression, and tamp down criticism of China and its associated regional friends.

Eurasian youths seek acceptance to the highly regarded universities of Beijing, Xi'an, Urumqi, and Kunming, whose degrees are recognized across the region. These schools offer substantial scholarships to the best and most promising students of the region and give a guarantee of employment in the local branches of Chinese state-owned enterprises. China's reputation as a center for learning extends beyond its universities, as the region's professional elites regularly benefit from training programs in government, law, and business, sponsored by Beijing inside and outside China. Students who were the first beneficiaries of BRI scholarships offered by Xi in 2013 are now senior officials in their respective governments. Police, intelligence, and military officers, from junior to senior ranks, continue to benefit from training programs organized and sponsored by China's Ministries of Public Security and State Security and the People's Liberation Army. In each of its embassies, China has stationed local liaison officers who facilitate cross-border security cooperation and intelligence sharing. With a growing corpus of alumni from Chinese schools and training programs working in local administrations, China's relations with its close and distant neighbors are very smooth. Increased economic cooperation and people-to-people exchanges, backed up by a sophisticated public diplomacy, have gradually changed perceptions of China. Beijing has, for example, finally prevailed over the last European resistance to lifting the embargo on arms sales that had been imposed after the 1989 Tiananmen incident.[101]

Global commercial and trade flows have drastically changed as BRI has accelerated Eurasia's seamless transportation and communication connectivity overland and decreased China's dependence on the maritime lines of communication for imports and exports. Between 2015 and 2030, trade volume between China and BRI countries has tripled. China imports agricultural products, including grain and fresh meat and produce to feed its population, as well as petroleum and liquefied natural gas, from Russia, Ukraine, the South Caucasus, Central Asian countries, and the Middle East, both by land and by sea, via the Indian Ocean through Pakistan and Myanmar.

Countries along the belt and road are tied to China both at the regional level and by a series of bilateral cooperation arrangements. They

---

[101] This eventuality is envisaged in a 2015 study commissioned by the European Parliament's Policy Department. See *China's Foreign Policy and External Relations* (Brussels: Policy Department, Directorate-General for External Policies, 2015), 37–39, http://www.europarl.europa.eu/RegData/etudes/STUD/2015/549057/EXPO_STU(2015)549057_EN.pdf.

have also negotiated and concluded a comprehensive regional agreement in order to facilitate unimpeded intraregional trade of goods and services, as well as financial integration and people-to-people exchanges.[102] The Regional Comprehensive Economic Partnership has now integrated not only the original participants (ASEAN, Australia, China, India, Japan, New Zealand, and South Korea) but also South Asian, Central Asian, and West Asian economies. Taken together, the economies of this Eurasian trade area exceed the EU and North American economies. As one Chinese general predicted in 2015, does the region "use dollars or euros for trade? Probably not! Think about it. Is the dollar's hegemony over a third of the global economy still hegemony?"[103] Financial transactions among BRI countries are now made in renminbi, thanks to the China International Payment System (CIPS) that has displaced the Society for Worldwide Interbank Financial Telecommunication (SWIFT) system across much of Eurasia. Tariffs and other barriers to trade in goods and services have decreased to facilitate commerce among the members of the Eurasian trade area, but there are no requirements in terms of protections for labor, human rights, and the environment.

When they have disputes with China, BRI countries cannot appeal to any supranational legal mechanism but must instead deal on a bilateral basis with Beijing. The Chinese government has been "actively educating businesses and investors on the benefits of arbitration in relation to any cross-border disputes" arising out of BRI.[104] China now controls the regional dispute-resolution and arbitration system, based in Hong Kong, which operates outside of the International Centre for Settlement of Investment Disputes established in Washington, D.C., in 1965.[105] Beijing appoints the arbitration court's prosecutors, judges, and attorneys. Like China's domestic judiciary system, it does not comply with Western standards of due process.

Political cooperation and consultation are taking place at multiple levels, through the Shanghai Cooperation Organisation for Central Asia, Iran, and Russia; ASEAN +1 for Southeast Asia; the China–Arab States Cooperation Forum for the Middle-East; and the 16+1 format for Central

---

[102] Zeng Lingliang, "Conceptual Analysis of China's Belt and Road Initiative: A Road towards a Regional Community of Common Destiny," *Chinese Journal of International Law* 15, no. 3 (2016): par. 44.

[103] Qiao Liang, "Quanqiu shiye xia de da zhanlüe gouxiang" [Grand Strategy Concept under Global Vision], in *Gaibian shijie jingji dili de Yidai Yilu* [Belt and Road: Transforming the Global Geo-Economy] (Shanghai: Jiaotong University Press, 2015), 51–65.

[104] Kanishk Verghese, "Opportunity Beckons," Asian Legal Business, January 28, 2016.

[105] Wang Qiao, "Common Values Lead the Way on Belt and Road," *China Daily*, February 21, 2017, http://www.chinadaily.com.cn/bizchina/2017-02/21/content_28278298_2.htm.

and Eastern Europe. Taken together, these mechanisms form a sort of hub-and-spoke structure that links the region to China, its biggest political, economic, and military power.[106] Other groupings are not positioned as "affiliates" or "subordinates" to China's BRI but instead "overlap with each other geographically and functionally, with no political contradictions and conflicts."[107] Maintaining several cooperation mechanisms allows Beijing to "adapt to the diversity of development paths in the region, and accommodate the diversity of local politics and culture."[108]

Since the launch of BRI, China has been expanding its influence outward in concentric rings, starting with its immediate neighborhood of weaker, smaller states. As U.S. alliances at both ends of Eurasia grew weaker due to the United States' lack of sustained strategic commitment and increased introversion, China incrementally drew into line the most advanced industrial countries, including Japan, South Korea, Australia, and the nations of Western Europe, by offering them more financial and economic incentives. Beijing deals with regional powers according to a hierarchy that is visible in the way it labels its different bilateral partnerships, depending on the level of cooperation—e.g., friendly partnership, friendly cooperative partnership, comprehensive friendly cooperative partnership, strategic partnership, and comprehensive strategic cooperative partnership.[109] The investment and assistance programs financed and controlled by China give it significant leverage in terms of influence over its neighbors, as Beijing can give and take back as it pleases. Enmeshed within a web of cooperation at all levels, and with no credible alternative sources of investment and aid in sight, regional countries are reluctant to oppose Beijing. Countries that have tried to challenge China's core interests, or refused to align their vote with it in the United Nations, have been put under severe pressure both economically and politically when China threatened to constrict trade and cooperation. Wary that they might be punished and isolated, most countries silently acquiesce to Beijing's diplomatic priorities.

In the security domain, too, regional powers deal with each other primarily through cooperative arrangements with China. CICA has become

---

[106] Arase, "China's Two Silk Roads."

[107] Zhao Huasheng, "Strategic Position and Role of the SCO in the Silk Road Economic Belt," *China Watch* 6, no. 6 (2015): 31–35, http://fudan-uc.ucsd.edu/_files/china-watch/ChinaWatch_Vol.06-2015.pdf.

[108] Li Xiangyang (presentation at the U.S.-China Belt and Road Forum, Washington, D.C., November 30, 2016).

[109] Such a hierarchical differentiation is already in place. See Peter Wood's map at https://www.p-wood.co/2016/09/18/chinas-foreign-relations; and Nigel Inkster, "Coming to Terms with Chinese Power," *Survival* 58, no. 1 (2016): 209–16.

the main platform for security dialogue and cooperation, covering the whole of Eurasia and providing the regional security cooperation architecture.[110] It addresses both traditional and nontraditional security challenges (terrorism, transnational crimes, environmental security, cybersecurity, energy and resource security, and natural disasters). Such shared concerns have created opportunities for the development of concrete military and security cooperation between China and its neighbors, including security forces training, regular joint military exercises, and joint counterterrorism operations.[111] CICA members "abide by the basic norms governing international relations such as respecting sovereignty, independence and territorial integrity and non-interference in internal affairs, respect the social systems and development paths chosen by countries on their own, and fully respect and accommodate the legitimate security concerns of all parties."[112] In addition, CICA members have increased their cooperation with Beijing on law enforcement and have agreed to locate, detain, and extradite political dissidents or "irritants," such as Uighur and Tibetan refugees or the family members of corrupt officials.[113]

In all, BRI has created around China a dense "network of cooperative countries and, even better, like-minded friends."[114] Neo-authoritarian regimes have long been seen by Beijing as friendlier, more predictable, and more susceptible to Chinese influence than democratic governments that might question agreements previously reached with Beijing or allow themselves to be manipulated by unnamed "third countries" that seek to encircle China and thwart its rise.[115] The rulers of these countries share the CCP's concerns about possible popular discontent and social unrest that could be exploited by "foreign hostile forces" in order to stage "color revolutions." To push back against the liberal peace model that used to be the cornerstone of U.S. foreign policy, Chinese diplomacy has consistently emphasized development as "the master key to regional security issues"

---

[110] Xi, "New Asian Security Concept for New Progress in Security Cooperation."

[111] Author's discussions at CASS, Beijing, November 2015. See also Feng Zhongping and Li Hongli, "Periphery Strategy Should Focus on Innovative Security Cooperation," *Contemporary International Relations* 23, no. 6 (2013): 50–53.

[112] Xi, "New Asian Security Concept for New Progress in Security Cooperation."

[113] Shannon Tiezzi, "After Uyghur Controversy, China Praises Law Enforcement Co-op with Thailand," *Diplomat*, July 24, 2015, http://thediplomat.com/2015/07/after-uyghur-controversy-china-praises-law-enforcement-co-op-with-thailand; and Weichi Sun and Huang Jingjing, "Hunt for Corrupt Officials Fleeing Overseas Meets Legal Barriers," *Global Times*, April 9, 2014, http://www.globaltimes.cn/content/853506.shtml.

[114] Zhang Feng, "China as a Global Force," *Asia and the Pacific Policy Studies* 3, no. 1 (2015): 125.

[115] Gao Junxian and Mao Yan, "China's New Silk Road: Where Does It Lead?" *Asian Perspective* 40, no. 1 (2016): 105–30.

and placed the "right to develop," instead of the right to individual freedom, as its core value.[116] Unlike Western countries, China does not impose any conditionality on its partners: no government transparency, anticorruption measures, or commitment to "good governance, economic freedom and investments in their citizens" is required in exchange for investment, economic assistance, and security cooperation.[117] By helping its authoritarian neighbors deliver economic growth, China has offered them ways to strengthen and preserve their rule.[118] Enhanced security cooperation has also allowed these countries to improve their social control techniques.

Western liberal ideas have been repelled, democracy has not spread across Eurasia, and China's periphery has been stabilized. China sits majestically enthroned, unchallenged at the top of a regional order in which other powers, bound by economic, political, and security dependence on Beijing, show deference and respect its interests.

Conclusion

As seen in chapter 1, the idea that Eurasian connectivity would lead to economic growth, which would, in turn, bring political changes, is not entirely new. The same "spillover logic" guides the BRI idea: the Chinese leadership hopes that it can use its leverage to "build a tight network of economic, cultural, political and security relations," with the ultimate goal of "socializ[ing] Asia and Europe into its own preferred view of global order."[119] Although the premises of BRI are the same, Beijing's endgame is very different from the one envisioned by the United Nations and several Western powers at the end of the Cold War—eventual political liberalization and integration of Eurasia into the liberal international order. The community of common destiny that the Chinese leadership would like to see emerge in Eurasia as a result of increased physical connectivity is not a group of

---

[116] Xi, "New Asian Security Concept for New Progress in Security Cooperation"; and Chang Jian, "Jiang Zhonghua wenming dui shijie renquan de gongxian shangsheng dao lilun gaodu" [The Chinese Civilization's Contribution to Global Human Rights Is Rising to Theoretical Heights], Xinhua, December 10, 2016, http://opinion.china.com.cn/opinion_77_154977.html. Chang is vice president of the Zhou Enlai School of Management at Nankai University.

[117] This is how the Millennium Challenge Corporation, an independent agency created by the U.S. Congress in 2004 that provides aid to poor countries, defines its mission. See the Millennium Challenge Corporation website, https://www.interaction.org/choose-to-invest-2017/mcc.

[118] Andrew J. Nathan, "China's Challenge," *Journal of Democracy* 26, no. 1 (2015): 156–70; and Octavia Bryant and Mark Chou, "China's New Silk Road: Autocracy Promotion in the New Asian Order?" *Democracy Theory* 3, no. 2 (2016): 114–24.

[119] William A. Callahan, "China's Belt and Road Initiative and the New Eurasian Order," Norwegian Institute of International Affairs, Policy Brief, 2016.

democracies interacting with each other according to a set of liberal rules and values such as good governance and the protection of human rights. The meaning of BRI's "inclusiveness" is that democracies are not prevented from joining, but also that neo-authoritarian states have the same access to Chinese investment and trade benefits as any other country, without political conditionality. Maintaining Eurasia's political and social diversity does not mean, however, that all countries are equal. Because of its size, civilization, and hard and soft power, China sees itself at the apex of the community it aims to create.

This new role for China as the regional hegemon is envisaged by its elites as an "extended projection of the Chinese civilizational identity."[120] The norms that BRI seems to want to project and apply under the guise of the Silk Road spirit are wrapped in a coat of neo-Confucian principles and elements of traditional Chinese wisdom that have been carefully selected to fit the broader purpose of rejecting universal rights and liberal norms. Rather than creating the basis for a new ideology or international order that would replace the current one with new institutions and rules, BRI might lead to Eurasia becoming an illiberal insert into the global order. The region would still trade and interact diplomatically with the rest of the world, but the influence of Western values and norms would be considerably diminished.

Will Asia's past become Asia's future? Even if the Chinese regime intends to use BRI to set the stage for a future Sinocentric Eurasian order, it must persuade other countries of the legitimacy of China's claim to leadership. The Silk Road values and norms that Beijing is crafting will have to demonstrate their universality in order to appeal to potential followers. The supposed moral superiority of the Chinese model extolled by the country's elites might not pass the test of other regional powers' opposition to Chinese hegemony. Smaller countries might also find it increasingly difficult to accept China's growing influence at their doorstep. As the next chapter will show, there are indeed many obstacles that might stand in the way of China's dream of re-emergence.

---

[120] Samuel P. Huntington, *The Clash of Civilizations and the Remaking of World Order* (New York: Simon and Schuster, 1996), 237.

Chapter 5

Hurdles on the Way

It would be very naive to assume that a plan as colossal in scope as BRI will unfold between now and 2049 without encountering significant obstacles. The Chinese government and strategic and intellectual elites are anything but naive. Much of China's strategic brainpower is employed to think about, assess, and analyze the nation's position in relation to its external environment and to "take the pulse" of the surrounding world. BRI has not escaped from this intense scrutiny. Strategic thinkers, international relations experts, businesspersons, and government officials all acknowledge the complexity of the Belt and Road strategy, as well as the many uncertainties and political, economic, and security challenges that lie ahead.[1] Ultimately, however, they believe that "risks and benefits go hand in hand,"[2] that "the depth and longevity of BRI's impact are proportional to the difficulties it will face to be achieved,"[3] and that "difficulties and challenges should not become reasons that stop us from pursuing a beautiful goal."[4]

The stakes are high: BRI is "an attempt and a pathway to transform China from a regional power with global influence into a global power with comprehensive strength." If the strategy to achieve this goal is effectively implemented, it may "remodel the 'American Asia-Pacific' into the 'periphery of China.'"[5] For China to achieve "modernization, there is only one way: Belt and Road....[W]e must not lose confidence or retreat."[6]

---

[1] Liu Li-juan, "The Belt and Road Initiative Working towards a Global Vision," *Journalism and Mass Communication* 6, no. 2 (2016): 60–66; and Zhong Sheng, "Open Up Bright Prospects through Active Action," Renmin Ribao, February 17, 2015.

[2] Du Debin and Ma Yahua, "'Yidai Yilu': Zhonghua minzu fuxing de diyuan da zhanlüe" ["Belt and Road": The Grand Geostrategy for China's National Rejuvenation], *Dili Yanjiu* 34, no. 6 (2015).

[3] Qiao Liang, "Yidai Yilu yu daguo guanxi guanli" [Belt and Road and Great Power Relationship Management], Sina, June 12, 2015, http://www.blog.sina.com.cn/s/blog_4ee8cf410102w1pv.html?refer=wbxg.

[4] Zhong, "Open Up Bright Prospects through Active Action."

[5] Xue Li, "Zhongguo 'Yidai Yilu' zhanlüe miandui de waijiao fengxian" [Diplomatic Risks Facing the Belt and Road Strategy], *Guoji Jingji Pinglun*, no. 2 (2015): 68–79.

[6] He Maochun, "'Yidai Yilu' zhanlüe mianlin de zhang'ai yu duice" ["Belt and Road" Strategy to Face Obstacles and Countermeasures], *Xinjiang Shifan Daxue Xuebao*, no. 3 (2015), http://www.uscnpm.com/model_item.html?action=view&table=article&id=8278.

In short, China has no choice but to confront and surmount the difficulties that will undoubtedly arise along the way.

Chinese policy analysts are trying to identify what could go wrong with BRI and to craft a set of recommendations to avoid the most obvious pitfalls.[7] Overall, they assess the existing risks quite realistically, but they also show a striking optimism that, over time, the fulfilment of BRI will by itself attenuate the challenges that it will encounter. Thus, "the mechanism of confrontation and wild competition will give way to long-term cooperation," and BRI will, as a matter of course, generate its own success.[8] A CCTV News report predicted that "regional economic cooperation will help alleviate the contradictions. With more cooperation, disputes will eventually disappear."[9] China just needs to "keep [its] intentions and desires good and consistent"; if it can do this, "no troubles or difficulties will be impossible to solve."[10]

Interestingly, no Chinese expert openly disapproves of BRI—the order has been given by the top leadership, and there is no point in advocating alternative strategies—but a few do offer words of caution. Shi Yinhong, a professor at Renmin University, warns, for example, that China may be opening "too many battlefields" and overstretching its capacities; he therefore calls for "strategic prudence."[11] General Qiao Liang worries that BRI could remain empty talk with no concrete results. But he hopes that this will not happen, because "if BRI fails, then it will be a heavy blow to the Chinese

---

[7] These analysts base their assessment on a careful study of foreign reactions to BRI, as well as on the field surveys conducted by research groups who have been dispatched around Eurasia and to the United States. See, for example, Hong Shihong, "Riben dui Zhongguo 'Yidai Yilu' de fanxing" [Japan's Reaction to China's "Belt and Road"], December 27, 2015, http://pit.ifeng.com/a/20151227/46850823_0.shtml; Wang Yiwei, "Jianpuzhai dui 'Yidai Yilu' de Shida Danxin" [Cambodia's Ten Worries about "Belt and Road"], *Guancha*, December 24, 2015, http://www.guancha.cn/WangYiWei/2015_12_24_345761.shtml; and Gong Ting, "'Yidai Yilu': Meiguo dui Zhongguo zhoubian waijiao gouxiang de jiedu" ["Belt and Road": U.S. Interpretations of China's Peripheral Diplomacy Concept], China Institute of International Studies (CIIS), December 19, 2014, ciis.org.cn/chinese/2014-12/19/content_7454821.htm.

[8] Igor Denisov, "China Going West: The Silk Road to Bring Beijing Out of the Shadows," *Russia in Global Affairs*, March 19, 2015, http://eng.globalaffairs.ru/number/China-Going-West-17371.

[9] "Closer to China: 'One Belt One Road,' International Affairs and Diplomacy," CCTV News, March 29, 2015, https://www.youtube.com/watch?v=itCNrlD2-Lw. See also Jiang Zhida, "'Yidai Yilu': Yi 'kongjian' huan 'shijian' de fazhan zhanlüe" ["Belt and Road": The Development Strategy That Turns "Space" into "Time"], *Heping yu Fazhan* 4 (2015).

[10] Qiao, "Yidai Yilu yu daguo guanxi guanli."

[11] Shi Yinhong, "'Yidai Yilu': Qiyuan shenshen" ["Belt and Road": Calling for Prudence], Institute of World Economics and Politics, Chinese Academy of Social Sciences (CASS), July 30, 2015, http://ejournal.iwep.org.cn/index.php?optionid=979&method=letters&auto_id=2569; and "Tuijin 'Yidai Yilu' jianshe yingyou shenshen xintai" [Patient Attitude Needed for Promoting "Belt and Road" Construction], *Renmin Wang*, July 5, 2015, http://world.people.com.cn/n/2015/0705/c1002-27256546.html.

economy and even to the great rejuvenation of the nation."[12] In a similar vein, an official from the Chinese Communist Party (CCP) International Liaison Department (ILD) underlines the risk of "overselling the concept" as BRI becomes associated with just about everything China is doing.[13] Xue Li cautions that if the strategy is implemented hastily, enormous projects might become incomplete or abandoned as useless "white elephants."[14] If not handled well, he notes, the United States could take advantage of China's problems for its own strategic purposes. Others point out that BRI will raise high expectations and caution that China will not be able to deliver "development miracles to the entire region."[15]

In private discussions, some experts are more forthright in their criticism of Xi Jinping's plans. For example, one Chinese observer remarked that Xi's "so-called strategic vision does not compare anywhere near Deng Xiaoping's," while others criticized the president's "arrogance" and "boundless ambition." The leadership wants to "achieve in fifteen years what would normally take a hundred years" and would like "to get everything too fast." This could be "a huge mistake." In five years, one senior scholar predicts, "everyone will be unhappy because the results will not be up to their expectations. The Chinese population will have lost faith in government because our investments will not have given the expected fruits. The next leadership will have to clean up the mess."[16]

This chapter will look at the four main challenges faced by BRI, as identified by Chinese experts, and evaluate the solutions they prescribe in response. The first section will describe how China could overcome its lack of experience in Eurasia's complex environment by improved understanding and better risk assessment. The second will discuss BRI's economic viability and consider options for mitigating investment risks. The third will focus on means of circumventing the potential negative reactions to BRI, both from great powers and smaller recipient countries. The fourth section will describe ways of reducing the security risks that could draw China into local quagmires.

---

[12] Qiao Liang, "Zhongguo lujun de fazhan fangxiang zhengque ma? Heli ma?" [Is the PLA Army's Development Direction Correct? Reasonable?], *PLA Daily*, May 7, 2015, http://military.china.com/important/11132797/20150507/19650325_all.html.

[13] Author's interview, Beijing, December 2016. The ILD oversees the party's foreign relations with other political parties. It also prepares foreign affairs and political memos for the CCP Politburo.

[14] Xue, "Zhongguo 'Yidai Yilu' zhanlüe miandui de waijiao fengxian."

[15] Author's interviews, Yinchuan, December 2016.

[16] Author's interviews, Beijing and Shanghai, November 2015 and December 2016.

Eurasia's Diversity and China's Lack of Experience

The diversity of the region encompassed by BRI is a function of the initiative's enormous geographic scope, extending as it does from the fringes of Western Europe to the Persian Gulf, East Africa's shores, the Indian Ocean, Russian expanses and Central Asian steppes, and Indochina. The complexity of this vast area is usually the first factor to be acknowledged by Chinese commentators as a potential obstacle to BRI's smooth implementation. The differences in economic development levels, sociopolitical systems, ethnicity, cultures, and religions are seen as immediate difficulties confronting the Chinese businesspersons and officials who have been called by the leadership to "go out" to the Belt and Road countries. China's overseas experience is not great, and executives and bureaucrats alike need to remedy their lack of "basic understanding of foreign political and economic history."[17] Even if the government is not naive about potential hurdles, having acknowledged the religious and territorial issues, "the reality is still more complicated than scholars and officials have imagined."[18]

Although Chinese leaders cannot reduce Eurasia's complexity, at the very least, Chinese commentators point out, they should try to improve their knowledge of the unique characteristics of the BRI countries. Research should be encouraged in many different fields, not just by academics and think-tank experts but also by companies that "need to strengthen [their] understanding and research on the basic dimensions of economic, social, legal, political, cultural, and religious aspects of these regions when [they] go out in Central Asia, South Asia, Southeast Asia, Africa, Central and Eastern Europe, the European Union, and others."[19] Research about foreign countries' sociopolitical conditions should be conducted in centers specifically dedicated to BRI, with the objective of providing recommendations to both government and corporate decision-makers.[20]

An official from the ILD acknowledges that it will take time "to adapt our system," train a new generation of translators and experts, change their

---

[17] Li Xing, "Sichouzhilu jingjidai, zhicheng 'Zhongguo meng' de zhanlüe, haishi celüe?" [Silk Road Economic Belt: Strategy or Tactic to Support the "China Dream"?], *Dongbeiya Luntan*, 2015, 85–92; and Gao Ke, "'Yidai Yilu' zhanlüe mianlin de tiaozhan yu yingdui celüe" [Challenges and Counterstrategies Facing "Belt and Road" Strategy], *Renmin Luntan*, April 26, 2016, http://www.cssn.cn/zzx/gjzzx_zzx/201604/t20160426_2983797.shtml.

[18] Liu, "The Belt and Road Initiative Working towards a Global Vision."

[19] "Ruhe zou hao Yidai Yilu jiaowiangyue" [How to Play Belt and Road as a Symphony], CIIS, March 24, 2015, http://www.ciis.org.cn/chinese/2015-03/24/content_7772711.htm.

[20] Gao, "'Yidai Yilu' zhanlüe mianlin de tiaozhan yu yingdui celüe"; and Liu, "The Belt and Road Initiative Working towards a Global Vision."

thinking and working mindset, and make appropriate preparations before having to confront increased risks overseas. According to him, "current international relations experts do not necessarily have knowledge that would be useful for businesses, or if they do, they do not usually interact with them."[21] Zhao Minghao notes that "better policy coordination among diverse governmental agencies [is] also essential for a successful grand diplomacy by China in marching westwards."[22] Chinese embassies should help companies seeking to do business locally in order to avoid the repetition of "incidents such as the Myitsone dam, where Chinese companies did not have a good sense of Myanmar's internal politics."[23] High-quality research should be used to inform "forward-looking thinking," enhanced strategic planning, and better risk assessment. A joint research mechanism should be established to enable effective dissemination of knowledge to both government and business entities.[24] Overcoming administrative divisions and making sure that the different actors involved in BRI (businesses, government, intellectuals, and media) coordinate their efforts are essential to the success of the initiative.[25] Better coordination does not necessarily mean micromanagement, however. As Huo Jianguo, the dean of the Ministry of Commerce Research Institute, points out, "top level design should not develop overly detailed plans, but establish principles, objectives and paths, and leave enough space to the markets and companies to do the work." The ultimate objective is to improve assessment, anticipate possible reactions, and "avoid being taken by surprise."[26]

As Chinese banks, businesses, and government officials venture out into new countries, operate in unfamiliar markets, and deal with challenging environments, knowledge of the local economic, political, and social conditions is essential to help them assess the risks and make informed decisions. Here, China obviously does not start from scratch. Intellectual resources abound, and since 2013, research centers specially dedicated to

---

[21] Author's interviews, Beijing, December 2016.

[22] Zhao Minghao, "'March Westwards' and a New Look on China's Grand Strategy," *Mediterranean Quarterly* 26, no. 1 (2015): 97–116.

[23] Author's interviews, Beijing, December 2016.

[24] Liu, "The Belt and Road Initiative Working towards a Global Vision"; and "'Yidai Yilu' jianshe zhong de fengxian guankong wenti" [The Issue of Risk Management in the Construction of "Belt and Road"], *Zhengzhi Jingji xue Pinglun* 6, no. 4 (2015): 190–203.

[25] Zhao Lei, "Zhe shi 'Yidai Yilu' zuida de tongdian" [This Is the Biggest Aching Point of "Belt and Road"], Sina, December 11, 2015, http://finance.sina.com.cn/zl/china/20151211/075123991283.shtml.

[26] Huo Jianguo, "'Yidai Yilu' shi zhanlüe gouxiang, bu shi 'gongcheng xiangmu'" ["Belt and Road" Is a Strategic Concept, Not an "Engineering Project"], *People's Daily*, March 19, 2015, http://finance.people.com.cn/money/n/2015/0319/c42877-26719589.html.

BRI have flourished. As seen in chapter 2, academics and other experts have responded enthusiastically to the central authorities' call to participate in the collective learning and counseling effort. Government-related entities such as the National Development and Reform Commission (NDRC), Export-Import Bank of China, and China National Petroleum Corporation (CNPC) also have been conducting regular BRI-related risk analysis.[27] The primary question remaining is therefore not about the availability of intellectual resources but about the effectiveness with which they can be deployed. In a country where whistle-blowing can be dangerous, it may be difficult for analysts working under the leadership of the party to report the truth if it does not fit with what the official authorities wish to hear.

Economic Viability

As opposed to Western commentaries, there are few Chinese analyses of the economic viability of BRI and of its potential to exacerbate China's domestic economic imbalances.[28] There are several possible explanations for this relative silence. Chinese commentators may find it difficult to overtly criticize the soundness of a plan that clearly bears Xi Jinping's mark, for fear of reprisal. It is also possible that such matters are indeed discussed and addressed but only behind closed doors so that the Chinese public does not start to raise questions about why China is investing its money abroad instead of in its own economy. If, as seen in chapter 3, the Chinese leadership genuinely believes that BRI is a solution to the country's economic problems, it becomes difficult to criticize the initiative as a source of more economic trouble to come. Finally, if the geopolitical motivations underlying BRI supersede the economic and commercial justifications, the leadership may not consider the possible lack of economic viability to be a deal-breaker. $1 trillion may simply be the price China has to pay in order to achieve its ultimate strategic objectives.

---

[27] Author's interviews, Beijing, December 2016.

[28] Skeptical Western views can be found, for example, in Jiayi Zhou, Karl Hallding, and Guoyi Han, "The Trouble with China's One Belt, One Road Strategy," *Diplomat*, June 26, 2015, http://thediplomat.com/2015/06/the-trouble-with-the-chinese-marshall-plan-strategy; "One Belt, One Road: Can China Overcome the Obstacles?" CCR Advisory Group, Newsletter, November 2016, https://ccradvisorygroup.com/one-belt-one-road-can-china-overcome-obstacles; "China's One Belt, One Road Initiative Brings Risks," Reuters, January 25, 2017, http://www.reuters.com/article/idUSFit987609; and Vikram Mansharamani, "China Is Spending Nearly $1 Trillion to Rebuild the Silk Road," *PBS NewsHour*, March 2, 2016, http://www.pbs.org/newshour/making-sense/china-is-spending-nearly-1-trillion-to-rebuild-the-silk-road.

As described in chapter 2, BRI is backed by the promise of huge sums of government money available for investments in countries that are less safe and likely less profitable than Japan or the economies of North America and Europe. Although as a rule infrastructure investments are not expected to provide short-term returns, the Chinese authorities are aware that such prospects might prove even less economically viable in BRI countries. An official from the Export-Import Bank of China laments: "We are left with the difficult projects, because the financially viable ones have already been finalized over the last 40 years. Some BRI projects are not financially viable in the short term, it is a fact."[29] Given that investing China's national wealth in "money-losing assets would violate the basic principles of foreign exchange reserves management," an expert from the Chinese Academy of Social Sciences (CASS) adds that China "must avoid doing this."[30] Earlier governmental investments in the construction of domestic infrastructure in the western and northeastern provinces of China "have failed to reach their expected goals," mainly because "financial returns were not the key investment concern," warns Huang Yiping, a professor at Peking University National School of Development.[31]

How should banks respond to the central government's demands for investments under BRI, knowing that there is a risk of low (or nonexistent) returns, while at the same time avoiding financial disaster for China? One solution is to mitigate the risks by sharing the burden with other actors. As Huang notes, "the Chinese government should not be the only one providing capital." Because "China alone cannot fill the infrastructure gap," local countries should help finance it, but more importantly "the United States should join the financing multilateral platform that China initiated."[32] The Asian Infrastructure Investment Bank (AIIB) is indeed seen by several experts as a convenient instrument to help mitigate the overall financial risk induced by infrastructure investment in poor BRI countries. A Peking University professor who works as a consultant for the NDRC explains, for example, that "before AIIB was created, China Development Bank used to 'invest' or rather 'donate' to emerging countries. Now, thanks to AIIB it has become easier to refuse to give them money, by placing the blame on AIIB

---

[29] Author's interviews, Beijing, December 2016.

[30] Xue, "Zhongguo 'Yidai Yilu' zhanlüe miandui de waijiao fengxian."

[31] Huang Yiping, "Keys to the 'Belt and Road' Strategy Succeeding," BiMBA Peking University National School of Development, http://en.bimba.edu.cn/index/NewsVoices/2015/0312/14415.html.

[32] Author's interviews with officials from the ILD's China Center for Contemporary World Studies and the National Development and Reform Commission (NDRC), Beijing, December 2016.

board members."³³ A prominent professor from Fudan University notes that "thanks to AIIB, for every dollar earned, we take back 30 cents; for every dollar lost, only 30% is lost for China. Overall, we can still earn money, it is impossible that we lose everywhere."³⁴

Chinese investments may ultimately prove detrimental to the country's welfare, but government-backing certainly provides some sense of financial security for China's state-owned enterprises (SOE), a situation that may encourage reckless decision-making. Economist Huang Yiping warns that in the past many SOEs failed to get profitable deals because they "did not have to shoulder any responsibilities," and their "blind spending" wasted foreign reserves. Private companies, on the other hand, may have encountered problems when investing abroad, but unlike SOEs "they learn from their experience quickly because they use their own money."³⁵ Because the subjugation of market forces to political demands heightens the risk that some projects will ultimately prove unprofitable, it would be preferable to let companies play a more active and autonomous role in choosing where they want to invest and operate. Huang advises, for example, that the government should continue to play a "leading role, but should not interfere too much in companies' decisions." For his part, Gao Ke, a fellow at CASS, notes that SOEs, which have become China's leading actors in investing overseas, might not be welcome in some countries for fear of their possible "unfair competition and even ulterior motives." Gao, therefore, recommends that the government speed up SOE reforms, especially those focused on improving transparency. BRI, he contends, is "not just an economic strategy, but the 'business card' China presents to the world," an opportunity for Chinese firms to showcase their reliability and seriousness. Hence, companies involved in BRI "should not only have a strong economic ability, but also excellent international public relations capabilities."³⁶ The dean of the Ministry of Commerce Research Institute advises that the top leadership introduce clear guidelines at the national level for companies to follow, with explicit "principles, objectives, and tasks."³⁷

---

³³ Author's interviews with officials from the NDRC, Beijing, December 2016.
³⁴ Author's interviews, Shanghai, December 2016.
³⁵ Huang, "Keys to the 'Belt and Road' Strategy Succeeding."
³⁶ Gao, "'Yidai Yilu' zhanlüe mianlin de tiaozhan yu yingdui celüe."
³⁷ Huo "'Yidai Yilu' shi zhanlüe gouxiang, bu shi 'gongcheng xiangmu.'"

The Misgivings of Great Powers and Local Countries

More widely discussed than BRI's economic viability are the potential negative reactions to the initiative, both from great powers such as the United States, India, Russia, and Japan and from smaller recipient countries. Chinese commentators believe that the other great powers will see BRI as a competitor to their own efforts to gain regional influence and will therefore try to undermine or oppose it. When looking at BRI's recipient countries, they see two main challenges: local political fluctuations and uneasiness about China's increased influence. The solutions envisaged have mainly to do with strategic communication, public diplomacy, and "political warfare" campaigns that provide reassuring narratives in order to influence public perception. Commentators also insist on the necessity of finding "synergies" or "convergences" between China's plans and local government priorities.

Challenges from Great Powers

When placed in the context of China's ambitions for regional preponderance, BRI faces an immediate challenge: great-power competition. General Qiao Liang notes, for example, that "what will really influence the smooth implementation of BRI from start to finish is the great-power relations that will be closely associated and concomitant with this undertaking.…Although we should not neglect any small country—because losing a horseshoe could make us lose the war—what we must first solve is our ability to effectively manage the major-power relations."[38] The United States, India, and Russia will inevitably see BRI as a potential challenge to their own regional influence. Washington will disapprove of the "revitalization of a Eurasian geopolitical plate," which would weaken its own overall geostrategic position. India, for its part, "believes the belt and road will hinder its Look East policy and is also concerned about the situation in the Indian Ocean." Meanwhile, "despite good relations with China, Russia still nurtures some misgivings about its weakening influence, possible competition over political, economic, and energy interests, and challenges to the Eurasian Economic Union."[39]

According to two Chinese geostrategists, "China's promotion and implementation of BRI, even if it is done through economic means, will strengthen its strategic presence in the area, thus challenging American vested interests and disrupting its global deployment. Hence, it is bound to

---

[38] Qiao, "Yidai Yilu yu daguo guanxi guanli."

[39] Jiang, "'Yidai Yilu': Yi 'kongjian' huan 'shijian' de fazhan zhanlüe."

be blocked by the U.S." In the Indian Ocean, the experts anticipate increased U.S. intervention in local internal affairs, in particular support for "local democratization process[es]," joint military training with India, pressure on Pakistan, and intentional "disruption of the China-Pakistan Economic Corridor." In the Silk Road Economic Belt region, the analysts see the potential for three main problems created by the U.S: "the war on terror and the color revolutions have been manufactured to create local chaos so that these countries do not have time to cooperate with China; they use historical, ethnic and religious issues to incite local fears of China; and they use Russia's opportunistic tendencies to crush the Sino-Russian strategic understanding in Central Asia."[40]

Some Chinese experts believe that whatever China is trying to achieve, the United States will always "oppose everything we do."[41] Washington's merciless machinations are everywhere, and if the BRI space is a "fiercely turbulent vortex," it is mainly because the United States is "trying to consolidate its position by means of color revolutions to fragment Eurasia." In addition, "many countries along the belt and road are allies to the U.S., which is an obstacle."[42] Systematic U.S. opposition to China's plans is inevitable and can be attributed to the "tragedy of great-power politics: after the Cold War, the U.S. gradually formed the consensus that Russia was incapable of resuscitating the Soviet Union and the only challenger to its hegemony was China."[43] But China also has some comparative advantages that can be played against the United States, especially in the financial domain:

> If the U.S. wants to work against China in [Central Asia], it will need to make a lot of effort to win [regional countries] one by one, which will come at a very high price....China can bring benefits to these countries, while the U.S. cannot. If you do not bring benefits to others, you cannot expect that just because you dislike China, or its ideology, or its political system, or because you see it as a challenger, you can simply ask other countries to help put pressure on China! China is not a challenger to these countries, why would they take the plague for you?[44]

---

[40] Du and Ma, "'Yidai Yilu': Zhonghua minzu fuxing de diyuan da zhanlüe."

[41] Qiao, "Zhongguo lujun de fazhan fangxiang zhengque ma? Heli ma?"

[42] Li Xiguang, "Zhongguo weihe yao buju 'Yidai Yilu' da zhanlüe?" [Why Does China Want to Lay Out the "Belt and Road" Strategy?], *Foreign Affairs Observer*, December 10, 2015, http://www.faobserver.com/NewsInfo.aspx?id=11595.

[43] Du and Ma, "'Yidai Yilu': Zhonghua minzu fuxing de diyuan da zhanlüe."

[44] Qiao Liang, "Quanqiu shiye xia de da zhanlüe gouxiang" [Grand Strategy Concept under Global Vision], in *Gaibian shijie jingji dili de Yidai Yilu* [Transforming the Global Geo-economy through Belt and Road]] (Shanghai: Jiaotong University Press, 2015), 51–65.

Other regional great powers such as Japan and India also have the capacity to limit China's strategic action. Both occupy "overlapping strategic space in continental Eurasia, but their power there is limited." More important, these two countries can "threaten sea lanes, as they guard the gateway to the Pacific Ocean and the Indian Ocean, respectively, especially if they continue to cooperate with the U.S." Chinese experts view the U.S.-Japan alliance as being "based on sea passage and pos[ing] a maritime threat to China: Ryukyu, Shimoji, and other reefs are used to install intelligence networks, submarines nets, and listening facilities to monitor China's vessels on their way to the Pacific Ocean." They believe that "the protection of southwestern routes is an excuse to expand toward the Indian Ocean, meddle in Malacca, and threaten the security of China's southern transportation lines. In the future, Japan will 'invite' other Southeast Asian countries to get involved in the South China Sea in order to contain the Maritime Silk Road."[45] Japan is seen as seeking "a more dominant role in Southeast Asia in the future, leading to a more intense competition with China in the region."[46] India, for its part, "wants to dominate the Indian Ocean along two maritime expansion rings: Andaman-Nicobar and the Bay of Bengal–Arabian Sea, which puts more pressure on the security of the Malacca Strait. In the future, a more confident India will actively interfere in the construction of the Maritime Silk Road."[47]

Finally, Chinese analysts acknowledge Russia's possible misgivings about BRI. Moscow is seen to be looking increasingly eastward and trying to strengthen its own influence in Eurasia, in particular through the Eurasian Economic Union (EEU). But Chinese experts are generally optimistic that Russia will not oppose BRI, both because the partnership between the two countries is particularly strong and because there is nothing much Moscow can do to block the initiative: "Russian elites might prefer not to see China's regional strategy succeed, but they cannot stop the historical trend of China's rise."[48] Specifically, Russia can do nothing to stop Central Asian countries from cooperating with China:

> Moscow cannot assist them economically, and Putin knows that if China is prevented from cooperating with Central Asia, other countries will fill the void. Moscow also understands that China has no intention of reducing Russia's regional power and influence, while it knows that other countries do have this intention. So, the Russians will continue to support BRI because it is the best

---

[45] Du and Ma, "'Yidai Yilu': Zhonghua minzu fuxing de diyuan da zhanlüe."
[46] Du Lan, "Southeast Asia and the Belt and Road" (presentation, Yinchuan, December 2016).
[47] Du and Ma, "'Yidai Yilu': Zhonghua minzu fuxing de diyuan da zhanlüe."
[48] Author's interviews, Beijing, November 2015.

strategy for them now. If they play against it, they will lose more than they will gain.[49]

Moscow's options thus appear extremely limited. Vladimir Putin finds himself having "no other choice" but to cooperate with China because Russia does not have sufficient financial and economic power to do otherwise.[50] If Moscow wants to "develop its energy market to the Asia-Pacific and reconstruct its economy not only on the exclusive basis of resources," it will inevitably need "China's huge and stable market demand, funding, and technical support."[51] Chinese analysts believe that China should use this as leverage to achieve Eurasian integration on its own terms. In the end, Beijing's partnership with Moscow is strong: "Both trust each other geopolitically, their border problems have been solved. There could be frictions because of trade, but that cannot make them become enemies. Maybe Russia sees that China's actions can serve Russia's interests too and that there is more to gain from cooperation than from competition." Such a calculation might explain why Putin agreed in May 2015 to sign a cooperation decree between the EEU and BRI.[52]

Challenges from Smaller Countries

Smaller countries along the belt and road can also be problematic for Beijing, either because of their political instability or because of their negative perceptions of China. In order to secure its projects under the BRI umbrella, Beijing favors high-level diplomacy. But this can put cooperation at risk whenever a new government comes to power.[53] In places where democracy prevails, the political process brings "a lot of uncertainty."[54] As local leaderships alternate on a regular basis, "their interest in implementing BRI also fluctuates" and they might suspend ongoing negotiations or question agreements previously reached.[55] These recurrent political changes are seen as potential impediments for the smooth implementation of BRI projects, even if sometimes they can play in China's favor, as in the Philippines, where the Duterte government adopted a more positive stance

---

[49] Author's interviews with officials from CIIS, the Ministry of Foreign Affairs' think tank, Beijing, November 2015.
[50] Author's interviews, Beijing and Shanghai, November 2015.
[51] "Ruhe zou hao Yidai Yilu jiaowiangyue."
[52] Author's interviews, Shanghai, November 2015.
[53] Gao, "'Yidai Yilu' zhanlüe mianlin de tiaozhan yu yingdui celüe."
[54] Ibid.
[55] Jiang, "'Yidai Yilu': Yi 'kongjian' huan 'shijian' de fazhan zhanlüe."

toward Beijing than its predecessors.[56] By contrast, Beijing sees authoritarian governments as friendlier, more predictable, and more capable of keeping local insurgent or extremist forces under control.[57] But they too can create uncertainty, especially when older autocrats pass away and a country enters a phase of political transition. When Uzbek leader Islam Karimov died in late 2016, Zhang Gaoli, member of the CCP Politburo Standing Committee and head of the Leading Small Group on Advancing the Development of the Belt and Road, was sent to attend his funeral, likely in order to secure continuity with the new leadership.[58] During his audience with Prime Minister Shavkat Mirziyoyev, Zhang underlined the necessity of continuing to "promote the Belt and Road initiative, and to enrich [the two countries'] all-round strategic partnership by prioritizing economy, trade, production capacity and security in bilateral cooperation."[59]

Smaller BRI countries are sometimes wary of an increased Chinese presence and influence:

> They worry that they will become too economically dependent on China. They fear that they may become a new kind of "banana republic" as large numbers of Chinese citizens flood in, and that official corruption will be on the rise.... Another challenge is that some of the countries along the Belt and Road are concerned about the environmental side-effects of big projects. Some fear that large-scale investments will change their culture, traditions, and lifestyles.[60]

Even if relations are good at the government and elite levels, the reactions of local populations and specific ethnic, racial, religious, or political groups cannot be ignored. They are indeed the key sources of possible "unexpected consequences," as Li Peilin, the vice president of CASS explained in a 2015 televised interview. As BRI makes progress in Eurasia, it will inevitably affect the local populations, both their way of life and their environment. China will have no control over how they react and how strongly they may resist the initiative. But Li is optimistic that

---

[56] Author's interviews with officials from the ILD, Beijing, December 2016.

[57] Gan Junxian and Mao Yan, "China's New Silk Road: Where Does It Lead?" *Asian Perspective* 40, no. 1 (2016): 105–30; and author's interviews, Shanghai, November 2015.

[58] Raffaello Pantucci, "Karimov's Death Seen from Beijing," China in Central Asia, September 9, 2016, http://chinaincentralasia.com/2016/09/09/karimovs-death-seen-from-beijing.

[59] "Chinese President's Special Envoy Attends Karimov's Funeral," Xinhua, April 9, 2016, http://www.globaltimes.cn/content/1004542.shtml.

[60] Xue Li, "'Yidai Yilu' zheshe de Zhongguo waijiao fengxian" [Chinese Diplomatic Risks Reflected from "Belt and Road"], *Financial Times* (Chinese edition), December 30, 2014, http://www.ftchinese.com/story/001059886?full=y.

over time "people will gradually understand the difference between China's opening up and the so-called neocolonialism."[61]

That recipient countries express doubts about BRI and how it might affect their own equilibrium does not come as a surprise to Chinese observers. Since the end of the Cold War, Beijing has become used to being the victim of the so-called China threat theory and has tried to find ways to counter foreign suspicions and negative perceptions of its rapid economic and military development.[62] Regional countries will naturally at first view an ambitious initiative like BRI with caution: "A country might act in good faith and still be perceived as a malicious threat by another. In Asia, smaller countries have adapted to China's rise, but their security instinct puts them on high alert mode."[63] Given that China's actions may give the impression that it is trying to dominate its neighbors, Beijing should "clarify [its] intentions, and foster mutual trust rather than suspicion."[64] But the success of BRI ultimately depends on regional countries' support and commitment. If the local people do not properly "understand China, it will breed some anti-Chinese sentiment, and the project will be caught in the middle of local conflicts and even canceled. This would be tantamount to a catastrophic blow for [China's] strategy."[65]

To dispel resistance to BRI, avoid misperception, and ease international suspicion, Chinese experts believe that Beijing must "sow the seeds of trust" with both words and deeds.[66] It can do this not only by increasing its strategic communication but also by taking into account other countries' wishes so that it becomes easier for them to accept BRI projects. China needs to build "a good understanding of BRI before starting a project, break the rumors of 'China's Marshall Plan' and 'China threat theory.'"[67] It must "persuade the countries along these routes that building the Silk Road Economic Belt and the 21st Century Maritime Silk Road will not harm their security but

---

[61] "Closer to China: 'One Belt One Road,'" International Affairs and Diplomacy."

[62] For a thorough discussion of the "China threat theory," see Yong Deng, "Reputation and the Security Dilemma: China Reacts to the China Threat Theory," in *New Directions in the Study of China's Foreign Policy*, ed. Alastair Iain Johnston and Robert S. Ross (Stanford: Stanford University Press, 2006), 186–214; and Simon Rabinovitch, "The Rise of an Image-Conscious China," *China Security* 4, no. 3 (2008): 33–47.

[63] Du and Ma, "'Yidai Yilu': Zhonghua minzu fuxing de diyuan da zhanlüe."

[64] Wu Zhicheng and Xing Haibing, "Strategic Planning for Its Neighboring Diplomacy," *Contemporary International Relations* 25, no. 2 (2015): 62–65.

[65] Gao, "'Yidai Yilu' zhanlüe mianlin de tiaozhan yu yingdui celüe."

[66] Gan Junxian, "Sichouzhilu fuxing jihua yu Zhongguo waijiao" [Planning for a Revival of the Silk Road and China's Diplomacy], *Dongbei Luntan* 19, no. 5 (2010): 65–73.

[67] Gao, "'Yidai Yilu' zhanlüe mianlin de tiaozhan yu yingdui celüe."

actually increase it, that the economic advantages exceed the disadvantages, and that their culture will not be impacted."[68] In order to persuade the world of China's benign intentions and win support for its political objectives, the country's propaganda apparatus is carefully crafting an official narrative around BRI targeting foreign public opinion.[69] In particular, it emphasizes "the 'mutually beneficial win-win' principle, so that the locals can really feel that BRI will bring positive changes to their lives."[70]

Despite intense efforts to develop an attractive and soothing story, this narrative does not automatically translate into greater acceptance from targeted countries. When assessing the impact of China's strategic communications, the ILD "found some gaps between China's understanding of BRI and external perceptions." The propaganda apparatus is still struggling to find formulas that will be more appealing to people outside China: one expert suggests that "globalization 2.0" or "connectivity" might sound better to foreign audiences than "Silk Road spirit."[71] Coating BRI with a globalization varnish could indeed present China as a seductive alternative to the emerging protectionist tendencies in Western democracies. Judging by his speech at the Davos summit, Xi Jinping has already started to present himself as "globalization's great defender," even though BRI is intended not "so much to collapse national boundaries as to pull neighboring countries into China's geopolitical orbit."[72]

In conjunction with increased political warfare, tangible results and early harvests are necessary for people to see the benefits of the initiative, which "will in turn enhance their support."[73] The Chinese government has thus started to look for synergies between BRI and local development strategies. Several examples of this search for converging interests can be found in the joint discussions leading to Kazakhstan's Nurly Zhol (Bright Path) economic policy announced in November 2014 and Mongolia's

---

[68] Xue, "Zhongguo 'Yidai Yilu' zhanlüe miandui de waijiao fengxian."

[69] Liu, "The Belt and Road Initiative Working towards a Global Vision"; and Liu Qibao, "Hongyang Silu jingshen dali xuanchuan 'Yidai Yilu'" [Vigorously Promote "Belt and Road's" Silk Road Spirit through Propaganda], Xinhua, January 4, 2015, http://news.xinhuanet.com/politics/2015-01/04/c_1113870928.htm.

[70] Gao, "'Yidai Yilu' zhanlüe mianlin de tiaozhan yu yingdui celüe."

[71] Author's interviews, Beijing, December 2016.

[72] Andrew Browne, "Xi Jinping in Davos, Making the Most of a Waning Era," *Wall Street Journal*, January 16, 2017, https://www.wsj.com/articles/xi-jinping-in-davos-making-the-most-of-a-waning-era-1484560806.

[73] Jiang, "'Yidai Yilu': Yi 'kongjian' huan 'shijian' de fazhan zhanlüe."

Steppe Road announced in September 2014,[74] as well as in dialogues with Russia's EEU and with the European Commission regarding its 315 billion euro investment plan.[75] China is also seeking to develop synergies with global institutions, as demonstrated by the signing of a letter of intent with the UN Economic and Social Commission for Asia and the Pacific in April 2016. The two sides promised to "jointly promote regional cooperation and the implementation of the OBOR initiative" and "make specific action plans and encourage relevant countries to synchronize their development strategies with the initiative."[76] The ILD is also weighing the possibility of increased cooperation with India in Afghanistan, given that both Beijing and New Delhi have "a considerable stake in keeping Afghanistan from becoming a failed state."[77] In addition, it is considering presenting BRI to the EU as a way to solve the refugee problems in Southern Europe.[78]

The United States is a significant factor in China's efforts to win foreign hearts and minds, and Chinese experts carefully scrutinize U.S. publications and declarations about BRI. Based on their observations, some recommend emphasizing the cooperative and nonexclusive character of the initiative to foreign audiences while downplaying its strategic or hegemonic intent and exploring venues for practical bilateral cooperation—for example, in the energy domain.[79] General Qiao Liang argues that China should "subtly" let the United States participate in BRI because whenever they are left out, the Americans "always play a disruptive role....If they were totally excluded from BRI, they would not spare any effort to suppress it, without scruples." He therefore advises letting "American investment banks, institutions, and technological businesses play a role, in order to completely tie them

---

[74] "China Is a Great Nation: Nursultan Nazarbayev," Tengrinews, September 4, 2015, https://en.tengrinews.kz/politics_sub/China-is-a-great-nation-Nursultan-Nazarbayev-261928; and Alicia J. Campi, "Mongolia's Place in China's 'One Belt, One Road,'" Jamestown Foundation, China Brief, August 18, 2015, https://jamestown.org/program/mongolias-place-in-chinas-one-belt-one-road.

[75] Russia and China signed a joint statement on cooperation on the construction of the EEU and Silk Road Economic Belt on May 8, 2015. See "Experts from China, Russia, Kazakhstan, Belarus, Armenia and Kyrgyzstan Discussed Prospects for Coherence of the EEU and the Silk Road Economic Belt," Skolkovo, September 2015, https://iems.skolkovo.ru/en/iems/events/468-2015-09-23. For more on the dialogue with the European Commission, see "China Focus on Belt and Road, Juncker Plan Synergies," Xinhua, February 18, 2016, http://www.chinadailyasia.com/nation/2016-02/18/content_15386616.html.

[76] "China-UNESCAP Deal to Boost Belt and Road Initiative Cooperation," Xinhua, April 13, 2016, http://www.scio.gov.cn/32618/Document/1474296/1474296.htm.

[77] Zhao, "'March Westwards' and a New Look on China's Grand Strategy."

[78] Author's interviews, Beijing, December 2016.

[79] Gong, "'Yidai Yilu': Meiguo dui Zhongguo zhoubian waijiao gouxiang de jiedu."

up with BRI. Once this binding-up has been achieved, the U.S. will act with restraint."[80]

Local Entrapments

Aside from various political risks associated with potential negative reactions to BRI, both from great powers and smaller countries, the Chinese initiative may also confront security risks that could draw China into local quagmires.[81] BRI's geographic scope extends over regions that form an "arc of instability" where the security situation has been increasingly volatile due to ethnic and religious violence, territorial disputes, and destabilizing spillovers from conflicts in Syria, Yemen, and Afghanistan.[82] In particular, terrorist groups and violent local insurgencies are seen as potential major threats to the smooth implementation of regional infrastructure projects. As China gets involved in more regional projects, its interests will become more vulnerable to attack.[83] Chinese strategic planners have started to ponder such scenarios and believe that there is a higher risk that physical infrastructure (e.g., pipelines and railways) will be damaged by a bomb than that the United States will impose a maritime blockade in the western Pacific.[84]

Chinese companies are on the front lines of such security challenges. With the expansion of China's global outreach, nearly 30,000 Chinese companies now operate abroad and face increasing security risks, including from terrorist attacks. Since 2010, they have been involved in 345 security incidents outside China, and the general trend is upward.[85] Businesses have to come up with strategies to limit the potential risks to the safety of both personnel and physical infrastructure. Along with making sure that their own employees "follow strict rules,"[86] working with locals appears to be the preferred approach: "invest locally, operate locally, integrate into the

---

[80] Qiao, "Zhongguo lujun de fazhan fangxiang zhengque ma? Heli ma?"

[81] Author's interviews, Beijing, December 2016.

[82] Du and Ma, "'Yidai Yilu': Zhonghua minzu fuxing de diyuan da zhanlüe"; and Jiang, "'Yidai Yilu': Yi 'kongjian' huan 'shijian' de fazhan zhanlüe."

[83] Author's interviews, Shanghai, November 2015.

[84] Author's interviews with officials from the China Institutes of Contemporary International Relations, Beijing, November 2015.

[85] Chen Xiangyang, "2016, ruhe weihu Zhongguo guojia anquan?" [How to Maintain China's National Security in 2016?] Cfisnet, January 4, 2016, http://comment.cfisnet.com/2016/0104/1303593.html; and Jonas Parello-Plesner and Mathieu Duchâtel, *China's Strong Arm: Protecting Citizens and Assets Abroad* (London: International Institute for Strategic Studies, 2015).

[86] Author's interviews with officials from the China National Petroleum Corporation (CNPC), Beijing, December 2016.

local community" is how some SOEs now describe their plan for operating in developing countries.[87] CNPC, for example, hires locals to patrol its pipelines and has implemented programs that are meant to provide local communities with water wells and medical clinics. The company also reaches out to local governments to assist with social development: "if in this neighborhood people have jobs, terrorism will not be a problem anymore. The priority is to create jobs, make money, so that the local government can collect taxes that will in turn help provide for security." Similarly, the China Chamber of Commerce of Metals, Minerals, and Chemicals Importers and Exporters has engaged directly with Pakistani government officials: "We organized several workshops with them and told them they should pay attention to projects related to civil society. If they could create more jobs, Taliban men would have better things to do than to create conflict. Living conditions can be improved by Chinese investments, so that the overall social conditions can be improved."[88] The idea is that if the local population and authorities have a personal stake in keeping the Chinese businesses operating locally, "the risks [that they will] be antagonistic to our projects will be significantly reduced."[89]

In the past, local outreach was usually not China's preferred way of doing business, but this practice seems to be evolving as both Chinese companies and political leaders acknowledge that local actors have an impact on the smooth implementation of BRI. One official provided the following observation:

> Traditionally we like to deal with the governments, with the ruling party, with the rich local people....We need to continue to talk with both the government and the ruling party, but also with the opposition, and more importantly we need to deal with the tribal elders along the belt. Their influence is often much more important than that of the opposition or ruling parties. If we have been able to accomplish things in areas under Taliban rule in Afghanistan and in Pakistan, it has been by working through the elders; going through government channels basically never helped accomplish anything. Our ministries, companies, cannot ignore these important relationships within the region.[90]

Chinese firms operating in risky environments are also increasingly hiring private security companies. BRI has been a boon for this emerging

---

[87] Author's interviews with officials from the China Chamber of Commerce of Metals, Minerals, and Chemicals Importers and Exporters (CCCMC), Beijing, December 2016

[88] Ibid.

[89] Author's interviews with officials from CNPC, Beijing, December 2016.

[90] Qiao, "Zhongguo lujun de fazhan fangxiang zhengque ma? Heli ma?"

Chinese industry.⁹¹ As of 2013, four thousand registered entities employed more than 4.3 million security personnel—most of them veterans of the People's Liberation Army (PLA) or the People's Armed Police Force—to offer personal protection and property patrol services. Chinese law prevents them from carrying lethal weapons, however, and the central government has also applied stringent regulations when they operate abroad out of "concern that armed contractors might accidentally provoke or escalate conflict with the locals—leading to diplomatic troubles."⁹² Foreign private security companies, such as the U.S firm Frontier Services Group (owned by the founder of Blackwater), have also started to pursue new opportunities offered by the growing demand for security along the belt and road.⁹³ Frontier Services Group set up two camps in China—one in Yunnan, one in Xinjiang—in order to "train and deploy an army of Chinese retired soldiers who can protect Chinese corporate and government strategic interests around the world, without having to involve the Chinese People's Liberation Army."⁹⁴

The Chinese government too is looking for ways to better protect its citizens and safeguard the nation's expanding overseas interests, but it remains wary of intervention. As a matter of policy, China is still strictly committed to the principle of noninterference in the domestic affairs of other countries and opposed to unilateral military intervention. It has historically been reluctant even to use coercive instruments accepted under international law, such as peacekeeping operations and sanctions. However, the growing overseas presence of Chinese assets and citizens—over one million Chinese nationals are now working abroad—and a series of violent incidents targeting Chinese workers in Africa and Asia have forced the leadership to think in more pragmatic terms about how to incrementally adapt its policy.⁹⁵ In the wake of the successful evacuation

---

[91] Xie Wenting, "Chinese Security Companies in Great Demand as Overseas Investment Surges," *Global Times*, June 23, 2016, http://www.globaltimes.cn/content/990161.shtml.

[92] Zi Yang, "China's Private Security Companies: Domestic and International Roles," Jamestown Foundation, China Brief, October 4, 2016, https://jamestown.org/program/chinas-private-security-companies-domestic-international-roles; and Alessandro Arduino, "Security in One Belt One Road: Singapore's Role in Training Expertise," S. Rajaratnam School of International Studies (RSIS), Commentary, no. 125, May 25, 2016, https://www.rsis.edu.sg/rsis-publication/rsis/co16125-security-in-one-belt-one-road-singapores-role-in-training-expertise/#.WMmKuhiZM3g.

[93] See, for example, Frontier Services Group, "Frontier Services Group Strategy Update," Press Release, December 5, 2016, http://202.66.146.82/listco/hk/frontier/press/p161205.pdf.

[94] Aram Roston, "Betsy DeVos's Brother, the Founder of Blackwater, Is Setting Up a Private Army for China, Sources Say," BuzzFeed, February 16, 2017, https://www.buzzfeed.com/aramroston/betsy-devoss-brother-is-setting-up-a-private-army-for-china.

[95] Mathieu Duchâtel, Olivier Bräuner, and Zhou Hang, *Protecting China's Overseas Interests: The Slow Shift Away from Non-interference*, SIPRI Policy Paper, no. 41 (Stockholm: Stockholm International Peace Research Institute, 2014), http://books.sipri.org/files/PP/SIPRIPP41.pdf.

of 35,000 Chinese citizens from Libya in March 2011, an operation historically unprecedented for China, the 18th Party Congress vowed in 2012 that China would "actively assume its international responsibilities and obligations, safeguard the international public security, oppose all forms of terrorism, actively support UN peacekeeping operations...[and] jointly safeguard the security of international passages."[96] The defense white paper published in 2013 mentioned for the first time the necessity of protecting nationals and interests overseas. China increasingly deploys troops to participate in UN peacekeeping operations in Africa, mainly where Chinese economic interests and personnel are at risk, such as in Mali and South Sudan. As an illustration of this renewed commitment to peacekeeping, Xi Jinping announced in his September 2015 speech at the UN General Assembly that China "planned to set up a United Nations permanent peacekeeping force of 8,000 troops and would provide $100 million to the African Union to create an immediate response unit capable of responding to emergencies." China is also committed to training 5,000 peacekeepers from other countries by 2020.[97]

A greater role for the Chinese military has also been envisaged. The PLA wishes to improve its power-projection capabilities, especially for overseas protection and rescue operations. To this end, China started to build a "logistical facility" in Djibouti in early 2016.[98] Although it has not been named as such by the Chinese authorities, this is bound to become China's first overseas military base. Some high-ranking officers have begun to think about the impact of BRI on the PLA's future development, reaching a variety of conclusions that reflect ongoing debates within the Chinese military.[99] But all agree that the PLA should protect Chinese interests along the belt and road.[100] Whereas PLA Navy representatives focus on the development of China's naval power and the protection of

---

[96] Chen, "2016, ruhe weihu Zhongguo guojia anquan?"

[97] Jane Perlez, "China Surprises UN with $100 Million and Thousands of Troops for Peacekeeping," *New York Times*, September 28, 2015, https://www.nytimes.com/interactive/projects/cp/reporters-notebook/xi-jinping-visit/china-surprisesu-n-with-100-million-and-thousands-of-troops-for-peacekeeping.

[98] Katrina Manson, "China Military to Set Up First Overseas Base in Horn of Africa," *Financial Times*, March 31, 2016, https://www.ft.com/content/59ad20d6-f74b-11e5-803c-d27c7117d132.

[99] Sabine Mokry, "How the Belt and Road Initiative Globalizes China's National Security Policy," Mercator Institute for China Studies, November 15, 2016, https://blog.merics.org/en/blog-post/2016/11/15/how-the-belt-and-road-initiative-globalizes-chinas-national-security-policy.

[100] Andrea Ghiselli, "The Belt, the Road and the PLA," Jamestown Foundation, China Brief, October 19, 2015.

the 21st Century Maritime Silk Road,[101] others have called publicly for the creation of an expeditionary force to address the Silk Road Economic Belt's security needs. Speaking to an audience of military officers at the National Defense University in Beijing, General Qiao Liang from the PLA Air Force framed the issue the following way:

> [W]hat we really need is a ground force expeditionary capacity....[W]ith BRI, the army's responsibility is not just to defend the homeland anymore, but to have the capacity to prepare for expeditions along the belt and road....A Chinese army of one million men to protect the country is not a problem. But stepping across the country's gates to go fight, is this a problem? Are we correctly developing the army right now?....[O]ur army's combat capability must be thought over again, we must strengthen its long-range strike capabilities and remote delivery capabilities. I think we are still far from recognizing it, and even further away from doing it. If the army cannot go outside the country, to support locals, or protect our interests, this is what we must think about today....If you do not start from your national interests and needs, and vaguely model yourself on the U.S. military, and assume that this is what your own army should look like, what will happen?...I believe BRI is a tremendous incentive for China's military reforms according to our national interests and needs.[102]

As General Qiao acknowledges, the PLA is still far away from having the capabilities necessary to project and deploy forces across the Eurasian continent. His speech also reflects a point of view that differs from what PLA Navy officers would advise. Whether on land or at sea, BRI's impact on the evolution of the Chinese military should not be underestimated, especially in times of important restructuring and reforms.[103] Meanwhile, Chinese elites keep looking for solutions that would allow possible future direct interventions wherever needed. Wang Yizhou, a professor at Peking University, has set the intellectual stage for modifying the principle of noninterference. The concept of "creative involvement" would supposedly allow overseas operations to safeguard Chinese interests without infringing on the legitimate interests of other countries.[104] An official from the ILD calls for China to use this concept in its dealings with the Middle East and

---

[101] See, for example, Li Jian, "Xin shidai huhuan xin de guojia haiyang guan" [The New Era Calls for a New National Oceanic Outlook] *Junshi Luntan*, April 25, 2017, http://www.81.cn/jfjbmap/content/1/2017-04/25/07/2017042507_pdf.pdf.

[102] Qiao, "Zhongguo lujun de fazhan fangxiang zhengque ma? Heli ma?"

[103] On PLA developments, see, for example, David M. Finkelstein, "Get Ready for the Second Phase of Chinese Military Reform," CNA, China Studies, January 2017, https://www.cna.org/CNA_files/PDF/DOP-2017-U-014677-Final.pdf; and Joe McReynolds, ed., *China's Evolving Military Strategy* (Washington, D.C.: Jamestown Foundation, 2016).

[104] According to Wang, such operations would be legitimate if they bear three characteristics: obeying the UN Charter, being invited by local people or a majority of political parties in the country, and conforming to the wishes of most neighbors. See "New Direction for China's Diplomacy," *Beijing Review*, March 8, 2012, http://www.bjreview.com.cn/expert/txt/2012-03/05/content_440505.htm.

North Africa: "China needs to be more attentive in studying the dynamics in that region and make 'creative involvements' to help resolve hotspot issues, mitigate tensions, stabilize post-crisis countries and respond to those countries' look east policy demands."[105] The central leadership is looking for "smart ways" to improve its response to security risks by "strengthening its own intelligence collection work in key countries, carrying out regular risk assessments, establishing early warning mechanisms in high risks areas, but also increasing its cooperation with belt and road countries in several domains such as counterterrorism, intelligence sharing, rescue operations, and law enforcement."[106]

China has started to enhance its security cooperation bilaterally, noticeably with Mongolia,[107] Afghanistan,[108] and Pakistan, where a special security division of 10,000–15,000 men specifically dedicated to the protection of the China-Pakistan economic corridor was set up by the Pakistani armed forces in April 2015.[109] In April 2016, China established a quadrilateral military consultative mechanism specifically dedicated to counterterrorism with Tajikistan, Afghanistan, and Pakistan. The purpose of this grouping is for the four countries to "coordinate with and support each other in a range of areas, including study and judgment of counter terrorism situation[s], confirmation of clues, intelligence sharing, anti-terrorist capability building, joint anti-terrorist training

---

[105] Zhao, "'March Westwards' and a New Look on China's Grand Strategy."

[106] Chen, "2016, ruhe weihu Zhongguo guojia anquan?" See also Gong Honglie, "How to Protect Chinese Nationals Overseas," *China Daily*, November 26, 2015, http://www.chinadaily.com.cn/opinion/2015-11/26/content_22519504.htm.

[107] "China, Mongolia Pledge Enhanced Security Cooperation," Xinhua, May 11, 2015, http://news.xinhuanet.com/english/2015-05/11/c_134229058.htm.

[108] Tang Shiyu, "Zhongguo-Afuhan guoji rendao zhuyi saolei yantao yu jiaoliu peixun ban jieye yishi juxing" [Completion Ceremony Held for China-Afghanistan International Humanitarian Land Mine Research, Exchange and Training Course], Phoenix Online, March 16, 2014, http://news.ifeng.com/a/20140516/40328780_0.shtml; and "Xi Pledges Closer China-Afghanistan Security Cooperation," Xinhua, July 10, 2015, http://news.xinhuanet.com/english/2015-07/10/c_134401664.htm. Reports of PLA soldiers patrolling inside Afghan territory have been denied by China's defense ministry, who noted that law-enforcement bodies from China and Afghanistan were "in accordance with a bilateral agreement on strengthening border law enforcement, conducting cooperation along the border so as to jointly carry out counter-terrorism and to fight against cross-border crime." See "China Again Dismisses Reports of Military Patrols in Afghanistan," Reuters, February 23, 2017, http://uk.reuters.com/article/uk-china-afghanistan-idUKKBN162132.

[109] It is not clear whether China will provide training and assistance to the Pakistan Army's Special Security Division. Pakistan's breakdowns of the $56 billion Chinese investments in the China-Pakistan economic corridor do not include security. I am grateful to Daniel S. Markey for this information. See also Saeed Shah and Josh Chin, "Pakistan to Create Security Force to Protect Chinese Workers," *Wall Street Journal*, April 22, 2015, https://www.wsj.com/articles/pakistan-to-create-security-force-to-protect-chinese-workers-1429701872; and Wang Xu, "Special Troops to Help Keep China-Pakistan Corridor Safe," *China Daily*, February 4, 2016, http://www.chinadaily.com.cn/china/2016-02/04/content_23385711.htm.

and personnel training."¹¹⁰ In Central Asia, Beijing seems to favor reinforced regional security cooperation through the already existing Shanghai Cooperation Organisation (SCO), possibly in conjunction with Russia's Collective Security Treaty Organization (CSTO).¹¹¹ This idea was welcomed in 2016 by Nikolai Bordyuzha, general secretary of the CSTO: "A broad Eurasian coalition is needed to fight international terrorism. Such a coalition could be created by Russia, China, the CSTO and SCO countries [and] could become a locomotive in the organization of the entire anti-terrorist fight."¹¹² New SCO members could also contribute to the capacities of their domestic security forces, thus "expanding the possibilities and range of information sharing, feedback, and mutual training."¹¹³

Conclusion

The range of hurdles that BRI could encounter is commensurate with the immense scope of its ambitions. China will need to make substantial additional efforts to tackle the economic, political, and security risks that will confront BRI as it unfolds across a Eurasian continent characterized by complexity, uncertainty, and instability. Even if Chinese officials claim that such challenges "will not put a stop to BRI because all the countries share a common aspiration to improve their livelihood," they also are aware that "it will take some time for us, and our companies, to learn."¹¹⁴ BRI's amorphous construct might prove a useful quality in this regard. As an official from the ILD explains, "it is not a fixed route: if one project is impossible, we will take another path! In the long run, we may even have breakthroughs where we thought we never would."¹¹⁵

But wishful thinking is not sound strategy. The leadership appears seriously committed to success; indeed, it seems to believe that failure is simply not an option for BRI. Yet Chinese companies and government

---

[110] "Afghanistan, China, Pakistan, Tajikistan Issue Joint Statement on Anti-terrorism," China Military Online, August 4, 2016, http://english.chinamil.com.cn/news-channels/2016-08/04/content_7191537.htm.

[111] Ji Minkui, "'Yidai Yilu' jianshe shi Zhong-Ha shuangfang fazhan jiyu" [Building the "Belt and Road" Is a Development Opportunity for Both China and Kazakhstan], China.org, December 16, 2014, http://www.qstheory.cn/international/2014-12/16/c_1113664308.htm.

[112] "Eurasia Needs Broad Anti-terror Coalition: CSTO Chief," Russia Beyond the Headlines, April 29, 2016, http://rbth.com/news/2016/04/29/eurasia-needs-broad-anti-terror-coalition-csto-chief_588889.

[113] Author's interviews, Shanghai, November 2015.

[114] Author's interviews with officials from the ILD, Beijing, December 2016.

[115] Ibid.

entities will not operate in a vacuum. The initiative's fate will ultimately depend in large part on actors that are not under Beijing's control—on local governments, communities, and even insurgent groups that China cannot force to bend to its will. There are several ways to surmount these obstacles, and all of them are being envisaged by China's elites: eschewing confrontation and bypassing obstacles, but also involving local and international stakeholders, sharing with them the burden of security and economic risks, and above all lulling them into acceptance of the idea that BRI is a wonderful opportunity that will be good for everyone.

If the leadership listens to the recommendations and advice offered by its experts and strategic thinkers, China will have to go through a series of important internal adaptations and transformations in order to secure BRI's success. It will need to nurture a new generation of regional experts, who understand local cultures and politics, speak local languages, and even more importantly, if at all possible, have the necessary leeway to give truthful assessments to the top leadership without fearing backlash. Better, more systematic, and more efficient coordination will be required among government agencies, as well as between the center and the provinces and between the central government and the various economic actors who are called to venture out along the belt and road. Chinese diplomacy will also be further affected. Since 2013, China's focus on its periphery instead of the United States has marked the beginning of a shift that may accelerate as BRI unfolds. More human resources will need to be devoted to Chinese embassies, consulates, defense attachés' offices, and covert intelligence operations across Eurasia. Chinese personnel will be given a clear mandate to expand the range and depth of cooperation with local countries and to identify potential local friends who can advance China's interests within their own governments, opposition parties, and communities. Chinese SOEs will have to better understand the local investment environment and pay closer attention to local concerns, and may even be pushed to adopt higher standards of transparency and compliance. Finally, China's propaganda apparatus will continue to actively contribute to a political warfare campaign that will need to develop themes such as globalization and interconnectivity that are sweeter to foreign ears than mere variations on obfuscated Chinese jargon.

Will BRI be the most brilliant grand strategy ever devised by a Chinese leader, bringing the nation to the pinnacle of economic and political power? Or will it turn out to be China's biggest foreign policy disaster, draining the country's financial resources and putting its security at risk? Foreign Minister Wang Yi said on the sidelines of the annual session of the

National People's Congress in 2015 that BRI is not a "solo" for China but a "'symphony' jointly performed by all countries."[116] Indeed, the prospects for the initiative's success lie not only in Beijing's capacity to properly navigate around the hurdles that will inevitably stand in its way, but also in the rest of the world's willingness to accept China's objectives and go along with its plans.

---

[116] "Wang Yi: 'Belt and Road' Is 'Symphony' Jointly Performed by All Countries," Ministry of Foreign Affairs of the People's Republic of China, February 2, 2015, http://www.fmprc.gov.cn/mfa_eng/zxxx_662805/t1234406.shtml.

Chapter 6

Political and Strategic Implications of the Belt and Road Initiative

With the Belt and Road Initiative (BRI), the Chinese leadership seeks to use old recipes to prepare for a future that vaguely resembles the glorious times of an imagined past. The image of a distant, quasi-mythical era, swathed in nostalgia, has been repurposed to fit the country's contemporary nationalistic narrative and geopolitical needs; in this vision, China sits at the peak of its political, economic, military, and cultural power. In pursuing this dream and attempting to prolong its economic miracle, China has chosen the well-trodden path of transcontinental transportation and infrastructure building, combined with heavy industrial production by national conglomerates, all supported by state capital, planning, and control. By proceeding in this way, the regime hopes to perpetuate the model of development it is most comfortable with, pushing further into the future the difficult decisions that will be required to achieve significant and systematic economic reform. While Beijing is selling the promise of economic development throughout the region, its main focus is on the benefits that it hopes BRI will bring to China, not simply in the realm of economics but most importantly in the geopolitical domain. More robust engagement of the entire Eurasian continent through BRI is intended to enable China to better use its growing economic clout to achieve its ultimate political aims. BRI is thus not merely a list of revamped construction projects but a grand strategy that serves China's vision for itself as the uncontested leading power in the region.

Will a trillion dollars of investment in regional infrastructure suffice to sustain China's economic growth, opening new markets, consolidating national champions, helping absorb excess capacity, and accelerating internationalization of the renminbi? Will BRI bring development and stability to poorer countries across Asia, contribute to preventing and thwarting local terrorism and insurgencies, and help China diversify and secure its energy supplies? Will the initiative reduce the contradictions and tensions with neighboring countries, increase China's influence along its broad periphery, and eventually tame U.S. hegemony? Will history come back full circle and restore the world's center of gravity to what historian

Peter Frankopan calls "the real crucible, the 'Mediterranean' in its literal meaning—the center of the world—[which] was not a sea separating Europe and North Africa, but right in the heart of Asia?"[1]

With BRI, the Chinese leadership is betting that the answer to each of these questions will be a resounding "yes." As the leadership is well aware, there will be many hurdles along the way. BRI is likely to provoke counteractions and will undoubtedly create unexpected consequences too, some of which could have a long-term impact, not only across the region but on China as well. Such an ambitious endeavor, mobilizing so many of China's national resources and accelerating its regional outreach all the way to the Middle East, the fringes of Western Europe, and the shores of East Africa, will inevitably compel Beijing to become more engaged in places where it has traditionally been largely absent. Growing pressure to take action to protect Chinese assets and citizens on foreign soil could also, over time, nudge the regime into modifying its noninterference policy and loosening restrictions on unilateral military intervention.

It remains to be seen whether BRI will bring "great peace for all under heaven" or help create a 21st-century version of a Sinocentric regional order across the Eurasian continent. What is clear, however, is that BRI is the centerpiece of Beijing's indirect strategy for regaining regional predominance against the backdrop of an intensified contest for supremacy with the United States.[2] If it succeeds, the implications would certainly be far-reaching: an integrated and interconnected Eurasian continent with enduring authoritarian political systems, where China's influence has grown to the point that it has muted any regional opposition and gained regional acquiescence; a new regional order with its distinctive political and economic institutions, whose rules and norms block the future spread of what the West claims as universal values; and a continental stronghold insulated to some degree from U.S. sea power. If this strategy succeeds, then, as Samuel Huntington foresaw two decades ago, China could eventually "compel the U.S. to accept what it has historically attempted to prevent: domination of a key region of the world by another power."[3]

Meanwhile, almost four years after BRI's launch, the initiative is still understudied and largely overlooked in the West. The main focus of the Western community of policymakers and strategic planners is still devoted

---

[1] Peter Frankopan, *The Silk Roads: A New History of the World* (New York: Alfred A. Knopf, 2016), xix.
[2] See Aaron L. Friedberg, *A Contest for Supremacy: China, America, and the Struggle for Mastery in Asia* (New York: Norton, 2011).
[3] Samuel P. Huntington, *Clash of Civilizations and the Remaking of World Order* (New York: Simon and Schuster, 1996), 237.

to maritime East Asia, where tensions in the East and South China Seas and on the Korean Peninsula have intensified significantly in recent years.[4] The comparative dearth of interest in BRI reflects both a lack of understanding of the strategic motivations that underpin the initiative and a serious underestimation of its potential implications, not only for the Eurasian continent but also for U.S. regional influence and the liberal international order writ large.

Will China Succeed Where the West Has Failed?

As the opening chapter of this book discussed, dreams of a seamlessly interconnected Eurasian continent are not new. The early post–Cold War period saw several multilateral and unilateral attempts to build transportation networks across the continent. These were launched by the United Nations, the European Union, and the Asian Development Bank, with the hope that new physical infrastructure would have a transformational impact on the economies and societies of the former Soviet states, eventually bringing with it an irresistible wave of sociopolitical liberalization and democratization. Along with their investments, the Western powers sought to promote the rule of law, good governance practices, respect for human rights, and the development of transparent and democratic political institutions. Improvements in these areas were seen as increasing the potential for regional stability. But across Eurasia, Western plans and projects were undermined by local despotic rulers and corrupt bureaucracies reluctant to relinquish their privileges. Although the iron curtain had disappeared, long-standing political tensions and competition among neighbors prevented further border softening and regional integration.

Will China succeed where the West has failed? Although BRI, like the post–Cold War interregional projects led by the West, aims to foster regional connectivity, Beijing does not require recipient countries to transform their sociopolitical systems in exchange for investment. That may be a very appealing proposition to autocratic rulers across Eurasia. Xi Jinping believes that "countries have different historical processes and realities," and that they have "the right to choose their own development path independently."[5]

---

[4] Analysis is also biased because of the "stovepiping" of regional expertise.

[5] See "Remarks by President Obama and President Xi of the People's Republic of China in Joint Press Conference," White House, Office of the Press Secretary, September 25, 2015, https://obamawhitehouse.archives.gov/the-press-office/2015/09/25/remarks-president-obama-and-president-xi-peoples-republic-china-joint.

Of course, Beijing is deeply uncomfortable with the idea of democratization, which the Chinese Communist Party (CCP) sees both as a source of instability in China's immediate neighborhood and as a threat to its own grip on power. Officially, China proclaims itself to be eager to build transport links, facilitate regional trade, and promote better understanding among people "based on the principles of equality and mutual benefit," without excluding any country on the basis of its political regime. The rhetoric and policies surrounding BRI also give priority to "development rights" over "freedom rights" and dismiss universal norms as "Western values" that must be rejected. There is thus a real possibility that through increased economic, political, and security cooperation, BRI will help strengthen what Alexander Cooley labels the "league of authoritarian gentlemen," who are championing the principle of noninterference and tight state control over society and will find it increasingly easy to push back against Western pressures for change.[6] Left unchecked, BRI may over time strengthen authoritarian practices across Eurasia, slowing the spread of universal values. As Nobel Peace Prize recipient Liu Xiaobo writes about CCP leaders:

> At home, they defend their dictatorial system any way they can, [whereas abroad] they have become a blood-transfusion machine for a host of other dictatorships.…When the "rise" of a large dictatorial state that commands rapidly increasing economic strength meets with no effective deterrence from outside, but only an attitude of appeasement from the international mainstream, and if the Communists succeed in once again leading China down a disastrously mistaken historical road, the results will not only be another catastrophe for the Chinese people, but likely also a disaster for the spread of liberal democracy in the world.[7]

The gradual creation of an integrated "community of common destiny" embodying supposed "Asian values," controlling information flows, and promoting intraregional trade using renminbi rather than dollars could eventually seal off much of Eurasia from outside influence and pressure.

Increased interconnectivity and unobstructed flows of goods and people, governed by regional institutions promoting economic development and financial linkages, could ultimately create a more prosperous Eurasia. But the regional connectivity promoted through BRI will create linkages that are intended principally to help advance China's strategic objectives. Tighter economic ties will allow Beijing to impose punitive costs on some

---

[6] Alexander Cooley, "The League of Authoritarian Gentlemen," *Foreign Policy*, January 30, 2013, http://foreignpolicy.com/2013/01/30/the-league-of-authoritarian-gentlemen.

[7] As quoted in Simon Leys, "He Told the Truth about China's Tyranny," *New York Review of Books*, February 9, 2012, http://www.nybooks.com/articles/2012/02/09/liu-xiaobo-he-told-truth-about-chinas-tyranny.

countries while rewarding friendly states with material benefits. Increased presence in its neighbors' economies will give China more opportunities for coercion, selectively applying "economic incentives and punishments designed to augment Beijing's diplomacy."[8] Beijing's use of economic pressure against Mongolia, Norway, and South Korea provides only the most recent examples of a trend that has been evident for over a decade, as China tries to leverage trade to bend other countries to its will.[9] As they are pulled ever more closely into China's economic orbit, BRI countries will find it increasingly difficult to challenge Beijing on political issues. This has already begun to happen, and not only in the poorer countries along China's borders. Eager for Chinese capital and fearful of provoking a backlash, several comparatively wealthy Western nations have recently scaled back criticism on issues such as human rights.[10]

Finally, tightened links between China and Europe through BRI could also affect U.S. relations with its traditional allies. As Europe is drawn closer to China, its relations with the United States will inevitably evolve. Beijing already has considerable experience in using divide-and-conquer tactics among European states, providing them with differentiated levels of cooperation and market access on the basis of the extent of their cooperation

---

[8] James Reilly, "China's Economic Statecraft: Turning Wealth into Power," Lowy Institute for International Policy, Analysis, November 2013, http://sydney.edu.au/arts/government_international_relations/downloads/documents/Reilly_China_Economic_Statecraft.pdf.

[9] China imposed fees on commodity imports from Mongolia after a November 2016 visit by the Dalai Lama. See "China Says Hopes Mongolia Learned Lesson after Dalai Lama Visit," Reuters, January 24, 2017, http://www.reuters.com/article/us-china-mongolia-dalailama-idUSKBN158197. It also shut down several Lotte stores across China because the South Korean firm allowed the U.S. Terminal High Altitude Area Defense system to be deployed on land it owns southeast of Seoul. See Eric B. Lorber, "Economic Coercion, with a Chinese Twist," *Foreign Policy*, February 28, 2017, http://foreignpolicy.com/2017/02/28/economic-coercion-china-united-states-sanctions-asia. After six years of frozen bilateral relations because of the Nobel Peace Prize awarded to Liu Xiaobo, China finally agreed to resume its ties with Norway in December 2016, after the latter issued a *mea culpa* and "deeply reflected upon the reasons why bilateral mutual trust was harmed." See "Norway, China Normalize Ties after Nobel Peace Prize Row," Reuters, December 19, 2016, http://www.reuters.com/article/us-norway-china-idUSKBN1480R4. The Norwegian government signed a joint statement with Beijing promising not to support future actions undermining China's interests. See Kenji Kawase, "Norway Tones Down Its China Criticism to Boost Business," *Nikkei Asian Review*, December 29, 2016, http://asia.nikkei.com/magazine/Agents-of-Change-in-2017/Business/Norway-tones-down-its-China-criticism-to-boost-business.

[10] See, for example, the reaction of French journalists to the government's weak response to Ursula Gauthier's expulsion from China in 2015, "The Expulsion from China of Our Colleague Ursula Gauthier Is Unjustifiable," *Le Monde*, December 30, 2015, http://www.lemonde.fr/idees/article/2015/12/30/the-expulsion-from-china-of-our-colleague-ursula-gauthier-is-unjustifiable_4839571_3232.html#AolBJe1gTDD4J8ZT.99. In March 2017, 21 EU countries, the EU, and the United States declined to sign a joint letter criticizing China over "credible claims" that lawyers and human rights activists have been tortured while in detention. See Simon Denyer and Emily Rauhala, "Eleven Countries Signed a Letter Slamming China for Torturing Lawyers. The U.S. Did Not," *Washington Post*, March 22, 2017, https://www.washingtonpost.com/news/worldviews/wp/2017/03/22/eleven-countries-signed-a-letter-slamming-china-for-torturing-lawyers-the-u-s-did-not/?utm_term=.72ee39f1596e.

with Chinese political goals. Over time, China's growing economic clout could persuade some European nations that there is more to gain from accommodating its interests than from challenging them. It will then become easier for Beijing to drive a wedge between the transatlantic allies. The decision by European countries and U.S. allies in the Asia-Pacific to join the Asian Infrastructure Investment Bank (AIIB) despite U.S. objections is an example of the divisions that could become more common in the future as a result of BRI. At a time of the United States' retrenchment and possible withdrawal from its global role, U.S. allies are now pondering whether they should heed Beijing's invitation to get onboard the "Chinese development train," endorse BRI, and take a ride on the power shift to Asia instead of continuing to side with a declining friend. Poorly managed transatlantic differences could lead to a situation in which, as Henry Kissinger warns, "the United States, separated from Europe, would become, geopolitically, an island off the shores of Eurasia resembling nineteenth-century Britain vis-à-vis Europe."[11]

To Go Along…?

In his January 2017 speech at the World Economic Forum in Davos, Xi Jinping claimed that since BRI's launch, "over 100 organizations have given warm responses and support to the initiative. More than 40 countries and international organizations have signed cooperation agreements with China, and our circle of friends along the 'Belt and Road' is growing bigger."[12] The number of countries that have chosen to welcome BRI or to work with China in implementing it has indeed increased over time. In March 2017 the UN Security Council even included the concept in Resolution 2344, related to the extension of the UN Assistance Mission in Afghanistan, a step that Ambassador Liu Jieyi praised as "showing the consensus of the

---

[11] Henry Kissinger, *Does America Need a Foreign Policy? Toward a Diplomacy for the 21st Century* (New York: Simon and Schuster, 2001), 52.

[12] Xi Jinping (speech at the World Economic Forum, Davos, January 17, 2017), https://www.weforum.org/agenda/2017/01/full-text-of-xi-jinping-keynote-at-the-world-economic-forum.

international community on embracing the concept, and manifesting huge Chinese contributions to global governance."[13]

BRI's allure is all the more mesmerizing as, in the words of one Asian academic, the "Euro-American world grapples with the somber aftereffects of Brexit and the installation of a pugnacious Trump Presidency." As Peter Chang explains, "at a time when the West is building walls in an inward retreat, the East is constructing gateways in an outward advance, to embrace globalization, through the One Belt One Road initiative, the brainchild of President Xi Jinping."[14] In this context, BRI and its promises of unimpeded trade and a seamlessly interconnected Eurasian continent appear as one of the most appealing options for European and Asian democracies seeking to push back against isolationist tendencies while enhancing their own prospects for growth and prosperity. A report by the Brussels-based think tank Bruegel looks, for example, at how the reduction of transportation costs thanks to BRI might help foster EU trade.[15] The opportunities offered, even for businesses that do not belong to BRI, might also seem too great to pass up. Andrew Robb, the former Australian minister for trade, believes that BRI can bring opportunities for Australian businesses that have competitive advantages and expertise in infrastructure construction and management.[16] Similarly, former U.S. ambassador Chas W. Freeman Jr. believes that U.S. companies could benefit from BRI projects, since they "represent an unprecedented set of business opportunities on a wider scale than most yet seem to have grasped." He also calls for greater U.S. involvement in BRI: "If our government does not help make the rules, our interests will be ignored.

---

[13] The UN Security Council "welcomes and urges further efforts to strengthen the process of regional economic cooperation, including measures to facilitate regional connectivity, trade and transit, including through regional development initiatives such as the Silk Road Economic Belt and the 21st-Century Maritime Silk Road (the Belt and Road) Initiative, and regional development projects." See "Security Council Authorizes Year-Long Mandate Extension for United Nations Assistance Mission in Afghanistan, Adopting Resolution 2344 (2017)," United Nations, March 17, 2017, https://www.un.org/press/en/2017/sc12756.doc.htm; and "Chinese Landmark Concept Put into UN Security Council Resolution for First Time," Xinhua, March 18, 2017, http://news.xinhuanet.com/english/2017-03/18/c_136139045.htm.

[14] Peter Chang, "The Civilizational Fissures Beneath China's OBOR," *Malay Mail Online*, January 25, 2017, http://www.themalaymailonline.com/what-you-think/article/the-civilisational-fissures-beneath-chinas-obor-peter-chang.

[15] Alicia Garcia Herrero and Jianwei Xu, "China's Belt and Road Initiative: Can Europe Expect Trade Gains?" Bruegel, Working Paper, no. 5, 2016, http://bruegel.org/wp-content/uploads/2016/09/WP-05-2016.pdf.

[16] Will Koulouris, "Belt and Road Initiative Heralds New Era in Cooperation for Australia and China," Xinhua, March 24, 2017, http://news.xinhuanet.com/english/2017-03/24/c_136155106.htm. Robb's enthusiasm for the Chinese initiative may have to do with the fact that soon after leaving parliament he was appointed as a senior economic adviser to Landbridge Group, the Chinese operator of the port of Darwin. See Philip Wen, "Andrew Robb Defends Landbridge Appointment as 'Commercial Arrangement,'" *Western Advocate*, October 31, 2016, http://www.westernadvocate.com.au/story/4263282/andrew-robb-defends-landbridge-appointment-as-commercial-arrangement/?cs=12.

If our companies cannot get into the game Asians and Europeans have begun without us, they cannot hope to score. What is at stake is decades of enormous business opportunities....If we don't, others will." Ambassador Freeman likewise describes the U.S. reluctance to join the AIIB as "a foolish forfeiture of U.S. influence."[17]

Other prominent American figures also strongly advocate greater U.S. involvement in BRI and have urged Washington to join the Chinese-led infrastructure investment bank.[18] Former ambassador to China Jon Huntsman, for example, worries that "for the United States to stand back and pretend that it doesn't exist or that we shouldn't somehow connect and influence its outcome, I think, is a huge missed opportunity." As he goes on to explain, "we had a choice: you can either be within the organization and help shape its outcome or you can stay out and try to get others to kind of stay out as well. Well that strategy failed."[19]

"Shaping the outcome from within" also seems to be the reason that European countries are willing to cooperate with Beijing under the BRI umbrella. A recent report from the Stockholm International Peace Research Institute notes that engagement with China will help "cooperatively shape the future security landscape in line with the EU's stated priorities in relation to global governance, state-societal resilience and cooperative regional orders." The report concedes that it might be complicated to find workable complementarities because of the EU's emphasis on "a more rigorous international and formalized rules-based approach to investment, human rights and democracy in its political engagements, and good governance in its state-building endeavors." But the authors express hope that the EU will nevertheless be able to "influence China on a range of these issues to take a human security- rather than regime-centric security approach."[20]

---

[17] Charles W. Freeman, "The Geoeconomic Implications of China's Belt and Road Initiative" (remarks to a conference of the University of San Francisco's China Business Studies Initiative, San Francisco, February 8, 2017), http://chasfreeman.net/the-geoeconomic-implications-of-chinas-belt-and-road-initiative.

[18] See, for example, James Woolsey, the former CIA director and senior adviser to then president-elect Donald Trump, as quoted in "One Belt, One Road Seen as Bilateral Plus," *China Daily*, December 1, 2016, http://usa.chinadaily.com.cn/epaper/2016-12/01/content_27537506.htm. See also Francis Fukuyama, "Exporting the Chinese Model," New Europe, January 5, 2016, https://www.neweurope.eu/article/exporting-the-chinese-model; and Gal Luft, "It Takes a Road—China's One Belt One Road Initiative: An American Response to the New Silk Road," Institute for the Analysis of Global Security, November 2016.

[19] "China's One Belt One Road Strategy: Continental and Oceanic Energy Superhighways?" Atlantic Council, Global Energy Forum, January 12, 2017, http://www.atlanticcouncil.org/news/transcripts/session-2-china-s-one-belt-one-road-strategy.

[20] Richard Ghiasy and Jiayi Zhou, "The Silk Road Economic Belt: Considering Security Implications and EU-China Cooperation Prospects," Stockholm International Peace Research Institute, February 2017, 51, https://www.sipri.org/publications/2017/other-publications/silk-road-economic-belt.

Socializing China with the objective of encouraging its eventual political liberalization has been at the heart of Western engagement with that country for more than three decades, but the results are somewhat underwhelming. That BRI would now be the main instrument to help coax China into more liberalization seems like a well-intended but ill-considered fantasy. As William Callahan notes, "we should switch from asking how the EU can socialize China to consider how Brussels needs to work with a Beijing that is trying to socialize Europe."[21] To unquestioningly endorse and fully participate in BRI would help Beijing build something that directly contradicts the West's decades-long efforts to nudge post-Communist states toward democratization. Seeing BRI only as a business opportunity for Western companies bears the risk of seeking short-term (and uncertain) monetary gains without taking account of the possible negative impacts on the longevity of the West's geopolitical and normative preeminence.

Or Not to Go Along...?

As former Russian ambassador Vitaly Vorobyov notes, "the real perception of and consent for this project, let alone participation in it, implies an awareness of its essence and goals."[22] At a minimum, an exhaustive assessment of BRI's drivers, manifestations, and objectives appears to be a basic requirement for prudent policy. The first order of business for the United States and its allies is to become aware of what is at stake with BRI. A careful study of Chinese writings and discussions about BRI—as this monograph has sought to provide—can help unveil the initiative in all of its facets and look beyond the official narrative relayed by state propaganda. The question confronting Western governments is not whether they should launch a virulent anti-BRI campaign or try to actively sabotage Beijing's efforts. These options are unrealistic and costly in every conceivable way. The challenge facing Western countries is rather to find ways to maximize the benefits and minimize the harms that BRI can bring, not only to themselves but to the nations of Eurasia.

In the early phase of the BRI launch, most countries around the world adopted a wait-and-see approach and tried to simply understand

---

[21] William A. Callahan, "China's Belt and Road Initiative and the New Eurasian Order," Norwegian Institute of International Affairs, Policy Brief, no. 22, 2016, https://brage.bibsys.no/xmlui/handle/11250/2401876.

[22] Vitaly Vorobyov, "Beijing's New Foreign Policy: Is China to Build a New Economic Silk Road?" *Russia in Global Affairs*, March 21, 2014, http://eng.globalaffairs.ru/number/Beijings-New-Foreign-Policy-16503.

the initiative. BRI was both ill-defined and extremely ambitious, and it needed to be assessed in the light of individual countries' national interests. Reports started to emerge from U.S. and European think tanks, chambers of commerce, and government organizations in early 2016,[23] but the serious study of BRI in the West remains in its infancy. Now that the initiative is entering its fourth year, greater effort must be made to ponder its impact, evaluate its possible risks and opportunities, and formulate appropriate policies in response.

More attention should be paid to specific projects in order to better understand China's *modus operandi*, identifying key actors in the decision-making process, both in China and locally, as well as examining the contractual terms, financial conditions, environmental standards, and local impact of various projects. Outside actors—both governments and NGOs—have a crucial role to play in collecting and publicizing such information to compensate for Beijing's lack of transparency. If projects will increase local debt burdens, create severe environmental degradation, harm local communities, or reduce the autonomy of national governments, Beijing should be systematically held to account. Shedding light on the inner workings of BRI can not only help participants better assess risks and potential benefits but also apply pressure on China to revise its actions in ways that are more in accordance with the interests of local countries.[24]

In addition to shining a spotlight on China's activities, the democracies must strive to remain engaged, politically and economically, with countries along the belt and road so that they are not left alone to manage relations as best they can with their much bigger, stronger, and wealthier neighbor. This will not be easy. Weighed down by their own economic difficulties, politically divided, and increasingly turned inward, the Western democracies do not presently have the money to match China's massive proposed spending on programs. They will have to pool their resources and concentrate their efforts wherever they can do the most good. Rather than allowing BRI countries to be drawn ever more deeply into a Chinese-dominated system and sphere of influence, the United States and its friends and allies need to continue to make themselves available as a counterweight and, where possible, an alternative to Chinese-led plans and projects.

BRI signifies a relative shift in China's strategic focus toward the Eurasian continent, as well as a renewed ambition to compete with the United

---

[23] See the appendix for a note on sources.

[24] Raffaello Pantucci, "Building Support for the Belt and Road," European Council on Foreign Relations, Commentary, March 8, 2016, http://www.ecfr.eu/article/commentary_building_support_for_the_belt_and_road6023.

States for regional preponderance, albeit in an indirect way. Accordingly, Washington and its allies will need to think more holistically about their regional objectives and strategies, expand their geostrategic horizons beyond maritime East Asia to the entire Eurasian continent, and recalibrate their approach in terms of both hard and soft power.

The United States and its Asian and European allies still share the same worldview, based on a common set of values that include economic and political freedom, openness, democracy, transparency, accountability, respect for human rights, the empowerment of civil society, and good governance. Liberal democracies should use to full advantage the strengths and synergies they naturally enjoy in order to formulate an effective and coordinated response to BRI. This process should start with a sharing of assessments of Beijing's actions and motives and collective deliberation about a possible common response. The democracies must combine their efforts in a more systematic way to defend the open, rules-based international order and to push back against Beijing's political warfare campaign that deprives concepts such as "openness" and "globalization" of their original substance and meaning.

Responding to BRI will require strategic patience. At least for the moment, China has the initiative, and its programs have acquired an undeniable momentum. But Beijing's ambition to reshape the economic and political map of Eurasia is still in its early stages, and there will be many twists and bumps in the road ahead. Liberal democracies should learn from Chinese wisdom and look for ways to go with the "propensity of things," remaining flexible and ready to continue to advance their own vision for a truly open and integrated Eurasia. This includes finding ways to take advantage of the challenges China will inevitably encounter as BRI unfolds.

BRI is a laboratory for China's future global role and posture. It gives us the opportunity to observe how China defines its strategic goals and sets out to shape its neighborhood, including with a new set of norms that fit its interests better than a scorned U.S.-led world order. In other words, Beijing is offering us a full-scale test of its ambitions as a great power and of its intention to transform the regional political and strategic landscape. BRI is intended to consign the United States' Pacific century to oblivion: for those who care to listen, the initiative provides the strongest evidence to date of what it would really mean to enter a Chinese Eurasian century.

Appendix: Note on Sources

This study is an attempt to describe the Belt and Road Initiative (BRI) as it is conceived by its architects. However, in a country such as the People's Republic of China (PRC) where information flows are tightly monitored and controlled, gaining direct access to the core leadership's thought on major political issues such as BRI (either through meetings with top political officials or via access to internal documents) remains an almost impossible task for outside observers. This study therefore relies on other sources: interviews in China and the United States with mid-ranking Chinese Communist Party (CCP) and government officials, representatives from state-owned enterprises, university scholars, and think-tank researchers, as well as extensive readings of Chinese media, civilian, and military punditry and academic publications in both Chinese and English.[1]

Using these written sources "requires close attention to authorship and affiliation to determine the importance and authority of the publication," says Peter Mattis, an astute analyst of the People's Liberation Army (PLA).[2] In their dissection of Chinese signaling ahead of military conflict and crisis, Alice Miller and Paul Godwin also note that not all Chinese sources are equally authoritative and establish a hierarchy of leadership statements depending mostly on institutional ranking.[3] Michael D. Swaine uses a similar hierarchical classification of Chinese sources, distinguishing among authoritative sources, authoritative statements, authoritative commentaries, quasi-authoritative sources, and non-authoritative sources.[4] Authoritative sources are those "explicitly speaking for the regime." These include Ministry of Foreign Affairs (MFA) and National Defense statements as well as briefings and remarks by senior civilian and military officials appearing in the military newspapers the *People's Daily* and *Liberation Army Daily*. Authoritative statements include, "in descending order of authority, PRC

---

[1] My various attempts to meet with military officials from either the National Defense University or the Academy of Military Sciences were met with unambiguous resistance; one of my interlocutors justified his refusal by stating that BRI "is not a military topic."

[2] Peter Mattis, "Observations on PLA Studies," China Policy Institute, September 30, 2015, https://cpianalysis.org/2015/09/30/observations-on-pla-studies.

[3] Paul H.B. Godwin and Alice L. Miller, "China's Forbearance Has Limits: Chinese Threat and Retaliation Signaling and Its Implications for a Sino-American Military Confrontation," Center for the Study of Chinese Military Affairs Institute for National Strategic Studies, China Strategic Perspectives, no. 6, April 2013.

[4] Michael D. Swaine, "Chinese Leadership and Elite Responses to the U.S. Pacific Pivot," Hoover Institution, China Leadership Monitor, no. 38, Summer 2012, http://carnegieendowment.org/files/CLM38MS.pdf.

government and CCP statements, MFA statements, MFA spokesperson statements, and MFA daily press briefings." Authoritative commentaries include, "in descending order, 'editorial department articles,' editorials, and commentator articles" published in the *People's Daily* and *Liberation Army Daily*. Quasi-authoritative sources include articles in the *People's Daily* that "convey the view of an important PRC organization." Finally, non-authoritative sources include "low-level commentary and signed articles appearing in a wide variety of PRC and Hong Kong media [that] convey notable yet decidedly non-authoritative views."[5]

Sources that explicitly speak for the regime are crucial because they relay the official party line. When studied in the context of foreign or military affairs, these sources are particularly significant because they generally attempt to shape the perception of domestic or foreign audiences and, when targeted at outsiders, can serve a deterrent or signaling purpose. Underneath what appears on the authoritative surface, a vibrant nonofficial—but still meaningful—discussion is also going on. Over the past few years, the political leadership has relied increasingly on the collective brainpower of a talented pool of scholars and analysts to improve the quality of strategic decision-making.[6] When they speak or write, these experts express opinions and views that are not equivalent to government statements but that may nevertheless contribute to high-level policy deliberations. The collective output of the experts on any given topic indicates what is important to the Chinese leadership. Silence is also revealing: not one BRI-related publication, for example, rejects the initiative as a foolish idea. As Linda Jakobson and Dean Knox note, "genuinely independent think tanks in the Western sense do not exist in an authoritarian state like China because public dissemination of what the authorities consider unsanctioned thought is not permitted."[7]

The "thickening of the Chinese elites" creates a double challenge for outside observers who are faced with voluminous quantities of publications and have to assess their relative importance and weight.[8]

---

[5] Swaine, "Chinese Leadership and Elite Responses to the U.S. Pacific Pivot."

[6] Yun Sun, "Chinese National Security Decision-Making: Processes and Challenges," Brookings Institution, Center for Northeast Asian Policy Studies, May 2013, https://www.brookings.edu/wp-content/uploads/2016/06/chinese-national-security-decisionmaking-sun-paper.pdf; and Linda Jakobson and Dean Knox, *New Foreign Policy Actors in China*, SIPRI Policy Paper, no. 26 (Stockholm: Stockholm International Peace Research Institute [SIPRI], 2010), http://books.sipri.org/files/PP/SIPRIPP26.pdf.

[7] Jakobson and Knox, *New Foreign Policy Actors in China*, 38.

[8] As described in Joseph Fewsmith and Stanley Rosen, "The Domestic Context of Chinese Foreign Policy: Does Public Opinion Matter?" in *The Making of Chinese Foreign and Security Policy in the Era of Reform*, ed. David M. Lampton (Stanford: Stanford University Press, 2001), 152.

The identity and affiliation of the authors can give an indication of their influence within the system, but, as Jakobson and Knox note, "a formal affiliation is not a prerequisite for those who serve in an advisory capacity: some advisors have gained prominence simply through their association with members of the CCP Politburo or the foreign affairs leading small group."[9] Articles written in foreign languages by Chinese experts are generally meant to shape the perception of a targeted audience and should be analyzed with that in mind. Many of the hundreds of Chinese-language articles on BRI do little more than parrot or extol the party line, without expressing any opinion or offering original perspectives. Others clearly reflect deeper thinking and express views that can, at first, appear slightly off the official tracks. The quality and sophistication of the views they express are undoubtedly the mark of real strategic thinkers' work. Such comparative audacity is generally permitted from prominent individuals who have proved their loyalty and their value to the leadership. However, "even they must stay within the permissible limits in their public writings and speeches."[10]

According to the China Academic Journals Full-text Database, in 2014 Chinese scholars published 492 articles on BRI-related topics; one year later, the number had jumped to more than 8,400 articles. Western analysts were slower to take notice of the initiative. Outside China, two researchers identified an emerging Chinese shift to the Silk Road region as early as 2013. In January of that year, Stimson Center scholar Yun Sun wrote an essay commenting on Wang Jisi's 2012 "March Westwards" article, and in December 2013, Justyna Szczudlik-Tatar wrote a report for the Polish Institute of International Affairs entitled "China's New Silk Road Diplomacy."[11] Most Western studies of BRI have appeared since 2015, with Europeans researchers so far producing the great majority of the

---

[9] Jakobson and Knox, *New Foreign Policy Actors in China*, 34.

[10] Ibid., 38.

[11] Yun Sun, "March West: China's Response to the U.S. Rebalancing," Brookings Institution, Up Front, January 31, 2013, https://www.brookings.edu/blog/up-front/2013/01/31/march-west-chinas-response-to-the-u-s-rebalancing; and Justyna Szczudlik-Tatar, "China's New Silk Road Diplomacy," Polish Institute of International Affairs (PISM), Policy Paper, no. 34 (82), December 2013, https://www.pism.pl/files/?id_plik=15818.

available literature.¹² The volume of work by U.S.-based scholars has thus far been comparatively low.¹³ In Australia, two reports stand out: the Australian Parliamentary Library Briefing Book on BRI written by Geoff Wade in

---

12. Camille Brugier, "China's Way: The New Silk Road," European Union Institute for Security Studies, Brief, no. 14, May 16, 2014; Marcin Kaczmarski, "The New Silk Road: A Versatile Instrument in China's Policy," Centre for Eastern Studies, Commentary, no. 161, February 9, 2015; Frans-Paul van der Putten and Minke Meijnders, "China, Europe and the Maritime Silk Road," Clingendael Institute, Clingendael Report, March 2015; Mario Esteban and Miguel Otero-Iglesias, "What Are the Prospects for the New Chinese-Led Silk Road and Asian Infrastructure Investment Bank?" Real Instituto Elcano, April 17, 2015; François Godement, "'One Belt, One Road': China's Great Leap Outward," European Council on Foreign Relations, China Analysis, June 2015; Alice Ekman, "China in Asia: What Is Behind the New Silk Roads?" Institut français des relations internationales (IFRI), July 2015; Justyna Szczudlik-Tatar, "'One Belt, One Road': Mapping China's New Diplomatic Strategy," PISM, Bulletin, no. 67 (799), July 2, 2015; Zhang Yunling et al., "China's New Silk Roads: What's Driving Beijing's 'Pivot to the West,'" Global Asia 10, no. 3 (2015); Jikkie Verlare and Frans-Paul van der Putten, "'One Belt, One Road': An Opportunity for the EU's Security Strategy," Clingendael Institute, Policy Brief, December 2015; Sarah Lain and Raffaello Pantucci, "Security and Stability along the Silk Road," Royal United Services Institute, Workshop Report, February 2016; "Tomorrow's Silk Road: Assessing an EU-China Free Trade Agreement," Centre for European Policy Studies, April 2016; Christina Müller-Markus, "One Belt, One Road: The Chinese Dream and Its Impact on Europe," Barcelona Centre for International Affairs, May 2016; Jeanne L. Wilson, "The Eurasian Economic Union and China's Silk Road: Implications for the Russian-Chinese Relationship," European Politics and Society 17, no. 1 (2016): 113–32; Peter Ferdinand, "Westward Ho—The China Dream and 'One Belt, One Road': Chinese Foreign Policy under Xi Jinping," International Affairs 92, no. 4 (2016): 941–57; Marcin Kaczmarski and Witold Rodkiewicz, "Russia's Greater Eurasia and China's New Silk Road: Adaptation Instead of Competition," Centre for Eastern Studies, Commentary, no. 219, July 2016; William A. Callahan, "China's 'Asia Dream': The Belt Road Initiative and the New Regional Order," Asian Journal of Comparative Politics 1, no. 3 (2016): 226–43; William A. Callahan, "China's Belt and Road Initiative and the New Eurasian Order," Norwegian Institute of International Affairs, Policy Brief, no. 22, 2016; Nicola Casarini, "When All Roads Lead to Beijing: Assessing China's New Silk Road and Its Implications for Europe," International Spectator 51, no. 4 (2016): 95–108; Balázs Sárvári and Anna Szeidovitz, "The Political Economics of the New Silk Road," Baltic Journal of European Studies 6, no. 1 (2016): 3–27; "The Belt and Road Initiative: Backgrounder," Institute for Security and Development Policy, October 2016; Frans-Paul van der Putten et al., eds., "Europe and China's New Silk Road," European Think-Tank Network on China, December 2016; Peter Wolff, "China's 'Belt and Road' Initiative: Challenges and Opportunities," German Development Institute, 2016; Alice Ekman et al., "Three Years of China's New Silk Roads: From Words to (Re)action?" IFRI, February 2017; Richard Ghiasy and Jiayi Zhou, "The Silk Road Economic Belt: Security Implications and EU-China Cooperation Prospects," SIPRI, February 7, 2017; and Tom Miller, China's Asian Dream: Empire Building along the New Silk Road (London: Zed Books, 2017).

13. Michael D. Swaine, "Chinese Views and Commentary on the 'One Belt, One Road' Initiative," Hoover Institution, China Leadership Monitor, no. 47, Summer 2015; David Dollar, "China's Rise as a Regional and Global Power: The AIIB and the 'One Belt, One Road,'" Horizons, no. 4 (2015): 162–72; Theresa Fallon, "The New Silk Road: Xi Jinping's Grand Strategy for Eurasia," American Foreign Policy Interests 37, no. 3 (2015): 140–47; Thomas Zimmerman, "The New Silk Roads: China, the U.S., and the Future of Central Asia," New York University, Center on International Cooperation, October 2015; Simeon Djankov et al., "China's Belt and Road Initiative: Motives, Scope, and Challenges," Peterson Institute for International Economics, Briefing, March 2016; Christopher K. Johnson, "President Xi Jinping's 'Belt and Road' Initiative: A Practical Assessment of the Chinese Communist Party's Roadmap for China's Global Resurgence," Center for Strategic and International Studies (CSIS), March 28, 2016; Alexander Cooley, "The Emerging Political Economy of OBOR: The Challenges of Promoting Connectivity in Central Asia and Beyond," CSIS, October 2016; Gal Luft, "It Takes a Road—China's One Belt One Road Initiative: An American Response to the Silk Road," Institute for the Analysis of Global Security, November 2016; and Alek Chance, "American Perspectives on the Belt and Road Initiative: Sources of Concern, Possibilities for U.S.-China Cooperation," Institute for China-America Studies, November 2016.

September 2016 and Peter Cai's "Understanding China's Belt and Road Initiative" published by the Lowy Institute in March 2017.[14]

Other useful resources include the Center for Strategic and International Studies' Reconnecting Asia Program, which provides infographics, maps, and analysis of the infrastructure linkages that are reshaping the Asian continent; the Clingendael Institute's weekly update of media reports related to BRI; and the Mercator Institute for China Studies' online collection of studies and infographics. The Eurasian Vision website and newsletter are also dedicated to the transcontinental initiatives of the 21st century between Asia and Europe.

More broadly, this monograph benefited from the groundbreaking and essential work of scholars who have dedicated their research to the study of China's foreign policy, both from inside out and outside in, and did not wait for Xi Jinping to launch his initiative to show an interest in the Silk Road region. These scholars include Michael Clarke, Alexander Cooley, Evan Feigenbaum, John Garver, Andrew Kuchins, Marlène Laruelle, Bertil Lintner, Daniel Markey, Raffaello Pantucci, Andrew Small, S. Frederick Starr, Niklas Swanström, and Ashley Tellis.

---

[14] Geoff Wade, "China's 'One Belt, One Road' Initiative," Parliamentary Library Briefing Book (Australia), September 2016; and Peter Cai, "Understanding China's Belt and Road Initiative," Lowy Institute for International Policy, March 2017.

About the Author

Nadège Rolland is Senior Fellow for Political and Security Affairs at the National Bureau of Asian Research (NBR). Prior to joining NBR, she served as Senior Adviser to the French Ministry of Defense and was responsible for analyzing diplomatic, military, and domestic political developments across East Asia and for making policy recommendations to the minister and his cabinet office. From 2008 to 2014, Ms. Rolland served as Desk Officer for China and Adviser on Northeast Asia in the Ministry of Defense's Directorate for Strategic Affairs. From 2003 to 2005, she was a senior analyst of Asia-Pacific affairs at the French Defense Ministry's Directorate for Strategy, and between 1994 and 1998 she worked in the ministry as a China analyst. In these positions, she wrote reports for the defense minister and other senior government officials, coordinated interagency policy reviews, and directed an external research program on a wide range of topics, including China's military modernization, diplomatic strategy, leadership dynamics, and treatment of ethnic minorities. Ms. Rolland received a master of science in strategic studies from the S. Rajaratnam School of International Studies in Singapore. She also holds a BA on contemporary Asia and a master of science in Chinese language with distinction from the National Institute of Oriental Languages and Civilizations in Paris.